**MOTOROLA**
Series in Solid-State Electronics

MW00680791

# Understanding Small Microcontrollers

*James M. Sibigtroth*

**PTR Prentice Hall, Englewood Cliffs, N.J. 07632**

**MOTOROLA**
Series in Solid-State Electronics

**Library of Congress Cataloging-in-Publication Data**
Sibigtroth, James M.
  Understanding small microcontrollers / James M. Sibigtroth
        p.      cm.
  Includes index.
  ISBN 0-13-089129-0
  1. Programmable controllers. I. Title
  TJ223.P76S53 1993                                              93-1156
  004.165--dc20                                                  CIP

Acquisitions editor: Karen Gettmann
Editorial assistant: Barbara Alfieri
Cover Design: Wanda Lubelska
Cover design director: Eloise Starkweather
Copyeditor: Ray Sarch
Manufacturing buyer: Mary E. McCartney

  Published by PTR Prentice-Hall
A Simon & Schuster Company
Englewood Cliffs, New Jersey 07632

The publisher offers discounts on this book when ordered in bulk quantities. For more information, contact Corporate Sales Department, PTR Prentice Hall, 113 Sylvan Avenue, Englewood Cliffs, New Jersey 07632. Phone: 201-592-2863; FAX: 201-592-2249.

Printed in the United States of America

10  9  8  7  6  5  4  3  2  1

ISBN 0-13-089129-0

Prentice-Hall International (UK) Limited, *London*
Prentice-Hall of Australia Pty. Limited, *Sydney*
Prentice-Hall Canada Inc., *Toronto*
Prentice-Hall Hispanoamericana, S.A., *Mexico*
Prentice-Hall of India Private Limited, *New Delhi*
Prentice-Hall of Japan, Inc., *Tokyo*
Simon & Schuster Asia Pte. Ltd., *Singapore*
Editora Prentice-Hall do Brasil, Ltda., *Rio de Janeiro*

# Contents

# Listings

# List of Figures

# List of Tables

# About the Author

Jim Sibigtroth received his BSEE from the University of Illinois at Urbana-Champaign in May 1974. From 1974 to 1978 Jim worked for Eagle Signal Corp., doing hardware and software design of traffic control equipment. In 1978, he joined Motorola in Austin, Texas, to design microprocessor educational kits, including the MEK6802D5 and the MEK6809D4 kits. Jim was the system design project leader for the MC68HC11A8 and wrote the original specifications for the M68HC11 family. He also wrote the M68HC11 Reference Manual: Prentice Hall 1989 with disk, ISBN 0-13-566720-8; without disk, ISBN 0-13-566712-7. This book is considered the most authoritative source of information for the M68HC11 microcontroller. Jim has also developed seminar training materials and taught seminar classes on the M68HC11. More recently, he has developed training materials and taught seminar classes on fuzzy logic software techniques for small microcontrollers.

In 1990 Jim helped design the M68HC11EVBU evaluation board and worked with professor John Peatman and his students at Georgia Tech to develop the M68HC11EVB2 system. The 'EVB2 is used to teach senior-level college students about microcontrollers.

# Acknowledgement

I wish to express my appreciation to the following people for helping to make this textbook possible.

To Gordon Doughman for contributing Chapter 9 on MCU peripherals. Gordon is a field applications engineer for Motorola in Dayton, Ohio.

To Mark McQuilken and Tim Ahrens for initially encouraging me to write this textbook and for carefully reviewing the contents. Mark McQuilken was the technical marketing manager for the CSIC MCU division of Motorola in Austin, Texas. Tim Ahrens is the manager of CSIC Development Tools at Motorola in Austin.

To Robert Chretien, Mark Johnson, and Ed Csoltko for reviewing the contents for accuracy. Robert and Mark work in the CSIC MCU applications engineering group at Motorola in Austin. Ed Csoltko is the technical writing manager for CSIC MCU products at Motorola.

Software programs in this textbook were developed with the μASM assembler for Macintosh™ by Micro Dialects, Inc., Cincinnati, OH. All programs were also tested with the IASM assembler and 05KICS in-circuit simulator from P & E Microcomputer Sytems, Inc. in Boston, MA.

# About This Textbook

Welcome to the world of microcontrollers. This textbook will help you understand the inner workings of these small, general-purpose computers and then explain how to design microcontrollers into useful applications. This book places special emphasis on the smallest microcontrollers in the Motorola M68HC05 family, although the ideas apply to all microcontrollers -- even to the largest computers.

This textbook does not assume any prior knowledge of microprocessors or software programming. Students can use this book in an instructor-led technical class. Experienced engineers can also use this book to learn about microcontrollers.

The following paragraphs provide a brief description of each chapter and appendix of this textbook:

# 1 – What is a Microcontroller?

This chapter introduces the major elements that make up any computer system. This chapter discusses different kinds of computer systems and the features that distinguish microcontrollers from other types of computer systems.

# 2 – Computer Numbers and Codes

This chapter explores the numbering systems and special codes used by computers. Computers count in binary (base 2) instead of decimal (base 10). The American Standard Code for Information Interchange (ASCII) is another code that lets computers work with alphabetic information. Finally, computers use special coded instructions when they execute computer programs.

# 3 – Basic Logic Elements

Digital computers are made up of simple logic elements that perform Boolean logic functions such as AND, OR, NOT, and EXclusive-OR, as well as simple latches and transmission gates. This chapter discusses some of these basic logic elements and provides information about the voltage levels that drive these circuits.

# 4 – Computer Memory and Parallel I/O

Memory is a basic building block of all computers. This chapter discusses several different kinds of memory. The idea of parallel input-output (I/O) as a kind of memory is discussed. As the idea of a computer memory map is explained in detail, you will get your first view of the inner workings of a computer.

# 5 – Computer Architecture

This chapter describes the internal structure and operation of the M68HC05 central processing unit (CPU). This chapter will bring together the ideas that were presented in the first three chapters to show how computers operate. This detailed view of internal computer operations will make the subsequent discussions of software easier to understand.

# 6 – M68HC05 Instruction Set

This chapter begins with an overview of the M68HC05 CPU as seen by a programmer. Addressing modes are explained to show the different ways a program can specify the location of an operand. The instruction set is presented in three ways. First, instructions are grouped by addressing mode. Second, instructions are summarized by functional type. Finally, the whole instruction set is summarized alphabetically.

# 7 – Programming

Computers are not smart. They do only what the instructions in a program tell them to do. Computers know only how to perform a relatively small set of simple instructions. It is the endless combination of ways these instructions can be combined that allows computers to do so many different jobs. This chapter shows you how to prepare a set of instructions for the computer to execute. Assemblers and simulators are also discussed.

# 8 – The Paced Loop

This programming structure can be used as the basis for many microcontroller applications. Sub-tasks that are specific to an application can be written independently. These sub-tasks can then be added to the paced loop framework.

# 9 – On-Chip Peripheral Systems

Microcontrollers often include special-purpose peripheral systems. This chapter describes the 15-bit multifunction timer that is found on small M68HC05 microcontrollers. A complete design of a digital-to-analog converter is discussed, including a software program that uses this timer to produce a pulse width modulated (PWM) signal.

# A – Instruction Set Details

This appendix includes detailed descriptions of all M68HC05 instructions.

# B – Reference Tables

This appendix includes useful conversion tables.

# Glossary

Glossary items are highlighted as bold italic words or phrases where they first appear in the text. The glossary provides brief explanations of common terms and phrases. For additional information refer to the subject-matter index.

# Index

The index in this textbook is a subject-matter index rather than a simple keyword index.

# 1

# What is a Microcontroller?

This chapter sets the groundwork for a detailed exploration of the inner workings of a small microcontroller. We will see that the microcontroller is one of the most basic forms of computer system. Although much smaller than its cousins, personal computers and mainframe computers, microcontrollers are built from the same basic elements. In the simplest sense, computers produce a specific pattern of outputs based on current inputs and the instructions in a computer program.

Like most computers, microcontrollers are simply general-purpose instruction executors. The real star of a computer system is a program of instructions that are provided by a human programmer. This program instructs the computer to perform long sequences of very simple actions to accomplish useful tasks, as intended by the programmer.

# Overall View of a Computer System

Figure 1-1 is a high-level view of a *computer system*. By simply changing the types of input and output devices, this could be a view of a *personal computer*, a room-sized *mainframe computer*, or a simple microcontroller unit (MCU). The input and output (*I/O*) devices shown in the figure happen to be typical I/O devices found in a microcontroller computer system.

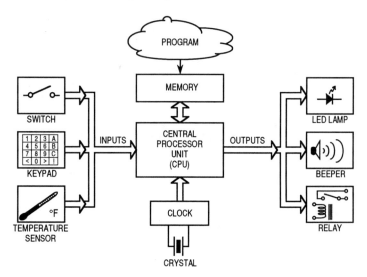

**Figure 1-1.**
Overall View of a Computer System

## Computer System Inputs

Input devices supply information to the computer system from the outside world. In a personal computer system, the most common input device is the typewriter-style keyboard. Mainframe computers use keyboards and punched-card readers as input devices. Microcontroller computer systems usually use much simpler input devices, such as individual switches or small keypads, although much more exotic input devices are found in many microcontroller-based systems. An example of an exotic input device for a microcontroller is the oxygen sensor in an automobile that measures the efficiency of combustion by sampling the exhaust gasses.

*What is a Microcontroller?*

Most microcontroller inputs can process only *digital* input signals at the same voltage levels as the main logic power source. The zero volt ground level is called $V_{SS}$ and the positive power source ($V_{DD}$) is typically 5 Vdc. A level of approximately zero volts indicates a *logic zero*; a voltage approximately equal to the positive power source indicates a *logic one* signal.

Of course the real world is full of *analog* signals, or signals that are some other voltage level. Some input devices translate signal voltages from some other level to the $V_{DD}$ and $V_{SS}$ levels needed for the microcontroller. Other input devices convert analog signals into digital signals (binary values made up of ones and zeros) that the computer can understand and manipulate. Some microcontrollers even include such analog-to-digital converter circuits on the same integrated circuit.

*Transducers* can be used to translate other real-world signals into logic-level signals that a microcontroller can understand and manipulate. Some examples include temperature transducers, pressure sensors, and light-level detectors. With such transducers, almost any physical property can be used as an input to a computer system.

## Computer System Outputs

Output devices are used to communicate information or actions from the computer system to the outside world. In a personal computer system, the most common output device is the *CRT* display. Microcontroller systems often use much simpler output devices, such as individual indicator lamps or beepers.

Translation circuits (sometimes built into the same integrated circuit as the microcomputer) convert digital signals into analog voltage levels. If necessary, other circuits can translate $V_{DD}$ and $V_{SS}$ levels (that are native to an MCU) into other voltage levels.

The "controller" in microcontroller comes from the fact that these small computer systems usually control something, as compared to a personal computer that usually processes information. In the case of the personal computer, most output is information (either displayed on a CRT screen or printed on paper). In a microcontroller system, most outputs are logic-level digital signals that drive display *LEDs* or electrical devices such as relays or motors.

## Central Processor Unit (CPU)

The *CPU* is at the center of every computer system. The job of the CPU is to obediently execute the program of instructions that were supplied by the programmer. A *computer program* instructs the CPU to *read* information from inputs, to read information from and write information to working memory, and to *write* information to outputs. Some program instructions involve simple decisions that cause the program to either continue with the next instruction or to skip to a new place in the program. In a later chapter, we will look closely at the set of available instructions for a particular microcontroller.

In mainframe and personal computers, there are actually layers of programs -- starting with internal programs -- that control the most basic operations of the computer. Another layer includes user programs that are loaded into the computer system memory when they are about to be used. This structure is very complex and would not be a good example to show a beginner how a computer works.

In a microcontroller, there is usually only one program at work in a particular control application. The M68HC05 CPU recognizes only about 60 different *instructions*, but these are representative of the instruction sets of any computer system. This kind of computer system is a good model for learning the basics of computer operation, because it is possible to know exactly what is happening at every tiny step as the CPU executes a program.

## Clock

With very few exceptions, computers use a small clock *oscillator* to trigger the CPU to move from one step in a sequence to the next. In the chapter on computer architecture, we will see that even the simple instructions of a microcontroller are broken down into a series of even more basic steps. Each of these tiny steps in the operation of the computer takes one cycle of the CPU clock.

*What is a Microcontroller?*

## Computer Memory

There are several kinds of computer memory that are used for various purposes in computer systems. The main kinds of memory found in microcontroller systems are read-only memory (*ROM*) and random access read/write memory (*RAM*). ROM is used mainly for programs and permanent data that must remain unchanged even when no power is applied to the microcontroller. RAM is used for temporary storage of data and intermediate calculation results during operation. Some microcontrollers include other kinds of memory, such as erasable programmable read-only memory (*EPROM*) and electrically erasable programmable read-only memory (*EEPROM*). We will learn more about these kinds of memory in a later chapter.

The smallest unit of computer memory is a single *bit* that can store a single value of zero or one. These bits are grouped into sets of 8 bits to make one *byte*. Larger computers further group bits into sets of 16 or 32 to make a unit called a *word*. The size of a word can be different for different computers, but a byte is always eight bits.

Personal computers work with very large programs and large amounts of data so they use special forms of memory called *mass storage* devices. Floppy disks, hard disks, and compact discs are memory devices of this type. It is not unusual to find several million bytes of RAM memory in a personal computer. Even this is not enough to hold the large programs and amounts of data used by personal computers. Therefore, most personal computers also include a hard disk with tens or even hundreds of millions of bytes of storage capacity. Compact discs, very similar to those used for popular music recordings, have a capacity of about 600 million bytes of read-only memory. Small microcontroller systems typically have a total of one thousand to 64 thousand bytes of memory.

## Computer Program

Figure 1-1 shows the program as a cloud, because it originates in the imagination of a computer programmer or engineer. This is comparable to an electrical engineer thinking up a new circuit or a mechanical engineer figuring out a new assembly. The components of a program are instructions from the instruction set of the CPU. Just as a circuit designer can build an adder circuit out of simple AND, OR, and NOT elements, a programmer can write a program to add numbers together out of simple instructions.

Programs are stored in the memory of a computer system where they can be sequentially executed by the CPU. In the chapter on programming, we will learn how to write programs and prepare them for loading into the memory of a computer.

# The Microcontroller

Now that we have discussed the various parts of a computer system, we are ready to talk about just what a microcontroller is. The top half of figure 1-2 shows a generic computer system with a portion enclosed in a dashed outline. This outlined portion is a microcontroller; the lower half of the figure is a block diagram showing its internal structure in greater detail. The crystal is not contained within the microcontroller but is a required part of the oscillator circuit. In some cases, a less expensive component such as a ceramic resonator or a resistor-capacitor (R-C) circuit may be used instead of this crystal.

A *microcontroller* can be defined as a complete computer system that includes a CPU, memory, a clock oscillator, and I/O, all on a single integrated circuit chip. When some of these elements (such as the I/O or memory) are missing, the integrated circuit would be called a *microprocessor*. The CPU in a personal computer is a microprocessor. The CPU in a mainframe computer is made up of many integrated circuits.

*What is a Microcontroller?*

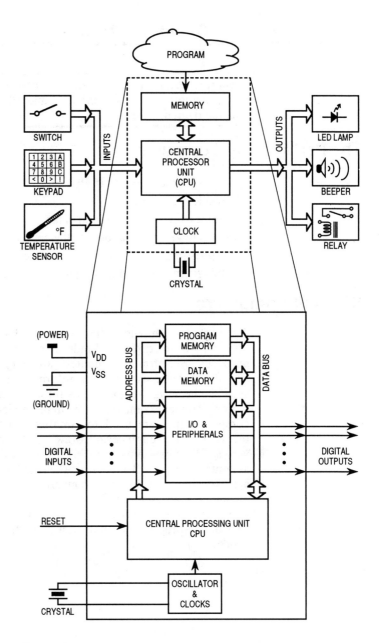

**Figure 1-2.**
Expanded View of a Microcontroller

# Chapter 1 Review

> A *microcontroller* is a complete computer system, including a CPU, memory, a clock oscillator, and I/O, all on a single integrated circuit chip.

## The Parts of any Computer

- A central processor unit (**CPU**)
- A **clock** to sequence the CPU
- **Memory** for instructions and data
- **Inputs** to get information into the computer system
- **Outputs** to get information out of the computer system
- A **program** to make the computer do something useful

## Kinds of Computers

Although all computers share the same basic elements and ideas, there are different kinds of computers for different purposes. Mainframe computers are very large computer systems that are used for big information processing jobs, such as checking the tax returns for all of the taxpayers in a region. Personal computers are small versions of mainframe computers that are used for smaller tasks, such as word processing and engineering drawing. Microcontrollers are very small single-chip computers that are used for such things as controlling a small appliance. The smallest microcontrollers are used for such things as converting the movements of a computer mouse into serial data for a personal computer. Very often, microcontrollers are *embedded* into a product and the user of the product may not even know there is a computer inside.

# 2

# Computer Numbers and Codes

Computers work best with information in a different form than people use. Humans typically work in the base 10 (decimal) numbering system (probably because we have ten fingers). Digital binary computers work in the base 2 (binary) numbering system because this allows all information to be represented by sets of digits, which can consist only of zeros or ones. In turn, a *one* or *zero* can be represented by the presence or absence of a logic voltage on a signal line or the on and off states of a simple switch. This chapter discusses binary, hexadecimal, octal, and binary-coded decimal (BCD) numbers that are commonly used by computers.

Computers also use special codes to represent alphabetic information and computer instructions. Understanding these codes will help you understand how computers can do so much with strings of ones and zeros.

# Binary and Hexadecimal Numbers

In *decimal* (*base 10*) numbers, the "weight" of each digit is ten times as great as the digit immediately to its right. The rightmost digit of a decimal integer is the ones place, the digit to its left is the tens digit, and so on. In *binary* (*base 2*) numbers, the weight of each digit is two times as great as the digit immediately to its right. The rightmost digit of the binary integer is the ones digit, the next digit to the left is the twos digit, next is the fours digit, then the eights digit, and so on.

Although computers are quite comfortable working with binary numbers of 8, 16, or even 32 binary digits, humans find it very inconvenient to work with so many digits at a time. The *base 16* (*hexadecimal*) numbering system offers a practical compromise. One hexadecimal digit can exactly represent four binary digits. Thus, an 8-bit binary number can be expressed by two hexadecimal digits.

The correspondence between a hexadecimal digit and the four binary digits it represents is simple enough that humans who work with computers readily learn to mentally translate between the two. In hexadecimal (base 16) numbers, the weight of each digit is 16 times as great as the digit immediately to its right. The rightmost digit of a hexadecimal integer is the ones place, the digit to its left is the sixteens digit, and so on.

Table 2-1 demonstrates the relationship between the decimal, binary, and hexadecimal representations of values. These three different numbering systems are just different ways to represent the same mathematical values. The letters A through F are used to represent the hexadecimal values corresponding to 10 through 15, because each hexadecimal digit can represent 16 different quantities; our customary numbers include only the 10 unique symbols (0 through 9). Thus, some other single-digit symbols had to be used to represent the hexadecimal values for 10 through 15.

**Table 2-1.**
Decimal, Binary, and Hexadecimal Equivalents

| Base 10 Decimal | Base 2 Binary | Base 16 Hexadecimal |
|---|---|---|
| 0 | 0000 | 0 |
| 1 | 0001 | 1 |
| 2 | 0010 | 2 |
| 3 | 0011 | 3 |
| 4 | 0100 | 4 |
| 5 | 0101 | 5 |
| 6 | 0110 | 6 |
| 7 | 0111 | 7 |
| 8 | 1000 | 8 |
| 9 | 1001 | 9 |
| 10 | 1010 | A |
| 11 | 1011 | B |
| 12 | 1100 | C |
| 13 | 1101 | D |
| 14 | 1110 | E |
| 15 | 1111 | F |
| 16 | 0001 0000 | 10 |
| 17 | 0001 0001 | 11 |
| 100 | 0110 0100 | 64 |
| 255 | 1111 1111 | FF |
| 1024 | 0100 0000 0000 | 400 |
| 65,535 | 1111 1111 1111 1111 | FFFF |

To avoid confusion about whether a number is hexadecimal or decimal, place a $ symbol before hexadecimal numbers. For example, 64 means decimal "sixty-four"; whereas, $64 means hexadecimal "six-four," which is equivalent to decimal 100. Some computer manufacturers follow hexadecimal values with a capital H (as in 64H).

Hexadecimal is a good way to express and discuss numeric information processed by computers because it is relatively easy for people to mentally convert between hexadecimal digits and their 4-bit binary equivalent. The hexadecimal notation is much more compact than binary while maintaining the binary connotations.

# ASCII Code

Computers must handle many kinds of information other than just numbers. Text (alphanumeric characters) and instructions must be encoded in such a way that the computer can understand this information. The most common code for text information is the American Standard Code for Information Interchange (*ASCII*). The ASCII code establishes a widely accepted correlation between alphanumeric characters and specific binary values. Using the ASCII code, $41 corresponds to capital A, $20 corresponds to a space character, etc. The ASCII code translates characters to 7-bit binary codes. In practice, however, the information is most often conveyed as 8-bit characters, with the most significant bit equal to zero. This standard code allows equipment made by various manufacturers to communicate with each other because all of the machines use this same code.

Table 2-2 shows the relationship between ASCII characters and hexadecimal values.

# Computer Operation Codes

Computers use another code to give instructions to the CPU. This code is called an operation code or *opcode*. Each opcode instructs the CPU to execute a very specific sequence of steps that accomplish an intended operation. Computers from different manufacturers use different sets of opcodes, because these opcodes are internally hard-wired in the CPU logic. The *instruction set* for a specific CPU is the set of all operations that the CPU knows how to perform. Opcodes are one representation of the instruction set and mnemonics are another. Even though the opcodes differ from one computer to another, all digital binary computers perform the same kinds of basic tasks in similar ways. The CPU in the MC68HC05 MCU can understand 62 basic instructions. Some of these basic instructions have several slight variations, each requiring a separate opcode. The instruction set of the MC68HC05 is represented by 210 unique instruction opcodes. We will discuss how the CPU actually executes instructions in another chapter. First, we need to understand a few more basic concepts.

*Computer Numbers and Codes*

**Table 2-2.**
ASCII to Hexadecimal Conversion

| Hex | ASCII | Hex | ASCII | Hex | ASCII | Hex | ASCII |
|-----|-------|-----|-------|-----|-------|-----|-------|
| $00 | NUL | $20 | SP space | $40 | @ | $60 | ` grave |
| $01 | SOH | $21 | ! | $41 | A | $61 | a |
| $02 | STX | $22 | " | $42 | B | $62 | b |
| $03 | ETX | $23 | # | $43 | C | $63 | c |
| $04 | EOT | $24 | $ | $44 | D | $64 | d |
| $05 | ENQ | $25 | % | $45 | E | $65 | e |
| $06 | ACK | $26 | & | $46 | F | $66 | f |
| $07 | BEL beep | $27 | ' apost. | $47 | G | $67 | g |
| $08 | BS back sp | $28 | ( | $48 | H | $68 | h |
| $09 | HT tab | $29 | ) | $49 | I | $69 | i |
| $0A | LF linefeed | $2A | * | $4A | J | $6A | j |
| $0B | VT | $2B | + | $4B | K | $6B | k |
| $0C | FF | $2C | , comma | $4C | L | $6C | l |
| $0D | CR return | $2D | - dash | $4D | M | $6D | m |
| $0E | SO | $2E | . period | $4E | N | $6E | n |
| $0F | SI | $2F | / | $4F | O | $6F | o |
| $10 | DLE | $30 | 0 | $50 | P | $70 | p |
| $11 | DC1 | $31 | 1 | $51 | Q | $71 | q |
| $12 | DC2 | $32 | 2 | $52 | R | $72 | r |
| $13 | DC3 | $33 | 3 | $53 | S | $73 | s |
| $14 | DC4 | $34 | 4 | $54 | T | $74 | t |
| $15 | NAK | $35 | 5 | $55 | U | $75 | u |
| $16 | SYN | $36 | 6 | $56 | V | $76 | v |
| $17 | ETB | $37 | 7 | $57 | W | $77 | w |
| $18 | CAN | $38 | 8 | $58 | X | $78 | x |
| $19 | EM | $39 | 9 | $59 | Y | $79 | y |
| $1A | SUB | $3A | : | $5A | Z | $7A | z |
| $1B | ESC | $3B | ; | $5B | [ | $7B | { |
| $1C | FS | $3C | < | $5C | \ | $7C | \| |
| $1D | GS | $3D | = | $5D | ] | $7D | } |
| $1E | RS | $3E | > | $5E | ^ | $7E | ~ |
| $1F | US | $3F | ? | $5F | _ under | $7F | DEL delete |

# Instruction Mnemonics and Assemblers

An opcode such as $4C is understood by the CPU, but it is not very meaningful to a human. To solve this problem, a system of *mnemonic* instruction equivalents is used. The $4C opcode corresponds to the INCA mnemonic, which is read "increment accumulator". Although there is printed information to show the correlation between mnemonic instructions and the opcodes they represent, this information is seldom used by a programmer, because the translation process is automatically handled by a separate computer program called an *assembler*. An assembler is a program that converts a program written in mnemonics into a list of *machine codes* (opcodes and other information) that can be used by a CPU.

An engineer develops a set of instructions for the computer in mnemonic form and then uses an assembler to translate these instructions into opcodes that the CPU can understand. We will discuss instructions, writing programs, and assemblers in other chapters. But you should understand that people prepare instructions for a computer in mnemonic form and the computer understands only opcodes. Thus, a translation step is required to change the mnemonics to opcodes, and this is the function of the assembler.

# Octal

Before leaving this discussion of number systems and codes, we will look at two additional codes you may have heard about. *Octal* (base 8) notation was used for some early computer work but is seldom used today. Octal notation uses the numbers 0 through 7 to represent sets of three binary digits in the same way hexadecimal is used to represent sets of four binary digits. The octal system had the advantage of using customary number symbols (unlike the hexadecimal symbols A through F discussed earlier).

Two disadvantages caused octal to be abandoned for the hexadecimal notation used today. First of all, most computers use 4, 8, 16, or 32 bits per word; these words do not break down nicely into sets of three bits. (Some early computers used 12-bit words that did break down into four sets of three bits each.) The second problem was that octal is not as

*Computer Numbers and Codes*

compact as hexadecimal. For example, the ASCII value for capital A is $1000001_2$ in binary, $41_{16}$ in hexadecimal, and $101_8$ in octal. (The subscript is the base. Base 10 is usually not shown as a subscript.) When a human is talking about the ASCII value for A, it is easier to say "four-one" than it is to say "one-zero-one."

Table 2-3 demonstrates the translation between octal and binary. The "direct binary" column shows the digit-by-digit translation of octal digits into sets of three binary bits. The leftmost (ninth) bit is shown in bold typeface. This bold zero is discarded to get the desired total of eight bits. The "8-bit binary" column has the same binary information as the direct binary column, except the bits are regrouped into sets of four. Each set of four bits translates exactly into one hexadecimal digit.

**Table 2-3.**
Octal, Binary, and Hexadecimal Equivalents

| Octal | Direct Binary | 8-Bit Binary | Hexadecimal |
|-------|---------------|--------------|-------------|
| 000 | **0**00 000 000 | 0000 0000 | $00 |
| 001 | **0**00 000 001 | 0000 0001 | $01 |
| 002 | **0**00 000 010 | 0000 0010 | $02 |
| 003 | **0**00 000 011 | 0000 0011 | $03 |
| 004 | **0**00 000 100 | 0000 0100 | $04 |
| 005 | **0**00 000 101 | 0000 0101 | $05 |
| 006 | **0**00 000 110 | 0000 0110 | $06 |
| 007 | **0**00 000 111 | 0000 0111 | $07 |
| 010 | **0**00 001 000 | 0000 1000 | $08 |
| 011 | **0**00 001 001 | 0000 1001 | $09 |
| 012 | **0**00 001 010 | 0000 1010 | $0A |
| 013 | **0**00 001 011 | 0000 1011 | $0B |
| 014 | **0**00 001 100 | 0000 1100 | $0C |
| 015 | **0**00 001 101 | 0000 1101 | $0D |
| 016 | **0**00 001 110 | 0000 1110 | $0E |
| 017 | **0**00 001 111 | 0000 1111 | $0F |
| 101 | **0**01 000 001 | 0100 0001 | $41 |
| 125 | **0**01 010 101 | 0101 0101 | $55 |
| 252 | **0**10 101 010 | 1010 1010 | $AA |
| 377 | **0**11 111 111 | 1111 1111 | $FF |

When mentally translating octal values to binary byte values, the octal value is represented by three octal digits. Each octal digit represents three binary bits, so there is one extra bit (3 digits × 3 bits = 9 bits). Since people typically work from left to right, it is easy to forget to throw away the leftmost extra bit from the leftmost octal digit and end up with an extra (ninth) bit. When translating from hexadecimal to binary, it is easier because each hexadecimal digit translates into exactly four binary bits. Two hexadecimal digits exactly match the eight binary bits in a byte.

# Binary-Coded Decimal

Binary-coded decimal (*BCD*) is a hybrid notation used to express decimal values in binary form. BCD uses four binary bits to represent each decimal digit. Since four binary digits can express 16 different mathematical values, there will be six bit-value combinations that are considered invalid (specifically, the hexadecimal values A through F). BCD values are shown with a $ sign because they are actually hexadecimal numbers that *represent* decimal quantities.

**Table 2-4.**
Decimal, BCD, and Binary Equivalents

| Decimal | BCD | Binary | Hexadecimal (reference) |
|---------|-----|--------|-------------------------|
| 0 | $0 | 0000 | $0 |
| 1 | $1 | 0001 | $1 |
| 2 | $2 | 0010 | $2 |
| 3 | $3 | 0011 | $3 |
| 4 | $4 | 0100 | $4 |
| 5 | $5 | 0101 | $5 |
| 6 | $6 | 0110 | $6 |
| 7 | $7 | 0111 | $7 |
| 8 | $8 | 1000 | $8 |
| 9 | $9 | 1001 | $9 |
| Invalid BCD Combinations | | 1010 | $A |
| | | 1011 | $B |
| | | 1100 | $C |
| | | 1101 | $D |
| | | 1110 | $E |
| | | 1111 | $F |
| 10 | $10 | 0001 0000 | $10 |
| 99 | $99 | 1001 1001 | $99 |

*Computer Numbers and Codes*

When the computer does a BCD add operation, it performs a binary addition and then adjusts the result back to BCD form. As a simple example, consider the following BCD addition.

$$9_{10} + 1_{10} = 10_{10}$$

The computer adds...

$$0000\ 1001_2 + 0000\ 0001_2 = 0000\ 1010_2$$

But $1010_2$ is equivalent to $A_{16}$, which is not a valid BCD value. When the computer finishes the calculation, a check is performed to see if the result is still a valid BCD value. If there was any carry from one BCD digit to another or if there was any invalid code, a sequence of steps would be performed to correct the result to proper BCD form. The $0000\ 1010_2$ is corrected to $0001\ 0000_2$ (BCD 10) in this example.

In most cases, it is inefficient to use BCD notation in computer calculations. It is better to change from decimal to binary as information is entered, do all computer calculations in binary, and change the binary result back to BCD or decimal, as needed, for display. Not all microcontrollers are capable of doing BCD calculations because they need a digit-to-digit carry indicator that is not present on all computers (though Motorola MCUs do have this half-carry indicator). Also, forcing the computer to emulate human behavior is inherently less efficient than allowing the computer to work in its native binary system.

# Chapter 2 Review

Computers have two logic levels (0 and 1), so they work in the binary numbering system. People have ten fingers, so they work in the decimal numbering system.

Hexadecimal numbers use the sixteen symbols 0 through 9 and A through F. Each hexadecimal digit can exactly represent a set of four binary digits. Table 2-1 shows the decimal, binary, and hexadecimal equivalents of various values. A $ symbol is used before a hexadecimal value to distinguish it from decimal numbers. (Alternatively, a capitol H may be used to follow a hexadecimal value.)

ASCII is a widely accepted code that allows alphanumeric information to be represented as binary values.

Each instruction or variation of an instruction has a unique opcode (binary value) that the CPU recognizes as a request to perform a specific instruction. CPUs from different manufacturers have different sets of opcodes.

Programmers specify instructions by a mnemonic such as "INCA." A computer program, called an assembler, translates mnemonic instructions into opcodes that the CPU can understand.

# 𝟛

# Basic Logic Elements

Digital computers are made up of relatively simple logic elements (sometimes called gates). These small circuits can be connected in various ways to manipulate logic-level signal voltages. Although this textbook is not intended to provide detailed information on logic design, some knowledge of the most basic logic elements will help you understand the inner workings of microcontrollers.

This chapter begins with a close look at the requirements for logic-level voltages. Transistors and interconnections for a typical *CMOS* microcontroller are discussed. A simple inverter, NAND gate, and NOR gate are explained. Finally, a transmission gate, a three-state buffer, and a flip-flop circuit are described. Virtually any part of a microcontroller can be explained in terms of these few simple logic elements.

# Logic Levels

Earlier, when we were discussing what a microcontroller is, we said a level of approximately zero volts indicates a logic zero and a voltage approximately equal to the positive power source indicates a logic one signal. To be more precise, there is a voltage level below which the microcontroller manufacturer guarantees that a signal will be recognized as a valid logic zero. Similarly, there is a voltage level above which the microcontroller manufacturer guarantees that a signal will be recognized as a valid logic one. When designing a microcontroller system, you should be sure that all signals conform to these specified limits, even under worst-case conditions.

Most modern microcontrollers use a technology called complementary metal-oxide semiconductor (CMOS). This means the circuits include both N-type and P-type transistors. Transistors will be explained in greater detail later in this chapter.

In a typical CMOS circuit, a logic zero input may be specified as 0.0 volts to 0.3 times $V_{DD}$. If $V_{DD}$ is 5.0 volts, this translates to the range 0.0 to 1.5 volts. A logic one input may be specified as 0.7 times $V_{DD}$ to $V_{DD}$. If $V_{DD}$ is 5.0 volts, this translates to the range 3.5 to 5.0 volts.

# CMOS Transistors

Figure 3-1 shows the symbols for an N-type and a P-type CMOS transistor. The exact characteristics of these transistors can be determined by the physical layout, size, and shape of the transistors. For the purposes of this textbook, they may be treated as simple switching devices.

**Figure 3-1.**
N-type and P-type CMOS Transistors

*Basic Logic Elements*

The N-type transistor in Figure 3-1 has its source terminal [3] connected to ground. In order for an N-type transistor to be *on* (conducting), its gate voltage [2] must be higher than its source voltage [3] by an amount known as a threshold. This N-type transistor is said to be *on* (conducts between terminals [1] and [3]) when there is a logic one voltage on its gate [2]. When the gate is at logic zero, this N-type transistor is said to be *off* and acts as an open circuit between terminals [1] and [3].

The P-type transistor in Figure 3-1 has its source terminal [4] connected to $V_{DD}$. In order for a P-type transistor to be *on*, its gate voltage [5] must be lower than its source voltage [4] by an amount known as a threshold. A P-type transistor is indicated by the small opened circle at its gate [5]. When there is a logic zero voltage on the gate [5] of this P-type transistor, it is said to be *on* and acts like there is a short circuit between terminals [4] and [6] . When the gate is at logic one, this P-type transistor is *off* and acts as an open circuit between terminals [4] and [6].

It is relatively easy to assemble thousands of N- and P-type transistors on a single microcontroller integrated circuit and to connect them in various ways to perform complex logical operations. In the following paragraphs, we will look at some of the most basic logic circuits that are found in a microcontroller.

# Simple Gates

The three most basic types of logic gates found in a microcontroller are the inverter, the NAND gate, and the NOR gate. A logic designer uses various combinations of these basic gates to form more-complex logic circuits, such as those that add two binary numbers together. This textbook is not intended to teach logic design techniques. These circuits are discussed to give you a better understanding of how a microcontroller operates on digital information.

## Inverter

Figure 3-2 shows the logic symbol, a CMOS equivalent circuit, and a truth table for an inverter. When a logic-level signal (0 or 1) is presented to the input [1] of an inverter, the opposite logic level appears at its output [2].

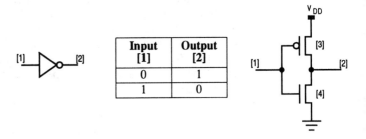

| Input [1] | Output [2] |
|-----------|------------|
| 0 | 1 |
| 1 | 0 |

**Figure 3-2.**
CMOS Inverter

Refer to the CMOS equivalent circuit at the right of Figure 3-2 for the following discussion: When input [1] is a logic 0, N transistor [4] is off and P transistor [3] is on, connecting output [2] to $V_{DD}$ (logic 1). When input [1] is a logic 1, P transistor [3] is off and N transistor [4] is on, connecting output [2] to ground (logic 0).

## NAND Gate

Figure 3-3 shows the logic symbol, a CMOS equivalent circuit, and a truth table for a CMOS NAND gate. When both input [1] and input [2] of the NAND gate are logic-level 1 signals, the output [3] will be a logic 0. If any of the inputs to a NAND gate are logic 0s, the output will be a logic 1.

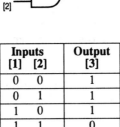

| Inputs [1] [2] | | Output [3] |
|------|------|------|
| 0 | 0 | 1 |
| 0 | 1 | 1 |
| 1 | 0 | 1 |
| 1 | 1 | 0 |

**Figure 3-3.**
CMOS NAND Gate

*Basic Logic Elements*

Refer to the CMOS equivalent circuit at the right of Figure
3-3 for the following discussion: When both inputs [1] and
[2] are logic 1s, P transistors [6] and [4] are both off and N
transistors [5] and [7] are both on, so output [3] is connected
to ground (logic 0). When input [1] is at logic 0, N transistor
[5] is off, which disconnects output [3] from ground
regardless of the condition of N transistor [7]. Also, when
input [1] is logic 0, P transistor [4] is on, connecting output
[3] to $V_{DD}$ (logic 1). Similarly when input [2] is logic 0, N
transistor [7] is off, which disconnects output [3] from
ground regardless of the condition of N transistor [5]. Also,
when input [2] is logic 0, P transistor [6] is on connecting
output [3] to $V_{DD}$ (logic 1).

Although this is a simple logical function, it shows how
CMOS transistors can be interconnected to perform Boolean
logic on simple logic-level signals. Boolean logic is a two-
valued (0 and 1) algebraic system based on mathematical
forms and relationships.

## NOR Gate

Figure 3-4 shows the logic symbol, a CMOS equivalent
circuit, and a truth table for a CMOS NOR gate. When
neither input [1] nor input [2] of a NOR gate are logic-level 1
signals, the output [3] will be a logic 1. If any input to a NOR
gate is a logic 1, the output will be a logic 0.

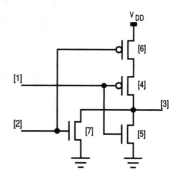

| Inputs [1] [2] | | Output [3] |
|:---:|:---:|:---:|
| 0 | 0 | 1 |
| 0 | 1 | 0 |
| 1 | 0 | 0 |
| 1 | 1 | 0 |

**Figure 3-4.**
CMOS NOR Gate

Refer to the CMOS equivalent circuit at the right of Figure
3-4 for the following discussion: When both inputs [1] and

[2] are logic 0s, N transistors [5] and [7] are both off and P transistors [4] and [6] are both on, so output [3] is connected to $V_{DD}$ (logic 1). When input [1] is at logic 1, P transistor [4] is off, which disconnects output [3] from $V_{DD}$ regardless of the condition of P transistor [6]. Also, when input [1] is logic 1, N transistor [5] is on, connecting output [3] to ground (logic 0). Similarly when input [2] is logic 1, P transistor [6] is off, which disconnects output [3] from $V_{DD}$ regardless of the condition of P transistor [4]. Also when input [2] is logic 1, N transistor [7] is on, connecting output [3] to ground (logic 0).

# Transmission Gates, Buffers, and Flip Flops

Microcontrollers include more-complex types of logic gates and functional elements than those shown in the previous section. In this section, we explore some of these more-complex structures. The first two structures, transmission gate and three-state buffer, introduce the idea of logically controlled high-impedance signals. The third, half flip flop, introduces a structure that can maintain a signal at its output even after the input signal has changed. Flip-flops are vital for a microcontroller to perform counting and sequencing tasks.

## Transmission Gate

Figure 3-5 shows the logic symbol, a CMOS equivalent circuit, and a truth table for a CMOS transmission gate. When control input [3] is a logic 1, the transmission gate is said to be on and whatever logic level is present on the input [1] is also seen at the output [2]. When the control input [3] is a logic 0, the transmission gate is said to be off and the output node [2] appears to be disconnected from everything (high impedance or Hi-Z).

| Control [3] | Input [1] | Output [2] |
|:---:|:---:|:---:|
| 0 | 0 | Hi-Z |
| 0 | 1 | Hi-Z |
| 1 | 0 | 0 |
| 1 | 1 | 1 |

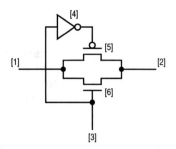

**Figure 3-5.**
CMOS Transmission Gate

Refer to the CMOS equivalent circuit at the right of Figure 3-5 for the following discussion: When control input [3] is logic 0, the gate of N transistor [6] will be logic 0 and the gate of P transistor [5] will be logic 1 ($V_{DD}$). There is no voltage between ground and $V_{DD}$ that would cause P transistor [5] or N transistor [6] to turn on, so there is no conduction between the input [1] and the output [2]. Since output node [2] is effectively isolated from everything, it is said to be high impedance.

When control input [3] is a logic 1, the transmission gate is said to be on and there appears to be a direct connection from the input [1] to the output [2]. If both control [3] and input [1] are at logic 1, P transistor [5] will be on and will form the connection between the input [1] and output [2]. Although the gate of N transistor [6] is a logic 1, the source [1] is also at the same voltage, so transistor [6] will be off. If control [3] is at logic 1 and input [1] is at logic 0, N transistor [6] will be on and will form the connection between the input [1] and output [2]. Although the gate of P transistor [5] is a logic 0, the source [1] is also at the same voltage, so transistor [5] will be off.

The transmission gate shown in Figure 3-5 is sometimes called an analog switch because it is capable of passing signals that fall between legal digital logic levels. For this discussion, we are interested only in digital logic-level signals, so we will refer to this structure as a transmission gate.

Transmission gates can form data multiplexers, as shown in Figure 3-6. When select signal [3] is a logic 1, transmission gate [6] is on and transmission gate [7] (because of inverter [5]) is off. Thus output [4] will have the same logic level as input [1], and signals on input [2] will not affect output [4]. When select signal [3] is a logic 0, transmission gate [7] is on and transmission gate [6] is off. Thus output [4] will have the same logic level as input [2] and signals on input [1] will not affect output [4].

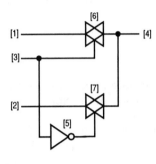

| Select [3] | Inputs [1] | [2] | Output [4] |
|:---:|:---:|:---:|:---:|
| 0 | 0 | 0 | 0 |
| 0 | 0 | 1 | 1 |
| 0 | 1 | 0 | 0 |
| 0 | 1 | 1 | 1 |
| 1 | 0 | 0 | 0 |
| 1 | 0 | 1 | 0 |
| 1 | 1 | 0 | 1 |
| 1 | 1 | 1 | 1 |

**Figure 3-6.**
2:1 Multiplexer

## Three-State Buffer

Figure 3-7 shows the logic symbol, a CMOS equivalent circuit, and a truth table for a CMOS three-state buffer. When control input [3] is a logic 0, the buffer is said to be off and output [2] is an isolated high impedance node. When control input [3] is a logic 1, the buffer is said to be on and whatever logic level is present on the input [1] is also seen at the output [2].

*Basic Logic Elements*

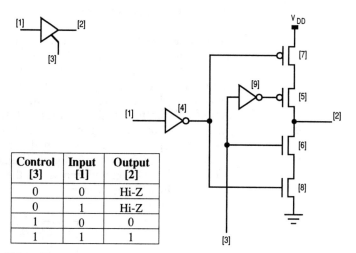

| Control [3] | Input [1] | Output [2] |
|:---:|:---:|:---:|
| 0 | 0 | Hi-Z |
| 0 | 1 | Hi-Z |
| 1 | 0 | 0 |
| 1 | 1 | 1 |

**Figure 3-7.**
Three-State Buffer

Refer to the CMOS equivalent circuit at the right of Figure 3-7 for the following discussion: When control input [3] is logic 0, the gate of N transistor [6] will be logic 0 and the gate of P transistor [5] through inverter [9], will be logic 1 ($V_{DD}$), so both transistors [5] and [6] are off. Since output node [2] is effectively isolated from everything, it is said to be high impedance.

When control input [3] is logic 1, the gate of N transistor 6 will be a logic one and the gate of P transistor [5] will be logic 0. If buffer input [1] is logic 0, the output of inverter [4] is logic 1, which turns on N transistor [8] and turns off P transistor [7]. With control [3] at logic 1 and input [1] at logic 0, buffer output [2] is connected to ground through N transistors [6] and [8], which are both on.

When control input [3] is logic 1, the gate of N transistor 6 will be a logic 1 and the gate of P transistor [5] will be logic 0. If buffer input [1] is logic 1, the output of inverter [4] is logic 0, which turns on P transistor [7] and turns off N transistor [8]. With control [3] and input [1] both at logic 1, buffer output [2] is connected to $V_{DD}$ through P transistors [7] and [5], which are both on.

## Half Flip Flop (HFF)

Figure 3-8 shows the logic symbol and a CMOS equivalent circuit for a half flip flop (HFF). When clock input [2] is a logic 1, transmission gate [9] is on and transmission gate [8] is off. The half flip flop is said to be transparent because input signal [1] passes directly to the Q [3] and Q-bar (Q̄) [4] outputs. When the clock [2] is logic 0, transmission gate [8] turns on and transmission gate [9] turns off. In this state, the half flip flop is said to be latched. Transmission gate [8], inverter [6] and inverter [7] form a stable "ring", and the Q [3] and Q-bar [4] outputs remain at the same logic level as when the clock changed from one to zero.

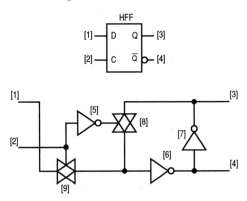

**Figure 3-8.**
Half Flip Flop

*Basic Logic Elements*

# Chapter 3 Review

Although we often think about logic levels being 0 volts or 5 volts, they are actually ranges of voltages that are guaranteed by the MCU manufacturer. For a specific MCU operating with $V_{DD}$ equal to 5.0 volts, a logic 0 could be 0.0 to 1.5 volts and a logic 1 might be 3.5 to 5.0 volts. Always refer to the data sheets for the MCU you are using to obtain the voltage ranges of logic 0 and logic 1.

CMOS MCUs are made up of thousands of N-type and P-type transistors. An N transistor is on (conducts from source to drain) when its gate is at a logic 1 and its source is at logic 0. A P transistor is on when its source is at logic 1 and its gate is at logic 0.

N and P transistors can be connected in various ways to perform logical operations. Inverters, NAND gates, and NOR gates are three types of simple logic gates. The output of an inverter is always the opposite logic-level of its input. The output of a NAND gate is logic 0 when all of its inputs are logic 1s. The output of a NOR gate is a logic 0 when any or all of its inputs are logic 1s.

The output of a transmission gate or a three-state buffer can be logic 0, logic 1, or high impedance. An output is high impedance when it appears not to be connected to anything (an open circuit).

A half flip flop (HFF) has a transparent condition and a latched condition. In the transparent condition (clock input equals logic 1), the Q output is always equal to the logic level presented at the input. In the latched condition (clock input equals logic 0), the output maintains the logic level that was present when the flip flop was last in the transparent condition. Changes in the input logic level, while the flip flop is latched, do not affect the output logic level.

# 4

# Computer Memory and Parallel I/O

Before the operation of a CPU can be discussed in detail, some conceptual knowledge of computer memory is required. In many beginning programming classes, memory is presented as being similar to a matrix of pigeonholes where you can save messages and other information. The pigeonholes we are referring to are like the mailboxes in a large apartment building. This is a good analogy but needs a little refinement if it is to be used to explain the inner workings of a CPU.

# Pigeonhole Analogy

The whole idea of memory is to be able to save information. Of course there is no point in saving information if you don't have a reliable way to recall that information when you need it. The array of mailboxes in a large apartment building could be used as a memory. You could put information into a mailbox with a certain apartment number on it. When you wanted to recall that information, you could go to the mailbox with that apartment number and retrieve the information. Next, we will carry this analogy further to explain just how a computer sees memory. We will confine our discussion to an 8-bit computer so that we can be very specific.

In an 8-bit CPU, each pigeonhole (or mailbox) can be thought of as containing a set of eight on/off switches. Unlike a pigeonhole, you cannot fit more information in by writing smaller, and there is no such thing as an empty pigeonhole (each of the eight switches is either on or off). The contents of a memory location can be unknown or undefined at a given time, just as the switches in the pigeonholes may be in unknown states until you set them the first time. The eight switches would be in a row where each switch represents a single binary digit (bit). A binary one corresponds to the switch being on, and a binary zero corresponds to the switch being off. Each pigeonhole (memory location) has a unique address, so that information can be stored and reliably retrieved.

In an apartment building, the addresses of the mailboxes might be 100–175 for the first floor, 200–275 for the second floor, etc. These are decimal numbers that have meaning for people. As we discussed earlier, computers work in the binary number system. A computer with four address wires could uniquely identify 16 addresses, because a set of four 1s and 0s can be arranged in 16 different combinations. This computer would identify the addresses of the 16 memory locations (mailboxes) with the hexadecimal values $0 through $F.

In the smallest MC68HC05 microcontrollers, there are ten address lines, so these computers can address 1,024 unique memory locations. The MC68HC11 general-purpose 8-bit microcontroller has 16 address lines, so it can address 65,536 unique memory locations.

*Computer Memory and Parallel I/O*

# How a Computer Sees Memory

An 8-bit computer with ten address lines sees memory as a row of 1,024, 8-bit values. The first memory location has the address $00\ 0000\ 0000_2$, and the last location has the address $11\ 1111\ 1111_2$. These 10-bit addresses are normally expressed as two 8-bit numbers that are in turn expressed as four hexadecimal digits. In hexadecimal notation, these addresses would range from \$0000 to \$03FF.

The computer specifies which memory location is being accessed (read from or written to) by putting a unique combination of ones and zeros on the ten address lines. The intention to read the location or write to the location is indicated by placing a one (read) or a zero (write) on a line called read/write (R/W). The information from or for the memory location is carried on eight data lines.

To a computer, any memory location can be written to or read from. Not all memory types can be written to, but it is the job of the programmer to know this, not the computer. If a programmer erroneously instructs the computer to write to a read-only memory, it will try to do so.

# Kilobytes, Megabytes, and Gigabytes

In the decimal world we sometimes express very small or very large numbers by including a prefix such as "milli-", "kilo-", etc., before the unit of measure. In the binary world we use similar prefixes to describe large amounts of memory. In the decimal system, the prefix "kilo-" means 1,000 (or $10^3$) times a value. In the binary system, the integer power of 2 that comes closest to $1,000_{10}$ is $2^{10}=1,024_{10}$. We say "kilobytes" but we mean "K bytes," which are multiples of $1,024_{10}$ bytes. Although this is sloppy scientific terminology, it has become a standard through years of use.

A megabyte is $2^{20}$ or $1,048,576_{10}$ bytes. A gigabyte is $2^{30}$ or $1,073,741,824_{10}$ bytes. A personal computer with 32 address lines can theoretically address 4 gigabytes ($4,294,967,296_{10}$) of memory. The small microcontrollers discussed in this textbook have about 512 bytes to 16 kilobytes of memory.

# Types of Memory

Computers use several kinds of information that require different types of memory. The instructions that control the operation of a microcontroller are stored in a ***nonvolatile*** memory, so the system does not have to be reprogrammed after power has been off. Working variables and intermediate results need to be stored in a memory that can be written (to) quickly and easily during system operation. It is not important to retain this kind of information when there is no power, so a ***volatile*** form of memory can be used. These types of memory are changed (written) and read only by the CPU in the computer.

Like memory information, input data is read by the CPU and output data is written by the CPU. I/O and control registers are a form of memory to the computer, but they are different from other kinds of memory because the information can be sensed and changed by circuits or devices other than the CPU.

## Random Access Memory (RAM)

RAM is a volatile form of memory that can be read or written by the CPU. As its name implies, RAM locations may be accessed in any order. This is the most common type of memory in a personal computer. RAM requires a relatively large area on an integrated-circuit chip. Because of this large chip area (and thus higher cost), usually only small amounts of RAM are included in microcontroller chips.

## Read-Only Memory (ROM)

ROM gets its information during the manufacturing process. The information must be provided by the customer before the integrated circuit that will contain this information is made. When the finished microcontroller is in use, this information can be read by the CPU but cannot be changed. ROM is a nonvolatile memory. ROM is the simplest, smallest, and least-expensive type of nonvolatile memory.

## Programmable ROM (PROM)

***PROM*** is similar to ROM, except that it can be programmed after the integrated circuit is made. Some variations of PROM include erasable PROM (***EPROM***), one-time-programmable

PROM (*OTPROM*), and electrically erasable PROM (*EEPROM*).

**EPROM**  EPROM can be erased by exposing it to an ultraviolet light source. Microcontrollers, with EPROM that can be erased, have a small quartz window that allows the integrated-circuit chip inside to be exposed to the ultraviolet light. The number of times an EPROM can be erased and reprogrammed is limited to a few hundred, depending on the particular device.

A special procedure is used to program information into an EPROM. Most EPROM microcontrollers also use an additional power supply, such as +12Vdc during the EPROM programming operation. The CPU cannot simply write information to an EPROM location the way it would write to a RAM location.

Some microcontrollers have built in EPROM programming circuits to enable the CPU in the microcontroller to program the EPROM. While the EPROM is being programmed, it is not connected to the CPU's address and data busses the way a normal memory would be. In the pigeonhole analogy, this would be like removing the entire rack of mailboxes and taking it to a warehouse where the boxes would be filled with information. While the mailboxes are away being programmed, the people at the apartment building cannot access the mailboxes.

Some EPROM microcontrollers (not the MC68HC705K1) have a special mode of operation that makes them appear to be an industry standard EPROM. These devices can be programmed with a general-purpose commercial EPROM programmer.

**OTP**  When an EPROM microcontroller is packaged in an opaque plastic package, it is called a one-time programmable or OTP microcontroller. Since ultraviolet light cannot pass through the package, the memory cannot be erased. The integrated-circuit chip inside an OTP MCU is identical to that in the quartz-window package. The plastic package is much less expensive than a ceramic package with a quartz window. OTP MCUs are ideal for quick turnaround, first-production runs and low-volume applications.

**EEPROM** EEPROM can be erased electrically by commands to a microcontroller. To program a new value into a memory location, you must first erase the location and then perform a series of programming steps. This is somewhat more complicated than changing a RAM location, which can simply be written to a new value by the CPU. The advantage of EEPROM is that it is nonvolatile. Unlike RAM memory, the number of times you can erase and reprogram an EEPROM location is limited (typically to 10,000). The number of times you can read an EEPROM location is not limited.

## I/O as a Memory Type

I/O status and control information is a type of memory location that allows the computer system to get information to or from the outside world. The simplest kinds of I/O memory locations are simple input ports and simple output ports. In an 8-bit MCU, a simple input port consists of eight pins that can be read by the CPU. A simple output port consists of eight pins that the CPU can control (write to). In practice, a simple output port location is usually implemented with eight *latches* and feedback paths that allow the CPU to read back what was previously written to the address of the output port.

Figure 4-1 shows the equivalent circuits for one bit of RAM, one bit of an input port, and one bit of a typical output port having readback capability. In an actual MCU, these circuits would be repeated eight times to make a single 8-bit RAM location, input port, or output port. The half flip-flops (HFF) in Figure 4-1 are simple transparent flip-flops. When the clock signal (C) is high, data passes freely from the D input to the Q and Q-bar outputs. When the clock input is low, data is latched at the Q and Q-bar outputs.

When the CPU stores a value to the address that corresponds to the RAM bit in Figure 4-1 (a), the WRITE signal is activated to latch the data from the data bus line into the flip-flop [1]. This latch is static and remembers the value written until a new value is written to this location (or power is removed). When the CPU reads the address of this RAM bit, the READ signal is activated, which enables the multiplexer at [2]. This multiplexer couples the data from the output of the flip-flop onto the data bus line. In an actual MCU, RAM bits are built with fewer transistors than shown here, but the operation is functionally equivalent to this circuit.

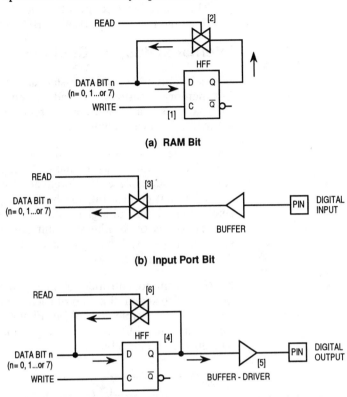

(a) RAM Bit

(b) Input Port Bit

(c) Output Port with Read-Back

**Figure 4-1.**
Memory and I/O Circuitry

When the CPU reads the address of the input port shown in Figure 4-1 (b), the READ signal is activated, which enables the multiplexer at [3]. The multiplexer couples the buffered data from the pin onto the data bus line. A write to this address would have no meaning.

When the CPU stores a value to the address that corresponds to the output port in Figure 4-1 (c), the WRITE signal is activated to latch the data from the data bus line into the flip-flop [4]. The output of this latch, which is buffered by the buffer driver at [5], appears as a digital level on the output pin.

When the CPU reads the address of this output port, the READ signal is activated, which enables the multiplexer at [6]. This multiplexer couples the data from the output of the flip-flop onto the data bus (DATA BIT n) line.

## Internal Status and Control Registers

Internal status and control registers are specialized versions of I/O memory locations. Instead of sensing and controlling external pins, status and control registers sense and control internal logic-level signals.

Look at Figure 4-1 and compare the RAM bit to the output port. The only difference is that the output bit has a buffer to connect the state of the flip-flop to an external pin. In the case of an internal control bit, the buffer output is connected to some internal control signal rather than an external pin. An internal status bit is like an input port bit, except that the signal that is sensed during a read is an internal signal rather than one from an external pin.

M68HC05 microcontrollers include general-purpose parallel I/O pins. The signal direction of each pin is programmable by a software-accessible control bit. Figure 4-2 shows the logic for a bidirectional I/O pin, including an output port latch and a data direction control bit.

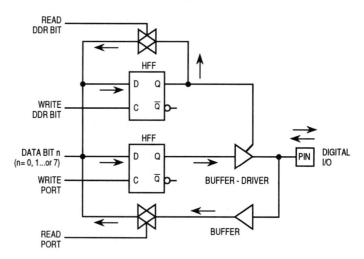

**Figure 4-2.**
I/O Port with Data Direction Control

*Computer Memory and Parallel I/O*

A port pin is configured as an output if its corresponding DDR (data direction register) bit is set to a logic 1. A pin is configured as an input if its corresponding DDR bit is cleared to a logic 0. At power-on or reset, all DDR bits are cleared, which configures all port pins as inputs. The DDRs are capable of being written to or read by the CPU.

# Memory Maps

Since there are a thousand or more memory locations in an MCU system, it is important to have a convenient way to keep track of where program information and control registers are located. A *memory map* is a pictorial representation of the total MCU memory space. Figure 4-3 is a typical memory map showing the memory resources in the MC68HC705K1.

The four-digit hexadecimal values along the left edge of Figure 4-3 are addresses beginning with $0000 at the top and increasing to $03FF at the bottom. $0000 corresponds to the first memory location (selected when the CPU drives all address lines of the internal address bus to logic 0). $03FF corresponds to the last memory location (selected when the CPU drives all ten address lines of the internal address bus to logic 1). The labels within the vertical rectangle identify what kind of memory (RAM, EPROM, I/O registers, etc.), resides in a particular area of memory.

Some areas, such as I/O registers, need to be shown in more detail because it is important to know the names of each location. The entire vertical rectangle can be interpreted as a row of 1,024 pigeonholes (memory locations). Each of these 1,024 locations contains eight bits of data, as shown in Figure 4-4.

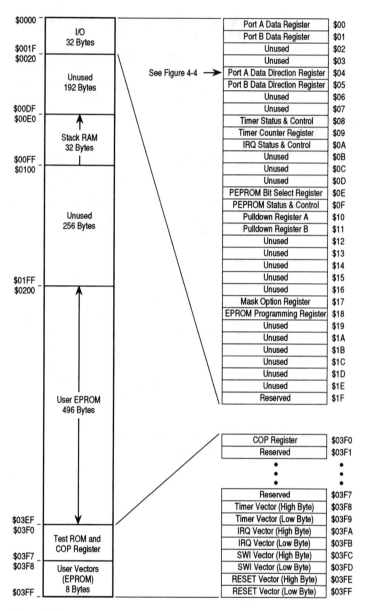

**Figure 4-3.**
Typical Memory Map

*Computer Memory and Parallel I/O*

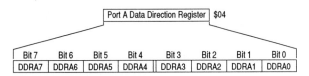

**Figure 4-4.**
Expanded Detail of One Memory Location

The first 256 memory locations ($0000 to $00FF) can be accessed by the computer in a special way, called direct addressing mode. Addressing modes are discussed in greater detail in Chapter 6. In direct addressing mode, the CPU assumes that the upper two hexadecimal digits of address are zeros; thus, only the two lower-order digits of the address need to be explicitly given in the instruction. On-chip I/O registers and 32 bytes of RAM are located in the $0000 to $00FF area of memory. In the memory map (Figure 4-3), the expansion of the I/O memory area identifies each register location with the two lower-order digits of its address rather than the full four-digit address. For example, the two-digit hexadecimal value $00 appears to the right of the port A data register, which is actually located at address $0000 in the memory map.

# Memory Peripherals

Memory can be a form of peripheral. The uses for different types of memory were discussed earlier, but the logic required to support these memories was not considered. ROM and RAM memories are straightforward and require no support logic other than address-select logic to distinguish one location from another. This select logic is provided on the same chip as the memory itself.

EPROM and EEPROM memories require support logic for programming (and erasure in the case of EEPROM). The peripheral support logic in the MC68HC705K1 is like having a PROM programmer built into the MCU. A control register includes control bits to select between programming and reading modes and to enable the high-voltage programming power supply.

We think of memory as an array of mailboxes. A computer views memory as a series of 8-bit values.

If a computer has $n$ address lines, it can uniquely address $2^n$ memory locations. A computer with ten address lines can address $2^{10}$, or $1,024_{10}$ locations.

One *kilobyte* (written *1K* byte) is equal to $1,024_{10}$ bytes.

## Kinds of Memory

- *RAM* Random access memory can be read or written by a CPU. Contents are remembered as long as power is applied.
- *ROM* Read-only memory can be read but not changed. The contents must be determined before the integrated circuit is manufactured. Loss of power does not affect ROM; it is nonvolatile.
- *EPROM* Erasable programmable ROM can be changed by erasing it with ultraviolet light and then programming it with a new value. The erasure and programming operations can be performed a limited number of times after the integrated circuit is manufactured. EPROM is nonvolatile.
- *OTP* The chip in a one-time-programmable EPROM is identical to that in an EPROM, but it is enclosed in an opaque package. Since ultraviolet light cannot get through the package, this memory cannot be erased once it is programmed.
- *EEPROM* Electrically erasable PROM can be changed using electrical signals and is nonvolatile. Typically, an EEPROM location can be erased and reprogrammed up to 10,000 times before it wears out.
- *I/O* I/O, control, and status registers are a special kind of memory. The information can be sensed and changed by circuits or devices other than the CPU.

> *Nonvolatile* memory remembers its contents even when there is no power.
>
> *Volatile* memory forgets its contents when power is turned off.

> A *memory map* is a pictorial view of all of the memory locations in a computer system.

The first 256 locations in a microcontroller system can be accessed in a special way called *direct addressing mode*. In this addressing mode, the CPU assumes the high-order byte of the address is $00, so it does not have to be explicitly given in a program (saving the space it would have taken and eliminating the clock cycle it would have required to fetch it).

Specialty memories, such as EPROM and EEPROM, can be considered peripherals in a computer system. Support circuitry and programming controls are required to modify the contents of these memories. Accessing them differs from simple memories such as RAM, which can be read or written in a single CPU clock cycle.

# 5

# Computer Architecture

This chapter will take us into the very heart of a computer to see what makes it tick. It will be a more detailed look than you normally need to *use* an MCU, but it will help you understand why some procedures are done in a certain way.

Everything the CPU does is broken down into sequences of simple steps. A clock oscillator generates a CPU clock that steps the CPU through these sequences. The CPU clock is very fast in human terms, so sequences seem to be happening almost instantaneously. By going through these sequences step by step, you will gain an understanding of how a computer executes programs. You will also gain valuable knowledge of a computer's capabilities and limitations.

# Computer Architecture

Motorola M68HC05 and M68HC11 *8-bit MCUs* have a specific organization that is called a Von Neumann architecture, after an American mathematician of the same name. In this architecture, a CPU and a memory array are interconnected by an address bus and a data bus. The *address bus* identifies which memory location is being accessed, and the *data bus* conveys information either from the CPU to the *memory location* (pigeonhole) or from the memory location to the CPU.

In the Motorola implementation of this architecture, there are a few special pigeonholes (called CPU registers) inside the CPU, that act as a small "scratch pad" and control panel for the CPU. These CPU registers are similar to memory in that information can be written into them and retained. However, it is important to remember that these registers are directly wired into the CPU and are not part of the addressable memory available to the CPU.

All information (other than that in the CPU registers) accessible to the CPU is "envisioned" (by the CPU) to be in a single row of a thousand or more pigeon holes. This organization is sometimes called a *memory-mapped I/O* system because the CPU treats all memory locations alike, whether they contain program instructions, *variable* data, or *input-output* (I/O) controls. There are other computer architectures, but this textbook is not intended to explore variations. Fortunately, the Motorola M68HC05 architecture we are discussing is believed to be one of the easiest to understand and use. This architecture encompasses the most important ideas of digital binary computers. Thus, the information presented in this textbook will be applicable even if you go on to study other architectures.

The number of wires in the address bus determines the total possible number of pigeonholes; the number of wires in the data bus determines the amount of information that can be stored in each pigeonhole. In the MC68HC705K1, the address bus has 10 lines, making a maximum of 1,024 separate pigeonholes. (In MCU jargon, you would say this CPU can access 1K locations.) Since the data bus size in the MC68HC705K1 is eight bits, each pigeonhole can hold one byte of information. One byte is eight binary digits, or two hexadecimal digits, or one ASCII character, or a decimal value from 0 to 255.

# CPU Registers

Different CPUs have different sets of CPU registers. The differences are primarily the number and size of the registers. Figure 5-1 shows the CPU registers found in an M68HC05. While this is a relatively simple set of CPU registers, it is representative and can be used to explain all of the fundamental CPU register concepts. This chapter provides a brief description of the M68HC05 registers as an introduction to CPU architecture in general. A separate chapter in this textbook addresses the instruction set of the M68HC05 and includes more detailed information about M68HC05 registers.

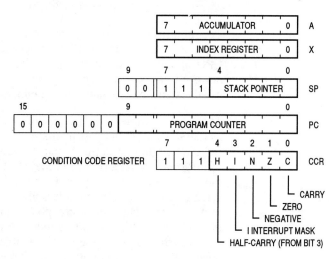

**Figure 5-1.**
M68HC05 CPU Registers

The A register, an 8-bit scratch-pad register, is also called an accumulator because it is often used to hold one of the *operands* or the result of an arithmetic operation.

The X register is an 8-bit index register, which can also serve as a simple scratch pad. The main purpose of an index register is to "point" at an area in memory where the CPU will load (read) or store (write) information. Sometimes an index register is called a *pointer register*. We will learn more about index registers when we discuss indexed addressing modes.

The program counter (PC) register is used by the CPU to keep track of the address of the next instruction to be executed. When the CPU is reset (starts up), the PC is loaded from a specific pair of memory locations called the *reset vector*. The reset vector locations contain the address of the first instruction that will be executed by the CPU. As instructions are executed, logic in the CPU increments the PC such that it always points to the next piece of information that the CPU will need. The number of bits in the PC exactly matches the number of wires in the address bus. This determines the total potentially available memory space that can be accessed by a CPU. In the case of an MC68HC705K1, the PC is 10 bits long; therefore, its CPU can access up to 1K (1,024) bytes of memory. Values for this register are expressed as four hexadecimal digits, where the upper-order six bits of the corresponding 16-bit binary address are always zeros.

The condition codes register (*CCR*) is an 8-bit register, holding status indicators that reflect the result of some prior CPU operation. The three high-order bits of this register are not used and always equal logic ones. *Branch instructions* use the status bits to make simple either/or decisions.

The stack pointer (*SP*) is used as a pointer to the next available location in a last-in-first-out (LIFO) stack. The *stack* can be thought of as a pile of cards, each holding a single byte of information. At any given time, the CPU can put a card on top of the stack or take a card off the stack. Cards within the stack cannot be picked up unless all the cards piled on top are removed first. The CPU accomplishes this stack effect by way of the SP. The SP points to a memory location (pigeonhole), which is thought of as the next available card. When the CPU pushes a piece of data onto the stack, the data value is written into the pigeonhole pointed to by the SP, and the SP is then decremented so it points at the next previous memory location. When the CPU pulls a piece of data off the stack, the SP is incremented so it points at the most recently used pigeonhole, and the data value is read from that pigeonhole. When the CPU is first started up, or after a reset stack pointer (RSP) instruction, the SP points to a specific memory location in RAM (a certain pigeonhole).

*Computer Architecture*

# Timing

A high-frequency *clock* source (typically derived from a crystal connected to the MCU) is used to control the sequencing of CPU instructions. Typical MCUs divide the basic crystal frequency by two or more to arrive at a bus-rate clock. Each memory read or write takes one bus-rate clock cycle. In the case of the MC68HC705K1 MCU, a 4-MHz (maximum) crystal oscillator clock is divided by two to arrive at a 2-MHz (maximum) internal processor clock. Each substep of an instruction takes one cycle of this internal bus-rate clock (500 ns). Most instructions take two to five of these substeps. Thus, the CPU is capable of executing more than 500,000 instructions every second.

# CPU View of a Program

Listing 5-1 shows a small example program that we will use in our discussion of a CPU. (The chapter on programming provides detailed information on how to write programs.) A program listing provides much more information than the CPU needs, because humans also need to read and understand programs. The first column in the listing shows four digit hexadecimal addresses. The next few columns show 8-bit values (the contents of individual memory locations). The rest of the information in the listing is for the benefit of humans who need to read the listing. The meaning of all this information will be discussed in greater detail in the chapter on programming.

Figure 5-2 is a memory map of the MC68HC705K1, showing how the example program fits in the memory of the MCU. This figure is the same as Figure 4-3, except that a different portion of the memory space has been expanded to show the contents of all locations in the example program.

Figure 5-2 shows that the CPU sees the example program as a linear sequence of binary codes, including instructions and *operands* in successive memory locations. An operand is any value other than the opcode that the CPU needs to complete the instruction. The CPU begins this program with its program counter (PC) pointing at the first byte in the program. Each instruction opcode tells the CPU how many (if any) and what type of operands go with that instruction. In this way, the CPU can remain aligned to instruction boundaries even though the mixture of opcodes and operands may look confusing to us.

**Listing 5-1.**
Example Program

```
        ***********************************************************
        * Simple 68HC05 Program Example                          *
        * Read state of switch at port A bit-0; 1=closed         *
        * When sw. closes, light LED for about 1 sec; LED on      *
        * when port A bit-7 = 0. Wait for sw release,            *
        * then repeat. Debounce sw 50mS on & off                 *
        * NOTE: Timing based on instruction execution times       *
        *  If using a simulator or crystal less than 4MHz,        *
        *  this routine will run slower than intended             *
        ***********************************************************
                $BASE   10T             ;Tell assembler to use decimal
                                        ;unless $ or % before value
0000            PORTA   EQU     $00     ;Direct address of port A
0004            DDRA    EQU     $04     ;Data direction control, port A
00E0            TEMP1   EQU     $E0     ;One byte temp storage location

0200                    ORG     $0200   ;Program will start at $0200

0200  A6 80     INIT    LDA     #$80    ;Begin initialization
0202  B7 00             STA     PORTA   ;So LED will be off
0204  B7 04             STA     DDRA    ;Set port A bit-7 as output
                * Rest of port A is configured as inputs

0206  B6 00     TOP     LDA     PORTA   ;Read sw at LSB of Port A
0208  A4 01             AND     #$01    ;To test bit-0
020A  27 FA             BEQ     TOP     ;Loop till Bit-0 = 1
020C  CD 02 23          JSR     DLY50   ;Delay about 50 mS to debounce
020F  1F 00             BCLR    7,PORTA ;Turn on LED (bit-7 to zero)
0211  A6 14             LDA     #20     ;Decimal 20 assembles to $14
0213  CD 02 23  DLYLP   JSR     DLY50   ;Delay 50 mS
0216  4A                DECA            ;Loop counter for 20 loops
0217  26 FA             BNE     DLYLP   ;20 times (20-19,19-18,...1-0)
0219  1E 00             BSET    7,PORTA ;Turn LED back off
021B  00 00 FD  OFFLP   BRSET   0,PORTA,OFFLP  ;Loop here till sw off
021E  CD 02 23          JSR     DLY50   ;Debounce release
0221  20 E3             BRA     TOP     ;Look for next sw closure


                ***
                * DLY50 - Subroutine to delay ~50mS
                * Save original accumulator value
                * but X will always be zero on return
                ***

0223  B7 E0     DLY50   STA     TEMP1   ;Save accumulator in RAM
0225  A6 41             LDA     #65     ;Do outer loop 32 times
0227  5F        OUTLP   CLRX            ;X used as inner loop count
0228  5A        INNRLP  DECX            ;0-FF, FF-FE,...1-0 256 loops
0229  26 FD             BNE     INNRLP  ;6cyc*256*500ns/cyc = 0.768ms
022B  4A                DECA            ;65-64, 64-63,...1-0
022C  26 F9             BNE     OUTLP   ;1545cyc*65*500ns/cyc=50.212ms
022E  B6 E0             LDA     TEMP1   ;Recover saved Accumulator val
0230  81                RTS             ;Return
```

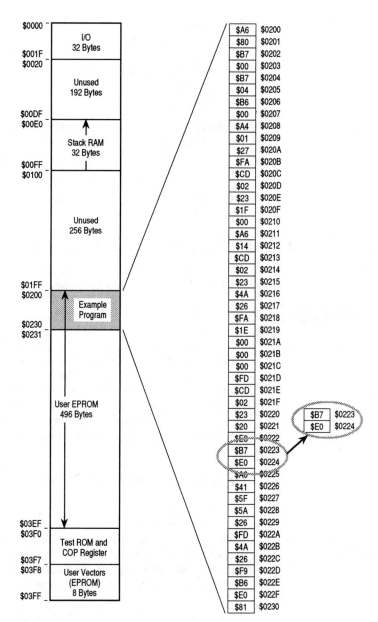

**Figure 5-2.**
Memory Map of Example Program

Most *application programs* would be located in ROM, EPROM, or OTPROM, although there is no special requirement that instructions must be in a ROM-type memory to execute. As far as the CPU is concerned, any program is just a series of binary bit patterns that are sequentially processed.

Carefully study the program listing in Listing 5-1 and the memory map of Figure 5-2. Find the first instruction of the DLY50 subroutine in Listing 5-1 and then find the same two bytes in Figure 5-2.

You should have found the following line from near the bottom of Listing 5-1.

```
0223  B7 E0     DLY50   STA    TEMP1    ;Save accumulator in RAM
```

The highlighted section of memory at the right side of Figure 5-2 is the area you should have identified.

# CPU Operation

This section will first discuss the detailed operation of CPU instructions and then explain how the CPU would execute an example program. The detailed descriptions of typical CPU instructions are intended to make you think like a CPU. We can then go through an example program using a teaching technique called "playing computer," in which you pretend you are the CPU interpreting and executing the instructions in a program.

## Detailed Operation of CPU Instructions

Before seeing how the CPU executes programs, it would help to know (in detail) how the CPU breaks down instructions into fundamental operations and performs these tiny steps to accomplish a desired instruction. As we will see, many small steps execute very quickly and very accurately within each instruction, but none of the small steps is very complicated.

The logic circuitry inside the CPU would seem straightforward to a design engineer accustomed to working with TTL logic or even relay logic. What sets the MCU and its CPU apart from these other forms of digital logic is the packing density. Very large scale integration (VLSI)

*Computer Architecture*

techniques have made it possible to fit the equivalent of thousands of TTL integrated circuits on a single silicon die. By arranging these logic gates to form a CPU, you can get a general-purpose instruction executor capable of acting as a universal *black box*. By placing different combinations of instructions in the device, it can perform virtually any definable function.

A typical instruction takes two to five cycles of the internal processor clock. Although it is not normally important to know exactly what happens during each of these execution cycles, it will help to go through a few instructions in detail to understand how the CPU works internally.

## STORE ACCUMULATOR (DIRECT ADDRESSING MODE)

Look up the STA instruction in Appendix A. In the table at the bottom of the page, we see that $B7 is the direct (DIR) addressing mode version of the store accumulator instruction. We also see that the instruction requires two bytes, one to specify the opcode ($B7) and the second to specify the *direct address* where the accumulator will be stored. (The two bytes are shown as "B7 dd" in the machine code column of the table.)

We will be discussing the addressing modes in more detail in another chapter, but the following brief description will help in understanding how the CPU executes this instruction. In direct addressing modes, the CPU assumes the address is in the range of $0000 through $00FF. Thus, there is no need to include the upper byte of the address of the operand in the instruction (since it is always $00).

The table at the bottom of the STA page (in Appendix A) shows that the direct addressing version of the STA instruction takes four CPU cycles to execute. During the first cycle, the CPU puts the value from the program counter on the internal address bus and reads the opcode $B7, which identifies the instruction as the direct addressing version of the STA instruction and advances the PC to the next memory location.

During the second cycle, the CPU places the value from the PC on the internal address bus and reads the low-order byte of the direct address ($00 for example). The CPU uses the third cycle of this STA instruction to internally construct the full address where the accumulator is to be stored, and advances the PC so it points to the next address in memory (the address of the opcode of the next instruction).

In this example, the CPU appends the assumed value $00 (because of direct addressing mode) to the $00 that was read during the second cycle of the instruction to arrive at the complete address $0000. During the fourth cycle of this instruction, the CPU places this constructed address ($0000) on the internal address bus, places the accumulator value on the internal data bus, and asserts the write signal. That is, the CPU writes the contents of the accumulator to $0000 during the fourth cycle of the STA instruction.

While the accumulator was being stored, the N and Z bits in the condition code register were set or cleared according to the data that was stored. The Boolean logic formulae for these bits appear near the middle of the instruction set page. The Z bit will be set if the value stored was $00; otherwise, the Z bit will be cleared. The N bit will be set if the most significant bit of the value stored was a logic 1; otherwise, N will be cleared.

**LOAD ACCUMULATOR (IMMEDIATE ADDRESSING MODE)** Next, look up the LDA instruction in the instruction set appendix A. The immediate addressing mode (IMM) version of this instruction appears as "A6 ii" in the machine code column of the table at the bottom of the page. This version of the instruction takes two internal processor clock cycles to execute.

The $A6 opcode tells the CPU to get the byte of data that immediately follows the opcode and put this value in the accumulator. During the first cycle of this instruction, the CPU reads the opcode $A6 and advances the PC to point to the next location in memory (the address of the immediate operand ii). During the second cycle of the instruction, the CPU reads the contents of the byte following the opcode into the accumulator and advances the PC to point at the next location in memory (i.e., the opcode byte of the next instruction).

While the accumulator was being loaded, the N and Z bits in the condition code register were set or cleared according to the data that was loaded into the accumulator. The Boolean logic formulae for these bits appear near the middle of the

*Computer Architecture*

instruction set page. The Z bit will be set if the value loaded into the accumulator was $00; otherwise, the Z bit will be cleared. The N bit will be set if the most significant bit of the value loaded was a logic 1; otherwise, N will be cleared.

The N (negative) condition code bit may be used to detect the sign of a *twos-complement* number. In twos-complement numbers, the most significant bit is used as a sign bit: one indicates a negative value and zero indicates a positive value. The N bit may also be used as a simple indication of the state of the most significant bit of a binary value.

**CONDITIONAL BRANCH**   Branch instructions allow the CPU to select one of two program flow paths, depending upon the state of a particular bit in memory or various condition code bits. If the condition checked by the branch instruction is true, program flow skips to a specified location in memory. If the condition checked by the branch is not true, the CPU continues to the instruction following the branch instruction. Decision blocks in a flowchart correspond to conditional branch instructions in the program.

Most branch instructions contain two bytes, one for the opcode and one for a relative offset byte. Branch on bit clear (BRCLR) and branch on bit set (BRSET) instructions require three bytes: the opcode, a one-byte direct address (to specify the memory location to be tested), and the relative offset byte.

The relative offset byte is interpreted by the CPU as a twos-complement signed value. If the branch condition checked is true, this signed offset is added to the PC, and the CPU reads its next instruction from this calculated new address. If the branch condition is not true, the CPU just continues to the next instruction after the branch instruction.

**SUBROUTINE CALLS AND RETURNS**   The jump-to-subroutine (JSR) and branch-to-subroutine (BSR) instructions automate the process of leaving the normal linear flow of a program to go off and execute a set of instructions and then return to where the normal flow left off. The set of instructions outside the normal program flow is called a subroutine. A JSR or BSR instruction is used to go from the running program to the subroutine. A return-from-subroutine (RTS) instruction is used, at the completion of the subroutine, to return to the program from which the subroutine was called.

Listing 5-2 shows lines of an assembler listing that will be used to demonstrate how the CPU executes a subroutine call. Assume that the stack pointer (SP) points to address $00FF when the CPU encounters the JSR instruction at location $0202. Assembler listings are described in greater detail in Chapter 7.

**Listing 5-2.**
Subroutine Call Example

```
  "      "   "              "              "
0200  A6 02       TOP    LDA    #$02      ;Load an immediate value
0202  CD 03 00           JSR    SUBBY     ;Go do a subroutine
0205  B7 E0              STA    $E0       ;Store accumulator to RAM
0207  "      "           "                "
  "      "   "           "                "
  "      "   "           "                "
0300  4A          SUBBY  DECA             ;Decrement accumulator
0301  26 FD              BNE    SUBBY     ;Loop till accumulator=0
0303  81                 RTS              ;Return to main program
```

Refer to Figure 5-3 during the following discussion. We will begin the explanation with the CPU executing the instruction "LDA #$02" at address $0200. The left side of the figure shows the normal program flow composed of TOP LDA #$02, JSR SUBBY, and STA $E0 (in that order) in consecutive memory locations. The right half of the figure shows subroutine instructions SUBBY DECA, BNE SUBBY, and RTS.

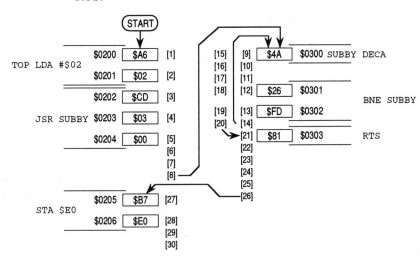

**Figure 5-3.**
Subroutine Call Sequence

The CPU clock cycle numbers (in brackets) will be used as references in the following explanation of this figure.

[1] CPU reads $A6 opcode from location $0200 (LDA immediate).

[2] CPU reads immediate data $02 from location $0201 into the accumulator.

[3] CPU reads $CD opcode from location $0202 (JSR extended).

[4] CPU reads high-order extended address $03 from $0203.

[5] CPU reads low-order extended address $00 from $0204.

[6] CPU builds full address of subroutine ($0300).

[7] CPU writes $05 to $00FF and decrements SP to $00FE. Another way to say this is "push low-order half of return address on stack."

[8] CPU writes $02 to $00FE and decrements SP to $00FD. Another way to say this is "push high-order half of return address on stack." The return address that was saved on the stack is $0205, which is the address of the instruction that follows the JSR instruction.

[9] CPU reads $4A opcode from location $0300. This is the first instruction of the called subroutine.

[10] The CPU uses its *ALU* to subtract one from the value in the accumulator.

[11] The ALU result (A − 1) is written back to the accumulator.

[12] CPU reads BNE opcode ($26) from location $0301.

[13] CPU reads *relative offset* ($FD) from $0302.

[14] During the LDA #$02 instruction at [1], the accumulator was loaded with the value 2; during the DECA instruction at [9], the accumulator was decremented to 1 (which is not equal to zero). Thus, at [14], the branch condition was true, and the twos-complement offset ($FD or −3) was added to the internal PC (which was $0303 at the time) to get the value $0300.

[15] through [19] are a repeat of cycles [9] through [13], except that when the DECA instruction at [15] was executed this time, the accumulator went from $01 to $00.

[20] Since the accumulator is now "equal to zero," the BNE [19] branch condition is not true, and the branch will not be taken.

[21] CPU reads the RTS opcode ($81) from $0303.

[22] Increment SP to $00FE.

[23] Read high-order return address ($02) from stack.

[24] Increment SP to $00FF.

[25] Read low-order return address ($05) from stack.

[26] Build recovered address $0205 and store in PC.

[27] CPU reads the STA direct opcode ($B7) from location $0205.

[28] CPU reads the low-order direct address ($E0) from location $0206.

[29] [30] The STA direct instruction takes a total of four cycles. During the last two cycles of the instruction, the CPU constructs the complete address where the accumulator will be stored by appending $00 (assumed value for the high-order half of the address due to direct addressing mode) to the $E0 read during [28]. The accumulator ($00 at this time) is then stored to this constructed address ($00E0).

# Playing Computer

*Playing computer* is a learning exercise where you pretend to be a CPU that is executing a program. Programmers often mentally check programs by playing computer as they read through a software routine. While playing computer, it is not necessary to break instructions down to individual processor cycles. Instead, an instruction is treated as a single complete operation rather than several detailed steps.

The following paragraphs demonstrate the process of playing computer by going through the subroutine-call exercise of Figure 5-3. The playing-computer approach to analyzing this sequence is much less detailed than the cycle-by-cycle analysis done earlier, but it accomplishes the same basic goal (i.e., it shows what happens as the CPU executes the sequence). After studying the chapter on programming, you should attempt the same thing with a larger program.

You begin the process by preparing a worksheet like that shown in Figure 5-4. This sheet includes the mnemonic program and the machine code to which it assembles. (You could alternatively choose to use a listing positioned next to the worksheet.) The worksheet also includes the CPU register names across the top of the sheet. There is ample room below to write new values as the registers change in the course of the program.

On this worksheet, there is an area for keeping track of the stack. After you become comfortable with how the stack works, you would probably leave this section off, but it will be instructive to leave it here for now.

As a value is saved on the stack, you will cross out any prior value and write the new value to its right in a horizontal row. You must also update (decrement) the SP value. Cross out any prior value and write the new value beneath it under the SP heading at the top of the worksheet. As a value is recovered from the stack, you would update (increment) the value of SP by crossing out the old value and writing the new value below it. You would then read the value from the location to which SP is now pointing and put it wherever it belongs in the CPU (e.g., in the upper or lower half of the PC).

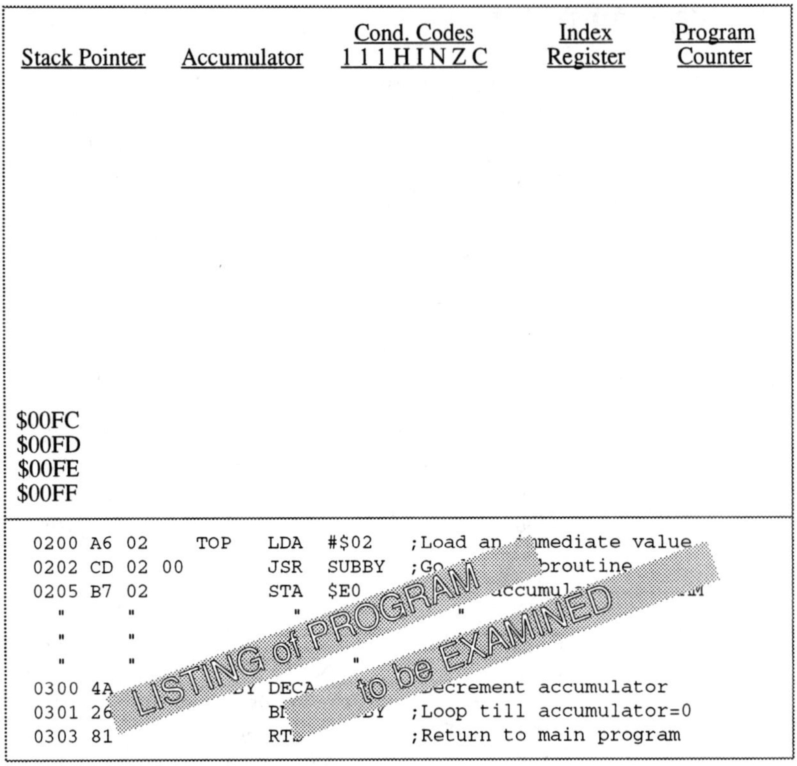

| Stack Pointer | Accumulator | Cond. Codes<br>1 1 1 H I N Z C | Index<br>Register | Program<br>Counter |
|---|---|---|---|---|
| | | | | |

$00FC
$00FD
$00FE
$00FF

```
0200 A6 02     TOP    LDA    #$02    ;Load an   mmediate value
0202 CD 02 00         JSR    SUBBY   ;Go        broutine
0205 B7 02            STA    $E0             ccumul          M
      "    "                 "                 "
      "    "                 "
      "    "                 "
0300 4A          Y DECA            ecrement accumulator
0301 26               BI        Y   ;Loop till accumulator=0
0303 81               RT            ;Return to main program
```

**Figure 5-4.**
Worksheet for Playing Computer

Figure 5-5 shows how the worksheet will look after working through the whole JSR sequence. Follow the numbers in square brackets as the process is explained. During the process, many values were written and later crossed out; a line has been drawn from the square bracket to either the value or the crossed-out mark to show to which item the reference number applies.

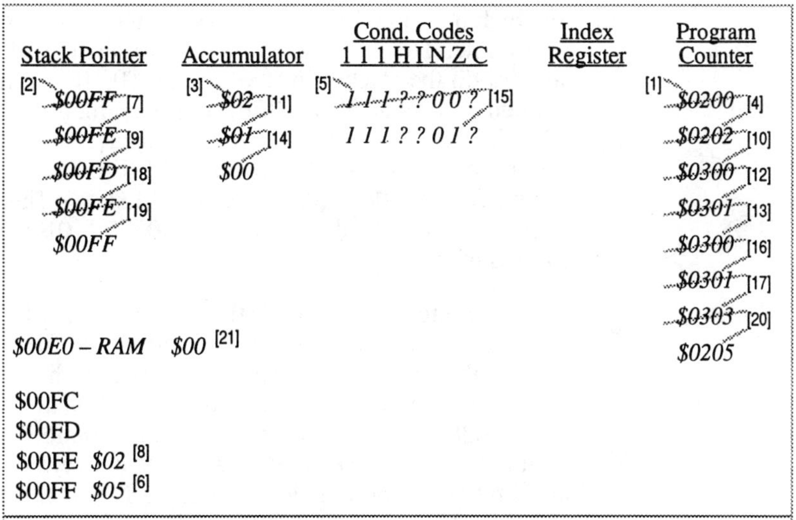

| Stack Pointer | Accumulator | Cond. Codes 1 1 1 H I N Z C | Index Register | Program Counter |
|---|---|---|---|---|
| [2] $00FF [7] | [3] $02 [11] | [5] 1 1 1 ? ? 0 0 ? [15] | | [1] $0200 [4] |
| $00FE [9] | $01 [14] | 1 1 1 ? ? 0 1 ? | | $0202 [10] |
| $00FD [18] | $00 | | | $0300 [12] |
| $00FE [19] | | | | $0301 [13] |
| $00FF | | | | $0300 [16] |
| | | | | $0301 [17] |
| | | | | $0303 [20] |
| | | | | $0205 |

$00E0 – RAM   $00 [21]

$0205

$00FC
$00FD
$00FE $02 [8]
$00FF $05 [6]

```
0200 A6 02    TOP    LDA   #$02    ;Load an immediate value
0202 CD 02 00        JSR   SUBBY   ;Go do a subroutine
0205 B7 02           STA   $E0     ;Store accumulator to RAM
  "    "            "     "        "
  "    "            "     "        "
  "    "            "     "        "
0300 4A       SUBBY  DECA          ;Decrement accumulator
0301 26 FD           BNE   SUBBY   ;Loop till accumulator=0
0303 81              RTS           ;Return to main program
```

**Figure 5-5.**
Completed Worksheet

Beginning the sequence, the PC should be pointing to $0200 [1] and the SP should be pointing to $00FF [2] (due to an earlier assumption). The CPU reads and executes the LDA #$02 instruction (load accumulator with the immediate value $02). Thus, you write $02 in the accumulator column [3] and replace the PC value [4] with $0202, which is the address of the next instruction. The load accumulator instruction affects the N and Z bits in the CCR. Since the value loaded was $02, both the Z bit and N bit would be cleared [5]. This information can be found in Appendix A. Since the other bits in the CCR are not affected by the LDA instruction, we have no way of knowing what they should be at this time. So we put question marks in the unknown positions for now [5].

Next, the CPU reads the JSR SUBBY instruction. Temporarily remember the value $0205, which is the address to which the CPU should come back after executing the called subroutine. The CPU saves the low-order half of the return address on the stack. Thus, you write $05 [6] at the location pointed to by the SP ($00FF) and decrement the SP [7] to $00FE. The CPU then saves the high-order half of the return address on the stack. You write $02 [8] to $00FE and again decrement the SP [9] (this time to $00FD). To finish the JSR instruction, you load the PC with $0300 [10], which is the address of the called subroutine.

The CPU fetches the next instruction. Since the PC is $0300, the CPU executes the DECA instruction, the first instruction in the subroutine. You cross out the $02 in the accumulator column and write the new value $01 [11]. You also change the PC to $0301 [12]. Because the DECA instruction changed the accumulator from $02 to $01 (which is not zero or negative), the Z bit and N bit remain clear. Since N and Z were already cleared at [5], you can leave them alone on the worksheet.

The CPU now executes the BNE SUBBY instruction. Since the Z bit is clear, the branch condition is met, and the CPU will take the branch. Cross out the $0301 under PC and write $0300 [13].

The CPU again executes the DECA instruction. The accumulator is now changed from $01 to $00 [14] (which is zero and not negative). Thus, the Z bit is set, and the N bit remains clear [15]. The PC advances to the next instruction [16].

The CPU now executes the BNE SUBBY instruction, but this time the branch condition is not true (Z is set now), so the branch will not be taken. The CPU simply falls to the next instruction (the RTS at $0303). Update the PC to $0303 [17].

The RTS instruction causes the CPU to recover the previously stacked PC. Pull the high-order half of the PC from the stack by incrementing the SP to $00FE [18] and by reading $02 from location $00FE. Next, pull the low-order half of the address from the stack by incrementing SP to $00FF [19] and by reading $05 from $00FF. The address recovered from the stack replaces the value in the PC [20].

The CPU now reads the STA $E0 instruction from location $0205. Program flow has returned to the main program

*Computer Architecture*

sequence where it left off when the subroutine was called. The STA (direct addressing mode) instruction writes the accumulator value to the direct address $E0 ($00E0), which is in the RAM of the MC68HC705K1. We can see from the worksheet that the current value in the accumulator is $00. Therefore, all eight bits of this RAM location will be cleared. Since the original worksheet did not have a place marked for recording this value in RAM, you would make a place and write $00 there [21].

For a larger program, the worksheet would have many more crossed out values by the time you are done. Playing computer on a worksheet like this is a good learning exercise. As a programmer gains experience, the process would be simplified. In the programming chapter, we will see a development tool called a simulator that automates the playing-computer process. The simulator is a computer program that runs on a personal computer. The current contents of registers and memory locations are displayed on the terminal display of the personal computer.

One of the first simplifications you could make to a manual worksheet would be to quit keeping track of the PC, because you learn to trust the CPU to take care of this for you. Another simplification is to stop keeping track of the condition codes. When a branch instruction that depends on a condition code bit is encountered, you can mentally work backwards to decide whether or not the branch should be taken.

Next, the storage of values on the stack would be skipped, although it is still a good idea to keep track of the SP value itself. It is fairly common to have programming errors resulting from incorrect values in the SP. A fundamental operating principle of the stack is that over a period of time, the same number of items must be removed from the stack as were put on the stack. Just as left parentheses must be matched with right parentheses in a mathematical formula, JSRs and BSRs must be matched one for one to subsequent RTSs in a program. Errors that cause this rule to be broken will appear as erroneous SP values while playing computer.

Even an experienced programmer will play computer occasionally to solve some difficult problem. The procedure the experienced programmer would use is much less formal than what was explained here, but it still amounts to placing yourself in the role of the CPU and working out what happens as the program is executed.

# Resets

Reset is used to force the MCU system to a known starting place (address). Peripheral systems and many control and status bits are also forced to a known state as a result of reset.

The following internal actions occur as the result of any MCU reset:

1) All data direction registers are cleared to zero (input)
2) Stack pointer forced to $00FF
3) I bit in the CCR set to 1 to inhibit maskable interrupts
4) External interrupt latch cleared
5) STOP latch cleared
6) WAIT latch cleared

As the computer system leaves reset, the program counter is loaded from the two highest memory locations ($03FE and $03FF in an MC68HC705K1). The value from $03FE is loaded into the high-order byte of the PC and the value from $03FF is loaded into the low-order byte of the PC. This is called "*fetching the reset vector*". At this point, the CPU begins to fetch and execute instructions, beginning at the address that was stored in the reset vector.

The following conditions can cause the MC68HC705K1 MCU to reset:

1) External, active-low input signal on the $\overline{\text{RESET}}$ pin
2) Internal power-on reset (POR)
3) Internal low-voltage inhibit (LVI)
4) Internal computer operating properly (COP) watchdog timed out
5) An attempt to execute an instruction from an illegal address

*Computer Architecture*

## RESET Pin

An external switch or circuit can be connected to this pin to allow a manual system reset.

## Power-On Reset

The power-on reset occurs when a positive transition is detected on $V_{DD}$. The power-on reset is used strictly for power turn-on conditions and should not be used to detect any drops in the power supply voltage. A low-voltage inhibit (LVI) circuit is provided to detect loss of power.

The power-on circuitry provides for a 4,064-cycle delay from the time that the oscillator becomes active. If the external RESET pin is low at the end of the 4,064-cycle delay time-out, the processor remains in the reset condition until RESET goes high.

## Low-Voltage Reset

The low-voltage inhibit (LVI) circuit is provided to trigger reset if $V_{DD}$ falls below 3.5 volts. Since the MC68HC705K1 can be used in 3-volt systems, there is a control bit that enables or disables the LVI reset function. This control bit is located in the nonvolatile mask option control register (MOR). This register is built out of EPROM bits so that the controls remain set or cleared even when there is no $V_{DD}$ power.

## Watchdog Timer Reset

The computer operating properly (COP) watchdog timer system is intended to detect software errors. When the COP is being used, software is responsible for keeping a free-running watchdog timer from timing out. If the watchdog timer does time out, it is an indication that software is no longer being executed in the intended sequence. Thus, a system reset is initiated.

A control bit in the nonvolatile mask option control register can be used to enable or disable the COP reset. If the COP is enabled, the operating program must periodically write a zero to the COPC bit in the COPR control register. Refer to the data sheet for the MC68HC705K1 for information about the COP time-out rate. Some members of the M68HC05 microcontroller family have different COP watchdog timer systems.

## Illegal Address Reset

If a program is written incorrectly, it is possible that the CPU will attempt to jump or branch to an address not in memory. If this happened, the CPU would continue to read data (though it would be unpredictable values) and attempt to act on it as if it were a program. These nonsense instructions could cause the CPU to write unexpected data to unexpected memory or register addresses. This situation is called program runaway.

To guard against this runaway condition, there is an illegal-address-detect circuit in the MC68HC705K1. If the CPU attempts to fetch an instruction from an address that is not in the EPROM ($0200 – $03FF) or RAM ($00E0 – $00FF), a reset is generated to force the program to start over.

# Interrupts

It is sometimes useful to interrupt normal processing to respond to some unusual event. The MC68HC705K1 may be interrupted by any of the following sources:

1) A logic 0 applied to the external interrupt ($\overline{\text{IRQ}}$) pin.
2) A logic 1 applied to any of the PA3–PA0 pins (provided the port interrupt function is enabled).
3) An overflow (TOF) or real-time interrupt (RTIF) request from the on-chip multifunctional timer system (if enabled).
4) The software interrupt (SWI) instruction.

If an interrupt comes while the CPU is executing an instruction, the instruction is completed before the CPU responds to the interrupt.

Interrupts can be inhibited by setting the I bit in the condition code register (CCR) or by clearing individual interrupt-enable control bits for each interrupt source. Reset forces the I bit to one and clears all local interrupt-enable bits to prevent interrupts during the initialization procedure. When the I bit is one, no interrupts (except the SWI instruction) are recognized. However, interrupt sources may still register a request that will be honored at some later time when the I bit is cleared.

*Computer Architecture*

Figure 5-6 shows how interrupts fit into the normal flow of CPU instructions. Interrupts cause the processor registers to be saved on the stack and the interrupt mask (I bit) to be set, to prevent additional interrupts until the present interrupt is finished. The appropriate interrupt vector then points to the starting address of the interrupt service routine (Table 5-1). Upon completion of the interrupt service routine, an RTI instruction (which is normally the last instruction of an interrupt service routine) causes the register contents to be recovered from the stack. Since the program counter is loaded with the value that was previously saved on the stack, processing continues from where it left off before the interrupt. Figure 5-7 shows that registers are restored from the stack in the opposite order they were saved.

**Table 5-1.**
Vector Addresses for Resets and Interrupts (MC68HC705K1)

| Reset or Interrupt Source | Vector Address |
|---|---|
| On-Chip Timer | $03F8, $03F9 |
| IRQ or Port A Pins | $03FA, $03FB |
| SWI Instruction | $03FC, $03FD |
| Reset (POR, LVI, Pin, COP, or Illegal Address) | $03FE, $03FF |

## External Interrupts

External interrupts come from the IRQ pin or from bits 3 to 0 of port A if port A is configured for port interrupts. In the MC68HC705K1 MCU, the IRQ pin sensitivity is software programmable. Either edge-sensitive triggering only, or negative edge- and level-sensitive triggering are available. The MC68HC705K1 MCU uses a bit in an option register at location $000A to configure the IRQ pin sensitivity. The IRQ pin is low true and the port A interrupts are high true. For additional information about interrupts, refer to the data sheet for the MC68HC705K1.

When an interrupt is recognized, the current state of the CPU is pushed onto the stack and the I bit is set. This masks further interrupts until the present one is serviced. The address of the external interrupt service routine is specified by the contents of memory locations $03FA and $03FB.

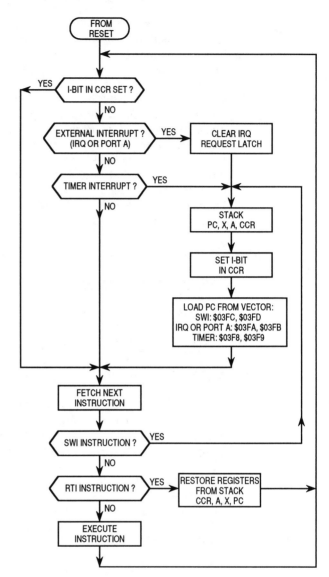

**Figure 5-6.**
Hardware Interrupt Flowchart

*Computer Architecture*

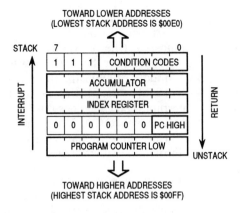

NOTE: When an interrupt occurs, CPU registers are saved on the stack in the order PCL, PCH, X, A, CCR. On a return from interrupt, registers are recovered from the stack in reverse order.

**Figure 5-7.**
Interrupt Stacking Order

## On-chip Peripheral Interrupts

Microcontrollers often include on-chip peripheral systems that can generate interrupts to the CPU. The timer system in the MC68HC705K1 is an example of such a peripheral. On-chip peripheral interrupts work just like external interrupts, except that there are normally separate interrupt vectors for each on-chip peripheral system.

## Software Interrupt (SWI)

The software interrupt is an executable instruction. The action of the SWI instruction is similar to the hardware interrupts. An SWI is executed regardless of the state of the interrupt mask (I bit) in the condition code register. The interrupt service routine address is specified by the contents of memory location $03FC and $03FD (in an MC68HC705K1).

## Interrupt Latency

Although we think of interrupts as if they cause the CPU to stop normal procesing immediately in order to respond to the interrupt request, this is not quite the case. There is a small delay from when an interrupt is requested until the CPU can actually respond. First, the CPU must finish any instruction that happens to be in progress at the time the interrupt is requested (the CPU would not know how to resume processing after the interrupt was handled if it had stopped in the middle of an instruction). Second, the CPU must make a record of what it was doing before it responded to the interrupt. The CPU does this by storing a copy of the contents of all its registers, including the program counter, on the stack. After the interrupt has been serviced, the CPU recovers this information in reverse order and normal processing resumes.

Interrupt latency is the total number of CPU cycles (time) from the initial interrupt request until the CPU starts to execute the first instruction of the interrupt service routine. This delay depends upon whether or not the I interrupt mask is set to one when the interrupt is requested. If the I bit is set, the delay could be indefinite and depends upon when an instruction clears the I bit so the interrupt can be recognized by the CPU. In the more normal case, where the I bit is clear when the interrupt is requested, the latency will consist of finishing the current instruction, saving the registers on the stack, and loading the interrupt vector (address of the interrupt service routine) into the program counter.

The longest instruction (execution time) in the M68HC05 is the multiply (MUL) instruction, which takes 11 bus cycles. If the CPU had just started to execute a MUL instruction when an interrupt was requested, a delay of up to 11 cycles would be experienced before the CPU could respond. It takes the CPU 9 bus cycles to save a copy of its registers on the stack and to fetch the interrupt vector. The total worst-case latency if I was clear and a MUL instruction just started would be 20 cycles (11+9).

The I bit is set to one as the CPU responds to an interrupt so that (normally) a new interrupt will not be recognized until the current one has been handled. In a system that has more than one source of interrupts, the execution time for the longest interrupt service routine must be calculated in order to determine the worst-case interrupt latency for the other interrupt sources.

*Computer Architecture*

## Nested Interrupts

In unusual cases, an interrupt service routine may take so long to execute that the worst-case latency for other interrupts in the system is too long. In such a case, instructions in the long interrupt service routine could clear the I bit to zero, thus allowing a new interrupt to be recognized before the first interrupt service routine is finished. If a new interrupt is requested while the CPU is already servicing an interrupt, it is called nesting. You must use great care if you allow interrupt nesting, because the stack must have enough space to hold more than one copy of the CPU registers. On small microcontrollers like the MC68HC05K1, the stack is small and nesting of interrupts is not recommended.

# Chapter 5 Review

In the M68HC05 architecture, there are five CPU registers that are directly connected within the CPU and are not part of the memory map. All other information available to the CPU is located in a series of 8-bit memory locations. A *memory map* shows the names and types of memory at all locations that are accessible to the CPU. The expression *memory mapped I/O* means that the CPU treats I/O and control registers exactly like any other kind of memory. (Some computer architectures separate the I/O registers from program memory space and use separate instructions to access I/O locations.)

To get started in a known place, a computer must be *reset*. Reset forces on-chip peripheral systems and I/O logic to known conditions and loads the program counter with a known starting address. The user specifies the desired starting location by placing the upper- and lower-order bytes of this address in the *reset vector* locations ($03FE and $03FF on the MC68HC705K1).

The CPU uses the *stack pointer* (SP) register to implement a last-in-first-out *stack* in RAM memory. This stack holds return addresses while the CPU is executing a subroutine, and holds the previous contents of all CPU registers while the CPU is executing an interrupt sequence. By recovering this information from the stack, the CPU can resume where it left off before the subroutine or interrupt was started.

Computers use a high-speed clock to step through each small substep of each operation. Although each instruction takes several cycles of this clock, it is so fast that operations seem to be instantaneous to a human. An MC68HC705K1 can execute about 500,000 instructions per second.

A CPU sees a program as a linear sequence of 8-bit binary numbers. Instruction *opcodes* and data are mixed in this sequence, but the CPU remains aligned to instruction boundaries because each opcode tells the CPU how many *operand* data bytes go with each instruction opcode.

*Playing computer* is a learning exercise where you pretend to be a CPU that is executing a program.

Reset can be caused by internal or external conditions. A reset pin allows an external action to initiate a reset. Voltage detection circuits can cause reset as power is applied or when power falls below some limit. A watchdog timer and an illegal-address-detect system can cause reset in the event software is not executing in the intended sequence.

Interrupts cause the CPU to temporarily stop main program processing to respond to the interrupt. All CPU registers are saved on the stack so the CPU can go back to where it left off in the main program as soon as the interrupt is serviced.

Interrupts can be inhibited globally by setting the I bit in the CCR, or locally by clearing enable control bits for each interrupt source. Requests can still be registered while interrupts are inhibited, so the CPU can respond as soon as the interrupts are re-enabled. SWI is an instruction and cannot be inhibited.

*Interrupt latency* is the delay from when an interrupt is requested to when the CPU begins executing the first instruction in the interrupt response program. When a CPU responds to a new interrupt while it is already processing an interrupt (which is not normally allowed), it is called a *nested interrupt*.

# 6

# M68HC05 Instruction Set

A computer's instruction set is its vocabulary. This chapter describes the CPU and instruction set of the M68HC05. Appendix A contains detailed descriptions of each M68HC05 instruction and can be used as a reference. This chapter discusses the same instructions in groups of functionally similar operations. The structure and addressing modes of the M68HC05 are also discussed. Addressing modes refer to the various ways a CPU can access operands for an instruction.

# M68HC05 Central Processor Unit (CPU)

The M68HC05 CPU is responsible for executing all software instructions in their programmed sequence for a specific application. A block diagram of a typical M68HC05 CPU is shown in Figure 6-1.

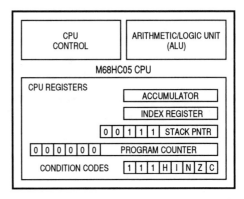

**Figure 6-1.**
M68HC05 CPU Block Diagram

## Arithmetic Logic Unit (ALU)

The arithmetic logic unit (*ALU*) performs the arithmetic and logical operations defined by the instruction set.

The various binary arithmetic operation circuits decode the current instruction and set up the ALU for the desired function. Most binary arithmetic is based on the addition algorithm, and subtraction is carried out as negative addition. Multiplication is not performed as a discrete instruction but as a chain of addition and shift operations within the ALU, under control of CPU control logic. The multiply instruction (MUL) requires 11 internal processor cycles to complete this chain of operations.

## CPU Control

The CPU control circuitry sequences the logic elements of the ALU to carry out the required operations. A central element of the CPU control section is the ***instruction decoder***. Each opcode is decoded to determine how many operands are needed and what sequence of steps will be required to

*M68HC05 Instruction Set*

complete the instruction. When one instruction is finished, the next opcode is read and decoded.

## CPU Registers

The CPU contains five registers, as shown in Figure 6-2. Registers in the CPU are memories inside the microprocessor (not part of the memory map). The set of registers in a CPU is sometimes called a *programming model*. An experienced programmer can tell a lot about a computer from its programming model.

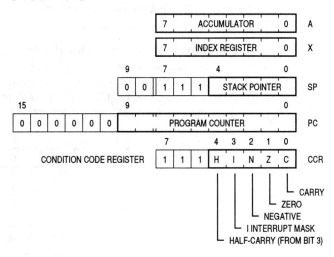

**Figure 6-2.**
Programming Model

**Accumulator (A)**   The accumulator is an 8-bit general-purpose register used to hold operands, results of the arithmetic calculations, and data manipulations. It is also directly accessible to the CPU for nonarithmetic operations. The accumulator is used during the execution of a program when the contents of some memory location are loaded into it. Also, the store instruction causes the contents of the accumulator to be stored at some prescribed memory location.

**Index Register (X)**   The index register is used for indexed modes of addressing or as an auxiliary accumulator. This 8-bit register can be loaded either directly or from memory, have its contents stored in memory, or its contents can be compared to memory.

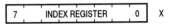

In indexed instructions, the X register provides an 8-bit value that is added to an instruction-provided base address to create an *effective address*. The instruction-provided value can be zero, one, or two bytes long.

**Condition Codes Register (CCR)**   The condition codes register contains an interrupt mask (I), and four status indicators "flags" that reflect the results of arithmetic and other operations of the CPU. The four flags are half-carry (H), negative (N), zero (Z), and carry/borrow (C).

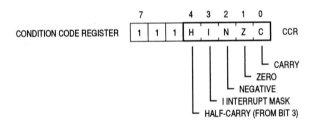

**Half-Carry Bit (H)**   The half-carry flag is used for binary-coded decimal (BCD) arithmetic operations and is affected by the ADD or ADC (add with carry) addition instructions. The H bit is set to a one when a carry occurs from the low-order hexadecimal digit in bits 3 to 0 and the high-order digit in bits 7 to 4. After the binary addition of two 2-digit BCD values, this half-carry bit is one piece of information needed to restore the result to a valid BCD value.

**Interrupt Mask Bit (I)**   The I bit is not a status flag but an interrupt mask bit that disables all maskable interrupt sources when the I bit is set (to 1). Interrupts are enabled when this bit is a zero. When any interrupt occurs, the I bit is automatically set after the registers are stacked but before the interrupt vector is fetched.

*M68HC05 Instruction Set*

If an external interrupt occurs while the I bit is set, the interrupt is latched and processed after the I bit is cleared. Therefore, an IRQ (interrupt request) that occurs while the I bit is set will not be lost.

After an interrupt has been serviced, a return from interrupt (RTI) instruction causes the registers to be restored to their previous values. Normally, the I bit would be zero after an RTI is executed. After any reset, I is set and can be cleared only by a software instruction.

**Negative (N)**   The N bit is set to one when the result of the last arithmetic, logical, or data manipulation is negative. Twos-complement signed values are considered negative if the most significant bit is a one.

The N bit has other uses: By assigning an often-tested flag bit to the MSB of a register or memory location, you can test this bit simply by loading the accumulator with the contents of that location.

**Zero (Z)**   The Z bit is set to one when the result of the last arithmetic, logical, or data manipulation is zero. A compare instruction subtracts a value from the memory location being tested. If the values were equal to each other before the compare, the Z bit will be set.

**Carry/Borrow (C)**   The C bit indicates whether or not there was a carry from an addition, or a borrow as a result of a subtraction. Shift and rotate instructions operate with and through the carry bit to facilitate multiple word shift operations. (See ASL, ASR, LSL, LSR, ROL, and ROR in appendix A.) The C bit is also affected during bit test and branch instructions. (See BRCLR and BRSET in appendix A.)

Figure 6-3 is an example of the way condition-code bits are affected by arithmetic operations.

Assume Initial Values in Accumulator and Condition Codes:

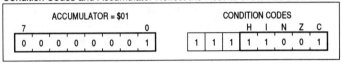

Execute the following Instruction:

```
---- AB 02        ADD   #2   Add 2 to Accumulator
```

Condition Codes and Accumulator Reflect the Results of the Add Instruction:

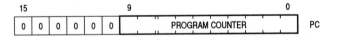

H - Set because there was a carry from bit 3 to bit 4 of the accumulator
I - No change
N - Clear because result is not negative (bit 7 of accumulator is 0)
Z - Clear because result is not zero
C - Set because there was a carry out of bit 7 of the accumulator

**Figure 6-3.**
How Condition Codes are Affected by Arithmetic Operations

The H bit is not meaningful after the above operation because the accumulator was not a valid BCD value before the operation.

**Program Counter (PC)**    The program counter is a 16-bit register that contains the address of the next instruction or instruction operand to be fetched by the processor. In most variations of the M68HC05, some of the upper bits of the program counter are not used and are always zero. The MC68HC705K1 uses only 10 bits of the program counter, so the upper six bits are always zero. The number of useful bits in the program counter exactly matches the number of address lines implemented in the computer system.

| 15 | | | | | | 9 | | | | | | | | | 0 | |
|---|---|---|---|---|---|---|---|---|---|---|---|---|---|---|---|---|
| 0 | 0 | 0 | 0 | 0 | 0 | PROGRAM COUNTER | | | | | | | | | | PC |

Normally, the program counter advances one memory location at a time as instructions and instruction operands are fetched.

*M68HC05 Instruction Set*

Jump, branch, and interrupt operations cause the program counter to be loaded with a memory address other than that of the next sequential location.

**Stack Pointer (SP)**   The stack pointer must have as many bits as there are address lines; in the MC68HC705K1, this means the SP is a 10-bit register. During an MCU reset or the reset-stack-pointer (RSP) instruction, the stack pointer is set to location $00FF. The stack pointer is then decremented as data is *pushed* (stored) onto the stack and incremented as data is *pulled* (recovered) from the stack.

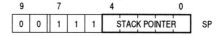

Many variations of the M68HC05 allow the stack to use up to 64 locations ($00FF to $00C0), but the smallest versions allow only 32 bytes of stack ($00FF to $00E0). In the MC68HC705K1, the five MSBs of the SP are permanently set to 00111. These five bits are appended to the five least-significant bits to produce an address within the range of $00FF to $00E0. Subroutines and interrupts may use up to 32 (decimal) locations. If 32 locations are exceeded, the stack pointer wraps around to $00FF and begins to write over previously stored information. A subroutine call uses two locations on the stack; an interrupt uses five.

# Addressing Modes

The power of any computer lies in its ability to access memory. The addressing modes of the CPU provide that capability. The *addressing mode* defines the manner in which an instruction will obtain the data required for its execution. Because of different addressing modes, an instruction may access the operand in one of several different ways. Each different addressing mode variation of an instruction must have a unique instruction opcode, so the 62 basic instructions of the M68HC05 CPU require 210 distinct instruction opcodes.

The M68HC05 CPU uses six addressing modes to reference memory. The six addressing modes are inherent, immediate, extended, direct, indexed (no offset, 8-bit offset, or 16-bit offset), and relative. In the smallest M68HC05 microcontrollers, all program variables and I/O registers fit in the $0000 to $00FF area of memory, so the most commonly used addressing mode is direct.

A general description and examples of the various modes of addressing are provided in the following paragraphs. The term *effective address* is used to indicate the memory address where the operand for an instruction is fetched or stored. A description of each instruction is available in Appendix A.

The information provided in the example program listings uses several symbols to identify the various types of numbers that occur in a program. Chapter 2 includes a description of computer numbers and codes. Special symbols used in listings include:

1. A blank or no symbol which indicates a decimal number. This number will be translated into a binary value before it is stored in memory to be used by the CPU.

2. A $ immediately preceding a number, which indicates that the number is hexadecimal; e.g., $24 is $24_{16}$ in hexadecimal, or the equivalent of $36_{10}$.

3. A #, which indicates an immediate operand; the number is found in the location following the opcode. A variety of symbols and expressions can be used following the # character. Since not all assemblers use the same syntax rules and special characters, refer to the documentation for the particular assembler that will be used.

| Prefix | Indicates the value that follows is... |
|---|---|
| None | Decimal |
| $ | Hexadecimal |
| @ | Octal |
| % | Binary |
| ' (apostrophe) | A single ASCII character |

For each addressing mode, an example instruction is explained in detail. These explanations describe what happens in the CPU during each processor clock cycle of the instruction. In these examples, numbers in brackets [ ] refer to a specific CPU clock cycle.

*M68HC05 Instruction Set*

# IMMEDIATE Addressing Mode

In the *immediate* addressing mode, the operand is contained in the byte immediately following the opcode. This mode is used when a value or constant is known at the time the program is written and does not change during program execution. These are two-byte instructions, one for the opcode and one for the immediate data byte.

**Example Program Listing:**

```
0200 A6 02   LDA   #$02    Load accumulator with
                           immediate value
```

**Execution Sequence:**

```
$0200   $A6   [1]
$0201   $02   [2]
```

**Explanation:**

[1]   CPU reads opcode $A6 — load accumulator with the value immediately following the opcode.

[2]   CPU then reads the immediate data $02 from location $0201 into the accumulator.

Table 6-1 lists all M68HC05 instructions that can use the immediate addressing mode.

**Table 6-1**
IMMEDIATE Addressing Mode Instructions

| Instruction | Mnemonic |
|---|---|
| Add with Carry | ADC |
| Add (without carry) | ADD |
| Logical AND | AND |
| Bit Test Memory with Accumulator | BIT |
| Compare Accumulator with Memory | CMP |
| Compare Index Register with Memory | CPX |
| Exclusive OR Memory with Accumulator | EOR |
| Load Accumulator from Memory | LDA |
| Load Index Register from Memory | LDX |
| Inclusive OR | ORA |
| Subtract with Carry | SBC |
| Subtract (without borrow) | SUB |

## INHERENT Addressing Mode

In the *inherent* addressing mode, all information required for the operation is already inherently known to the CPU, and no external operand from memory or from the program is needed. The operands (if any) are only CPU registers or stacked data values. These are always one-byte instructions.

**Example Program Listing:**

```
0200 4C      INCA          Increment accumulator
```

**Execution Sequence:**

```
$0200   $4C   [1], [2], [3]
```

**Explanation:**

[1]   CPU reads opcode $4C — increment accumulator

[2]   CPU adds one to the current accumulator value.

[3]   CPU stores the new value in the accumulator and adjusts condition-code flag bits, as necessary.

Table 6-2 lists all M68HC05 instructions that can use the inherent addressing mode.

**Table 6-2**
INHERENT Addressing Mode Instructions

| Instruction | Mnemonic |
|---|---|
| Arithmetic Shift Left | ASLA, ASLX |
| Arithmetic Shift Right | ASRA, ASRX |
| Clear Carry Bit | CLC |
| Clear Interrupt Mask Bit | CLI |
| Clear | CLRA, CLRX |
| Complement (invert all bits) | COMA, COMX |
| Decrement | DECA, DECX |
| Increment | INCA, INCX |
| Logical Shift Left | LSLA, LSLX |
| Logical Shift Right | LSRA, LSRX |
| Multiply | MUL |
| Negate (twos complement) | NEGA, NEGX |
| No Operation | NOP |
| Rotate Left thru Carry | ROLA, ROLX |
| Rotate Right thru Carry | RORA, RORX |
| Reset Stack Pointer | RSP |
| Return from Interrupt | RTI |
| Return from Subroutine | RTS |
| Set Carry Bit | SEC |
| Set Interrupt Mask Bit | SEI |
| Enable IRQ, STOP Oscillator | STOP |
| Software Interrupt | SWI |
| Transfer Accumulator to Index Register | TAX |
| Test for Negative or Zero | TSTA, TSTX |
| Transfer Index Register to Accumulator | TXA |
| Wait for Interrupt | WAIT |

## EXTENDED Addressing Mode

In the *extended* addressing mode, the address of the operand is contained in the two bytes following the opcode. Extended addressing may be used to reference any location in the MCU memory, including I/O, RAM, ROM, and EPROM. Extended addressing-mode instructions are three bytes, one for the opcode and two for the address of the operand.

**Example Program Listing:**

```
0200 C6 03 65   LDA   $0365 Load accumulator from
                            an extended address
```

**Execution Sequence:**

```
$0200   $C6.  [1]
$0201   $03   [2]
$0202   $65   [3] and [4]
```

**Explanation:**

[1]   CPU reads opcode $C6 — load accumulator using extended addressing mode.

[2]   CPU then reads $03 from location $0201 This $03 is interpreted as the high-order half of an address.

[3]   CPU then reads $65 from location $0202 This $65 is interpreted as the low-order half of an address.

[4]   CPU builds the complete extended address $0365 from the two previously read values. This address is placed on the address bus, and the CPU reads the data value from location $0365 into the accumulator.

*M68HC05 Instruction Set*

Table 6-3 lists all M68HC05 instructions that can use the extended addressing mode.

**Table 6-3**
EXTENDED Addressing Mode Instructions

| Instruction | Mnemonic |
|---|---|
| Add with Carry | ADC |
| Add (without carry) | ADD |
| Logical AND | AND |
| Bit Test Memory with Accumulator | BIT |
| Compare Accumulator with Memory | CMP |
| Compare Index Register with Memory | CPX |
| Exclusive OR Memory with Accumulator | EOR |
| Jump | JMP |
| Jump to Subroutine | JSR |
| Load Accumulator from Memory | LDA |
| Load Index Register from Memory | LDX |
| Inclusive OR | ORA |
| Subtract with Carry | SBC |
| Store Accumulator in Memory | STA |
| Store Index Register in Memory | STX |
| Subtract (without borrow) | SUB |

## DIRECT Addressing Mode

The *direct* addressing mode is similar to the extended addressing mode, except the upper byte of the operand address is assumed to be $00. Thus, only the lower byte of the operand address needs to be included in the instruction. Direct addressing allows you to efficiently address the lowest 256 bytes in memory. This area of memory is called the *direct page* and includes on-chip RAM and I/O registers. Direct addressing is efficient in both program memory space and execution time. Direct addressing mode instructions are usually two bytes, one for the opcode and one for the low-order byte of the operand address.

**Example Program Listing:**

```
0200  B6 E0     LDA  $E0     Load accumulator from
                             a direct page address
```

**Execution Sequence:**

```
$0200   $B6   [1]
$0201   $E0   [2] and [3]
```

**Explanation:**

[1]   CPU reads opcode $B6 — load accumulator using direct addressing mode.

[2]   CPU then reads $E0 from location $0201 This $E0 is interpreted as the low-order half of an address in the direct page ($0000 to $00FF).

[3]   CPU builds the complete direct address $00E0 from the assumed high-order value $00 and the previously read low-order address value. This address is placed on the address bus, and the CPU reads the data value from location $00E0 into the accumulator.

*M68HC05 Instruction Set*

Table 6-4 lists all M68HC05 instructions that can use the direct addressing mode.

**Table 6-4**
DIRECT Addressing Mode Instructions

| Instruction | Mnemonic |
|---|---|
| Add with Carry | ADC |
| Add (without carry) | ADD |
| Logical AND | AND |
| Arithmetic Shift Left | ASL |
| Arithmetic Shift Right | ASR |
| Clear Bit in Memory | BCLR |
| Bit Test Memory with Accumulator | BIT |
| Branch if Bit n is Clear | BRCLR |
| Branch if Bit n is Set | BRSET |
| Set Bit in Memory | BSET |
| Clear | CLR |
| Compare Accumulator with Memory | CMP |
| Complement (invert all bits) | COM |
| Compare Index Register with Memory | CPX |
| Decrement | DEC |
| Exclusive OR Memory with Accumulator | EOR |
| Increment | INC |
| Jump | JMP |
| Jump to Subroutine | JSR |
| Load Accumulator from Memory | LDA |
| Load Index Register from Memory | LDX |
| Logical Shift Left | LSL |
| Logical Shift Right | LSR |
| Negate (twos complement) | NEG |
| Inclusive OR | ORA |
| Rotate Left thru Carry | ROL |
| Rotate Right thru Carry | ROR |
| Subtract with Carry | SBC |
| Store Accumulator in Memory | STA |
| Store Index Register in Memory | STX |
| Subtract (without borrow) | SUB |
| Test for Negative or Zero | TST |

## INDEXED Addressing Mode

In the *indexed* addressing mode, the effective address is variable and depends upon two factors: 1) the current contents of the index register (X), and 2) the offset contained in the byte(s) following the opcode. Three types of indexed addressing are supported by the M68HC05 CPU: no offset, 8-bit offset, and 16-bit offset. A good assembler should use the indexed addressing mode that requires the least number of bytes to express the offset.

**Indexed/No Offset** In the indexed/no offset addressing mode, the effective address of the operand for the instruction is contained in the 8-bit index register. Thus, this addressing mode can access the first 256 memory locations ($0000 to $00FF). These instructions consist of one byte.

**Example Program Listing:**

```
0200 F6        LDA  0,X    Load A from address
                           pointed to by X
```

**Execution Sequence:**

$0200   $F6   [1], [2], and [3]

**Explanation:**

[1]   CPU reads opcode $F6 — load accumulator using indexed/no offset addressing mode.

[2]   CPU builds a complete address by adding $0000 to the contents of the 8-bit index register (X).

[3]   This address is placed on the address bus, and the CPU reads the data value from that location into the accumulator.

Table 6-5 lists all M68HC05 instructions that can use the indexed/no offset and indexed/8-bit offset addressing modes.

**Table 6-5**
INDEXED (No Offset or 8-Bit Offset) Addressing Mode Instructions

| Instruction | Mnemonic |
|---|---|
| Add with Carry | ADC |
| Add (without carry) | ADD |
| Logical AND | AND |
| Arithmetic Shift Left | ASL |
| Arithmetic Shift Right | ASR |
| Bit Test Memory with Accumulator | BIT |
| Clear | CLR |
| Compare Accumulator with Memory | CMP |
| Complement (invert all bits) | COM |
| Compare Index Register with Memory | CPX |
| Decrement | DEC |
| Exclusive OR Memory with Accumulator | EOR |
| Increment | INC |
| Jump | JMP |
| Jump to Subroutine | JSR |
| Load Accumulator from Memory | LDA |
| Load Index Register from Memory | LDX |
| Logical Shift Left | LSL |
| Logical Shift Right | LSR |
| Negate (twos complement) | NEG |
| Inclusive OR | ORA |
| Rotate Left thru Carry | ROL |
| Rotate Right thru Carry | ROR |
| Subtract with Carry | SBC |
| Store Accumulator in Memory | STA |
| Store Index Register in Memory | STX |
| Subtract (without borrow) | SUB |
| Test for Negative or Zero | TST |

**Indexed/8-Bit Offset**  In the indexed/8-bit offset addressing mode, the effective address is obtained by adding the contents of the byte following the opcode to the contents of the index register. The offset byte supplied in the instruction is an unsigned 8-bit integer. These are two-byte instructions, with the offset contained in the byte following the opcode. The content of the index register (X) is not changed.

**Example Program Listing:**

```
0200 E6 05     LDA  5,X     Load A with 6th item
                            in table, starting at X
```

**Execution Sequence:**

```
$0200   $E6   [1]
$0201   $05   [2], [3] and [4]
```

**Explanation:**

[1]  CPU reads opcode $E6 — load accumulator using indexed/8-bit offset addressing mode.

[2]  CPU reads 8-bit offset ($05) from address $0201.

[3]  CPU builds a complete address by adding the value just read ($05) to the contents of the 8-bit index register (X).

[4]  This address is placed on the address bus, and the CPU reads the data value from that location into the accumulator.

Table 6-5 lists all M68HC05 instructions that can use the indexed/no offset and indexed/8-bit offset addressing modes.

**Indexed/16-Bit Offset** In the indexed/16-bit offset addressing mode, the effective address of the operand for the instruction is the sum of the contents of the 8-bit index register and the two-byte address following the opcode. The content of the index register is not changed. These instructions are three bytes, one for the opcode and two for a 16-bit offset.

**Example Program Listing:**

```
0200 D6 03 77   LDA   $377,X   Load A with Xth item
                                in table at $0377.
```

**Execution Sequence:**

```
$0200   $D6   [1]
$0201   $03   [2]
$0201   $77   [3], [4] and [5]
```

**Explanation:**

[1]   CPU reads opcode $D6 — load accumulator using indexed/16-bit offset addressing mode.

[2]   CPU reads high-order half of 16-bit base address ($03) from address $0201.

[3]   CPU reads low-order half of 16-bit base address ($77) from address $0202.

[4]   CPU builds a complete address by adding the contents of the 8-bit index register (X) to the 16-bit base address just read.

[5]   This address is placed on the address bus, and the CPU reads the data value from that location into the accumulator.

Table 6-6 lists all M68HC05 instructions that can use the indexed/16-bit offset addressing mode.

**Table 6-6.**
INDEXED (16-Bit Offset) Addressing Mode Instructions

| Instruction | Mnemonic |
|---|---|
| Add with Carry | ADC |
| Add (without carry) | ADD |
| Logical AND | AND |
| Bit Test Memory with Accumulator | BIT |
| Compare Accumulator with Memory | CMP |
| Compare Index Register with Memory | CPX |
| Exclusive OR Memory with Accumulator | EOR |
| Jump | JMP |
| Jump to Subroutine | JSR |
| Load Accumulator from Memory | LDA |
| Load Index Register from Memory | LDX |
| Inclusive OR | ORA |
| Subtract with Carry | SBC |
| Store Accumulator in Memory | STA |
| Store Index Register in Memory | STX |
| Subtract (without borrow) | SUB |

# RELATIVE Addressing Mode

The *relative* addressing mode is used only for branch instructions. Branch instructions, other than the branching versions of bit-manipulation instructions, generate two machine-code bytes: one for the opcode and one for the relative offset. Because it is desirable to branch in either direction, the offset byte is a signed twos-complement offset with a range of −128 to +127 bytes (with respect to the address of the instruction immediately following the branch instruction). If the branch condition is true, the content of the 8-bit signed byte following the opcode (offset) is added to the contents of the program counter to form the effective branch address. Otherwise, control continues to the instruction immediately following the branch instruction.

A programmer specifies the destination of a branch as an absolute address (or label that refers to an absolute address). The assembler calculates the 8-bit signed relative offset, which is placed, after the branch opcode, in memory.

**Example Program Listing:**

```
0200 27 rr     BEQ  DEST   Branch to DEST if Z=1
                           (if equal or zero)
```

**Execution Sequence:**

```
$0200   $27   [1]
$0201   $rr   [2] and [3]
```

**Explanation:**

[1]  CPU reads opcode $27 — branch if Z=1. The Z condition code bit will be 1 if the result of the previous arithmetic or logical operation was zero.

[2]  CPU reads the offset value $rr from $0201. After this cycle, the program counter is pointing at the first byte of the next instruction ($0202).

[3]  If the Z bit is zero, nothing happens in this cycle and the program will just continue to the next instruction at $0202. If the Z bit is one, the CPU will add the signed offset $rr to the present value in the program counter to get the address of the branch destination. This causes program execution to continue from the new address (DEST).

Table 6-7 lists all M68HC05 instructions that can use the relative addressing mode.

**Table 6-7.**
RELATIVE Addressing Mode Instructions

| Instruction | Mnemonic |
|---|---|
| Branch if Carry Clear | BCC |
| Branch if Carry Set | BCS |
| Branch if Equal | BEQ |
| Branch if Half-Carry Clear | BHCC |
| Branch if Half-Carry Set | BHCS |
| Branch if Higher | BHI |
| Branch if Higher or Same | BHS |
| Branch if Interrupt Line is High | BIH |
| Branch if Interrupt Line is Low | BIL |
| Branch if Lower | BLO |
| Branch if Lower or Same | BLS |
| Branch if Interrupt Mask is Clear | BMC |
| Branch if Minus | BMI |
| Branch if Interrupt Mask is Set | BMS |
| Branch if Not Equal | BNE |
| Branch if Plus | BPL |
| Branch Always | BRA |
| Branch if Bit n is Clear | BRCLR |
| Branch if Bit n is Set | BRSET |
| Branch Never | BRN |
| Branch to Subroutine | BSR |

## Bit Test and Branch Instructions

These instructions use the direct addressing mode to specify the location being tested, and relative addressing to specify the branch destination. This textbook treats these instructions as direct addressing mode instructions. Some older Motorola documents call the addressing mode of these instructions BTB for "bit test and branch".

# Instructions Organized by Type

Tables 6-8 through 6-11 show a summary of the M68HC05 instruction set grouped by type of instruction.

*M68HC05 Instruction Set*

## Register/Memory Instructions

**Table 6-8.** Register/Memory Instructions

| Function | Mne | Immediate Machine Code | ~ | Direct Machine Code | ~ | Extended Machine Code | ~ | Indexed (no offset) Machine Code | ~ | Indexed (8-bit offset) Machine Code | ~ | Indexed (16-bit offset) Machine Code | ~ |
|---|---|---|---|---|---|---|---|---|---|---|---|---|---|
| Load A from Memory | LDA | A6 ii | 2 | B6 dd | 3 | C6 hh ll | 4 | F6 | 3 | E6 ff | 4 | D6 ee ff | 5 |
| Load X from Memory | LDX | AE ii | 2 | BE dd | 3 | CE hh ll | 4 | FE | 3 | EE ff | 4 | DE ee ff | 5 |
| Store A in Memory | STA | -- | - | B7 dd | 4 | C7 hh ll | 5 | F7 | 4 | E7 ff | 5 | D7 ee ff | 6 |
| Store X in Memory | STX | -- | - | BF dd | 4 | CF hh ll | 5 | FF | 4 | EF ff | 5 | DF ee ff | 6 |
| Add Memory to A | ADD | AB ii | 2 | BB dd | 3 | CB hh ll | 4 | FB | 3 | EB ff | 4 | DB ee ff | 5 |
| Add Memory and Carry to A | ADC | A9 ii | 2 | B9 dd | 3 | C9 hh ll | 4 | F9 | 3 | E9 ff | 4 | D9 ee ff | 5 |
| Subtract Memory from A | SUB | A0 ii | 2 | B0 dd | 3 | C0 hh ll | 4 | F0 | 3 | E0 ff | 4 | D0 ee ff | 5 |
| Subtract Memory from A with Borrow | SBC | A2 ii | 2 | B2 dd | 3 | C2 hh ll | 4 | F2 | 3 | E2 ff | 4 | D2 ee ff | 5 |
| AND Memory with A | AND | A4 ii | 2 | B4 dd | 3 | C4 hh ll | 4 | F4 | 3 | E4 ff | 4 | D4 ee ff | 5 |
| OR Memory with A | ORA | AA ii | 2 | BA dd | 3 | CA hh ll | 4 | FA | 3 | EA ff | 4 | DA ee ff | 5 |
| Exclusive OR Memory with A | EOR | A8 ii | 2 | B8 dd | 3 | C8 hh ll | 4 | F8 | 3 | E8 ff | 4 | D8 ee ff | 5 |
| Arithmetic Compare A with Memory | CMP | A1 ii | 2 | B1 dd | 3 | C1 hh ll | 4 | F1 | 3 | E1 ff | 4 | D1 ee ff | 5 |
| Arithmetic Compare X with Memory | CPX | A3 ii | 2 | B3 dd | 3 | C3 hh ll | 4 | F3 | 3 | E3 ff | 4 | D3 ee ff | 5 |
| Bit Test Memory with A (logical compare) | BIT | A5 ii | 2 | B5 dd | 3 | C5 hh ll | 4 | F5 | 3 | E5 ff | 4 | D5 ee ff | 5 |
| Jump Unconditional | JMP | -- | - | BC dd | 2 | CC hh ll | 3 | FC | 2 | EC ff | 3 | DC ee ff | 4 |
| Jump to Subroutine | JSR | -- | - | BD dd | 5 | CD hh ll | 6 | FD | 5 | ED ff | 6 | DD ee ff | 7 |

~ — Indicates execution time in cycles

*M68HC05 Instruction Set*

**6-23**

## Read-Modify-Write Instructions

**Table 6-9.**
Read-Modify-Write Instructions

| Function | Mne | Inherent (A) Machine Code | ~ | Inherent (B) Machine Code | ~ | Direct Machine Code | ~ | Indexed (no offset) Machine Code | ~ | Indexed (8-bit offset) Machine Code | ~ |
|---|---|---|---|---|---|---|---|---|---|---|---|
| Increment | INC | 4C | 3 | 5C | 3 | 3C dd | 5 | 7C | 5 | 6C ff | 6 |
| Decrement | DEC | 4A | 3 | 5A | 3 | 3A dd | 5 | 7A | 5 | 6A ff | 6 |
| Clear | CLR | 4F | 3 | 5F | 3 | 3F dd | 5 | 7F | 5 | 6F ff | 6 |
| Complement (invert all bits) | COM | 43 | 3 | 53 | 3 | 33 dd | 5 | 73 | 5 | 63 ff | 6 |
| Negate (2s complement) | NEG | 40 | 3 | 50 | 3 | 30 dd | 5 | 70 | 5 | 60 ff | 6 |
| Rotate Left thru Carry | ROL | 49 | 3 | 59 | 3 | 39 dd | 5 | 79 | 5 | 69 ff | 6 |
| Rotate Right thru Carry | ROR | 46 | 3 | 56 | 3 | 36 dd | 5 | 76 | 5 | 66 ff | 6 |
| Logical Shift Left | LSL | 48 | 3 | 58 | 3 | 38 dd | 5 | 78 | 5 | 68 ff | 6 |
| Logical Shift Right | LSR | 44 | 3 | 54 | 3 | 34 dd | 5 | 74 | 5 | 64 ff | 6 |
| Arithmetic Shift Right | ASR | 47 | 3 | 57 | 3 | 37 dd | 5 | 77 | 5 | 67 ff | 6 |
| Test for Negative or Zero | TST | 4D | 3 | 5D | 3 | 3D dd | 4 | 7D | 4 | 6D ff | 5 |
| Unsigned Multiply | MUL | 42 | 11 | - | - | - | - | - | - | - | - |

~ — Indicates execution time in cycles

*M68HC05 Instruction Set*

**Table 6-10.**
Branch Instructions

| Function | Mnemonic | Relative Addressing Mode Machine Code | ~ |
|---|---|---|---|
| Branch Always | BRA | 20 rr | 3 |
| Branch Never | BRN | 21 rr | 3 |
| Branch if Equal | BEQ | 27 rr | 3 |
| Branch if Not Equal | BNE | 26 rr | 3 |
| Branch if Plus | BPL | 2A rr | 3 |
| Branch if Minus | BMI | 2B rr | 3 |
| Branch if Carry Clear | BCC | 24 rr | 3 |
| Branch if Carry Set | BCS | 25 rr | 3 |
| Branch if Half-Carry Clear | BHCC | 28 rr | 3 |
| Branch if Half-Carry Set | BHCS | 29 rr | 3 |
| Branch if Higher | BHI | 22 rr | 3 |
| Branch if Higher or Same (same as BCC) | BHS | 24 rr | 3 |
| Branch if Lower (same as BCS) | BLO | 25 rr | 3 |
| Branch if Lower or Same | BLS | 23 rr | 3 |
| Branch if Interrupt Line is Low | BIL | 2E rr | 3 |
| Branch if Interrupt Line is High | BIH | 2F rr | 3 |
| Branch if Interrupt Mask is Clear | BMC | 2C rr | 3 |
| Branch if Interrupt Mask is Set | BMS | 2D rr | 3 |
| Branch if Bit n is Clear | BRCLR | 0x dd rr | 5 |
| Branch if Bit n is Set | BRSET | 0x dd rr | 5 |
| Branch to Subroutine | BSR | AD rr | 3 |

~ — Indicates execution time in cycles

**Table 6-11.**
Control Instructions

| Function | Mnemonic | Inherent Addressing Mode | |
|---|---|---|---|
| | | Machine Code | ~ |
| Clear Carry Bit | CLC | 98 | 2 |
| Set Carry Bit | SEC | 99 | 2 |
| Clear Interrupt Mask Bit | CLI | 9A | 2 |
| Set Interrupt Mask Bit | SEI | 9B | 2 |
| No Operation | NOP | 9D | 2 |
| Reset Stack Pointer | RSP | 9C | 2 |
| Return from Interrupt | RTI | 80 | 9 |
| Return from Subroutine | RTS | 81 | 6 |
| Stop Oscillator | STOP | 8E | 2 |
| Software Interrupt | SWI | 83 | 10 |
| Transfer A to X | TAX | 97 | 2 |
| Transfer X to A | TXA | 9F | 2 |
| Wait for Interrupt | WAIT | 8F | 2 |

~ — Indicates execution time in cycles

*M68HC05 Instruction Set*

# Instruction Set Summary

Computers use operation codes (opcodes) to give instructions to the CPU. The instruction set for a specific CPU is the set of all operations that the CPU knows how to perform. The CPU in the MC68HC705K1 MCU can understand 62 basic instructions, some of which have several variations that require separate opcodes. The M68HC05 instruction set is represented by 210 unique instruction opcodes.

The following table is an alphabetical listing of all M68HC05 instructions [The symbols are used in the instruction set summary (Table 6-12)]:

## Condition Code Symblols

| | | | |
|---|---|---|---|
| H — | Half Carry (Bit 4) | 0 — | Cleared |
| I — | Interrupt Mask (Bit 3) | 1 — | Set |
| N — | Negative (Bit 2) | Δ — | Test and Set if True, |
| Z — | Zero (Bit 1) | | (cleared otherwise) |
| C — | Carry/Borrow (Bit 0) | - — | Not Affected |

## Boolean Expression Symbols

| | | | |
|---|---|---|---|
| • — | Logical AND | A — | Accumulator |
| + — | Logical OR | X — | Index Register |
| ⊕ — | Exclusive OR | M — | Memory Location |
| ̄ — | Not (invert) | CCR — | Condition Codes |
| − — | Negate or Subtract | PC — | Program Counter |
| + — | Arithmetic Add | PCL — | PC (Low Byte) |
| × — | Multiply | PCH — | PC (High Byte) |
| ← — | is loaded with, "gets" | SP — | Stack Pointer |
| ( ) — | Contents of... | REL — | Relative Offset |

| Address Mode | Abbreviation | Operands | |
|---|---|---|---|
| Inherent | INH | *none* | |
| Immediate | IMM | ii | |
| Direct | DIR | dd | |
| (for bit tests) | | dd | rr |
| Extended | EXT | hh | ll |
| Indexed (no offset) | IX | *none* | |
| Indexed (8-bit offset) | IX1 | ff | |
| Indexed (16-bit offset) | IX2 | ee | ff |
| Relative | REL | rr | |

Table 6-12. Instruction Set Summary (Sheet 1 of 9)

| Source Form(s) | Operation | Description | Addr. Mode | Machine Coding Opcode | Machine Coding Operand(s) | Cyc. | H | I | N | Z | C |
|---|---|---|---|---|---|---|---|---|---|---|---|
| ADC #opr | Add with Carry | A ← (A) + (M) + C | IMM | A9 | ii | 2 | △ | - | △ | △ | △ |
| ADC opr | | | DIR | B9 | dd | 3 | | | | | |
| ADC opr | | | EXT | C9 | hh ll | 4 | | | | | |
| ADC opr,X | | | IX2 | D9 | ee ff | 5 | | | | | |
| ADC opr,X | | | IX1 | E9 | ff | 4 | | | | | |
| ADC ,X | | | IX | F9 | | 3 | | | | | |
| ADD #opr | Add without Carry | A ← (A) + (M) | IMM | AB | ii | 2 | △ | - | △ | △ | △ |
| ADD opr | | | DIR | BB | dd | 3 | | | | | |
| ADD opr | | | EXT | CB | hh ll | 4 | | | | | |
| ADD opr,X | | | IX2 | DB | ee ff | 5 | | | | | |
| ADD opr,X | | | IX1 | EB | ff | 4 | | | | | |
| ADD ,X | | | IX | FB | | 3 | | | | | |
| AND #opr | Logical AND | A ← (A) • (M) | IMM | A4 | ii | 2 | - | - | △ | △ | - |
| AND opr | | | DIR | B4 | dd | 3 | | | | | |
| AND opr | | | EXT | C4 | hh ll | 4 | | | | | |
| AND opr,X | | | IX2 | D4 | ee ff | 5 | | | | | |
| AND opr,X | | | IX1 | E4 | ff | 4 | | | | | |
| AND ,X | | | IX | F4 | | 3 | | | | | |
| ASL opr | Arithmetic Shift Left | C ← b7 ... b0 ← 0 | DIR | 38 | dd | 5 | - | - | △ | △ | △ |
| ASLA | | | INH | 48 | | 3 | | | | | |
| ASLX | | | INH | 58 | | 3 | | | | | |
| ASL opr,X | | | IX1 | 68 | ff | 6 | | | | | |
| ASL ,X | | | IX | 78 | | 5 | | | | | |
| ASR opr | Arithmetic Shift Right | b7 ... b0 → C | DIR | 37 | dd | 5 | - | - | △ | △ | △ |
| ASRA | | | INH | 47 | | 3 | | | | | |
| ASRX | | | INH | 57 | | 3 | | | | | |
| ASR opr,X | | | IX1 | 67 | ff | 6 | | | | | |
| ASR ,X | | | IX | 77 | | 5 | | | | | |

*M68HC05 Instruction Set*

**Table 6-12.** Instruction Set Summary (Sheet 2 of 9)

| Source Form(s) | Operation | Description | Addr. Mode | Machine Coding Opcode | Machine Coding Operand(s) | Cyc. | H | I | N | Z | C |
|---|---|---|---|---|---|---|---|---|---|---|---|
| BCC rel | Branch if Carry Clear | ? C = 0 | REL | 24 | rr | 3 | - | - | - | - | - |
| BCLR n, opr | Clear Bit n in Memory | Mn ← 0 | DIR b0 | 11 | dd | 5 | | | | | |
| | | | DIR b1 | 13 | dd | 5 | | | | | |
| | | | DIR b2 | 15 | dd | 5 | | | | | |
| | | | DIR b3 | 17 | dd | 5 | | | | | |
| | | | DIR b4 | 19 | dd | 5 | | | | | |
| | | | DIR b5 | 1B | dd | 5 | | | | | |
| | | | DIR b6 | 1D | dd | 5 | | | | | |
| | | | DIR b7 | 1F | dd | 5 | | | | | |
| BCS rel | Branch if Carry Set | ? C = 1 | REL | 25 | rr | 3 | - | - | - | - | - |
| BEQ rel | Branch if Equal | ? Z = 1 | REL | 27 | rr | 3 | - | - | - | - | - |
| BHCC rel | Branch if Half Carry Clear | ? H = 0 | REL | 28 | rr | 3 | - | - | - | - | - |
| BHCS rel | Branch if Half Carry Set | ? H = 1 | REL | 29 | rr | 3 | - | - | - | - | - |
| BHI rel | Branch if Higher | ? C + Z = 0 | REL | 22 | rr | 3 | - | - | - | - | - |
| BHS rel | Branch if Higher or Same | ? C = 0 | REL | 24 | rr | 3 | - | - | - | - | - |
| BIH rel | Branch if $\overline{IRQ}$ Pin is High | ? $\overline{IRQ}$ Pin High | REL | 2F | rr | 3 | - | - | - | - | - |
| BIL rel | Branch if $\overline{IRQ}$ Pin is Low | ? $\overline{IRQ}$ Pin Low | REL | 2E | rr | 3 | - | - | - | - | - |
| BIT #opr | Bit Test A with Memory | (A) • (M) | IMM | A5 | ii | 2 | - | - | Δ | Δ | - |
| BIT opr | | | DIR | B5 | dd | 3 | | | | | |
| BIT opr | | | EXT | C5 | hh ll | 4 | | | | | |
| BIT opr,X | | | IX2 | D5 | ee ff | 5 | | | | | |
| BIT opr,X | | | IX1 | E5 | ff | 4 | | | | | |
| BIT ,X | | | IX | F5 | | 3 | | | | | |
| BLO rel | Branch if Lower | ? C = 1 | REL | 25 | rr | 3 | - | - | - | - | - |
| BLS rel | Branch if Lower or Same | ? C + Z = 1 | REL | 23 | rr | 3 | - | - | - | - | - |
| BMC rel | Branch if I Mask Clear | ? I = 0 | REL | 2C | rr | 3 | - | - | - | - | - |
| BMI rel | Branch if Minus | ? N = 1 | REL | 2B | rr | 3 | - | - | - | - | - |

*M68HC05 Instruction Set*

**Table 6-12.** Instruction Set Summary (Sheet 3 of 9)

| Source Form(s) | Operation | Description | Addr. Mode | Machine Coding Opcode | Machine Coding Operand(s) | Cyc. | H | I | N | Z | C |
|---|---|---|---|---|---|---|---|---|---|---|---|
| BMS *rel* | Branch if I Mask Set | ? I = 0 | REL | 2D | rr | 3 | - | - | - | - | - |
| BNE *rel* | Branch if Not Equal | ? Z = 0 | REL | 26 | rr | 3 | - | - | - | - | - |
| BPL *rel* | Branch if Plus | ? N = 0 | REL | 2A | rr | 3 | - | - | - | - | - |
| BRA *rel* | Branch Always | ? 1 = 1 (always true) | REL | 20 | rr | 3 | - | - | - | - | - |
| BRCLR *n, opr, rel* | Branch if Bit n of M=0 | ? Bit n of M = 0 | DIR b0 | 01 | dd rr | 5 | - | - | - | - | Δ |
| | | | DIR b1 | 03 | dd rr | 5 | | | | | |
| | | | DIR b2 | 05 | dd rr | 5 | | | | | |
| | | | DIR b3 | 07 | dd rr | 5 | | | | | |
| | | | DIR b4 | 09 | dd rr | 5 | | | | | |
| | | | DIR b5 | 0B | dd rr | 5 | | | | | |
| | | | DIR b6 | 0D | dd rr | 5 | | | | | |
| | | | DIR b7 | 0F | dd rr | 5 | | | | | |
| BRN *rel* | Branch Never | ? 1 = 0 (never true) | REL | 21 | rr | 3 | - | - | - | - | - |
| BRSET *n, opr, rel* | Branch if Bit n of M=1 | ? Bit n of M = 1 | DIR b0 | 00 | dd rr | 5 | - | - | - | - | Δ |
| | | | DIR b1 | 02 | dd rr | 5 | | | | | |
| | | | DIR b2 | 04 | dd rr | 5 | | | | | |
| | | | DIR b3 | 06 | dd rr | 5 | | | | | |
| | | | DIR b4 | 08 | dd rr | 5 | | | | | |
| | | | DIR b5 | 0A | dd rr | 5 | | | | | |
| | | | DIR b6 | 0C | dd rr | 5 | | | | | |
| | | | DIR b7 | 0E | dd rr | 5 | | | | | |

**Table 6-12.** Instruction Set Summary (Sheet 4 of 9)

| Source Form(s) | Operation | Description | Addr. Mode | Machine Coding Opcode | Operand(s) | Cyc. | H | I | N | Z | C |
|---|---|---|---|---|---|---|---|---|---|---|---|
| BSET n, opr | Set Bit n in Memory | Mn ← 1 | DIR b0 | 10 | dd | 5 | – | – | – | – | – |
| | | | DIR b1 | 12 | dd | 5 | | | | | |
| | | | DIR b2 | 14 | dd | 5 | | | | | |
| | | | DIR b3 | 16 | dd | 5 | | | | | |
| | | | DIR b4 | 18 | dd | 5 | | | | | |
| | | | DIR b5 | 1A | dd | 5 | | | | | |
| | | | DIR b6 | 1C | dd | 5 | | | | | |
| | | | DIR b7 | 1E | dd | 5 | | | | | |
| BSR rel | Branch to Subroutine | PC←(PC)+2 push (PCL); SP=SP–1 push (PCH); SP=SP–1 PC←(PC)+REL | REL | AD | rr | 6 | – | – | – | – | – |
| CLC | Clear Carry Bit | C ← 0 | INH | 98 | | 2 | – | – | – | – | 0 |
| CLI | Clear Interrupt Mask Bit | I ← 0 | INH | 9A | | 2 | – | 0 | – | – | – |
| CLR opr | Clear | M ← 00 | DIR | 3F | dd | 5 | – | – | 0 | 1 | – |
| CLRA | | A ← 00 | INH | 4F | | 3 | | | | | |
| CLRX | | X ← 00 | INH | 5F | | 3 | | | | | |
| CLR opr,X | | M ← 00 | IX1 | 6F | ff | 6 | | | | | |
| CLR ,X | | M ← 00 | IX | 7F | | 5 | | | | | |
| CMP #opr | Compare A with Memory | (A) – (M) | IMM | A1 | ii | 2 | – | – | Δ | Δ | Δ |
| CMP opr | | | DIR | B1 | dd | 3 | | | | | |
| CMP opr | | | EXT | C1 | hh ll | 4 | | | | | |
| CMP opr,X | | | IX2 | D1 | ee ff | 5 | | | | | |
| CMP opr,X | | | IX1 | E1 | ff | 4 | | | | | |
| CMP ,X | | | IX | F1 | | 3 | | | | | |

**Table 6-12.** Instruction Set Summary (Sheet 5 of 9)

| Source Form(s) | Operation | Description | Addr. Mode | Machine Coding Opcode | Machine Coding Operand(s) | Cyc. | H | I | N | Z | C |
|---|---|---|---|---|---|---|---|---|---|---|---|
| COM *opr* | 1's Complement (invert all bits) | M ← $\overline{M}$ = $FF – (M) | DIR | 33 | dd | 5 | – | – | △ | △ | 1 |
| COMA | | A ← $\overline{A}$ | INH | 43 | | 3 | | | | | |
| COMX | | X ← $\overline{X}$ | INH | 53 | | 3 | | | | | |
| COM *opr*,X | | M ← $\overline{M}$ | IX1 | 63 | ff | 6 | | | | | |
| COM ,X | | M ← $\overline{M}$ | IX | 73 | | 5 | | | | | |
| CPX #*opr* | Compare X with Memory | (X) – (M) | IMM | A3 | ii | 2 | – | – | △ | △ | △ |
| CPX *opr* | | | DIR | B3 | dd | 3 | | | | | |
| CPX *opr* | | | EXT | C3 | hh ll | 4 | | | | | |
| CPX *opr*,X | | | IX2 | D3 | ee ff | 5 | | | | | |
| CPX *opr*,X | | | IX1 | E3 | ff | 4 | | | | | |
| CPX ,X | | | IX | F3 | | 3 | | | | | |
| DEC *opr* | Decrement | M ← (M) – 1 | DIR | 3A | dd | 5 | – | – | △ | △ | – |
| DECA | | A ← (A) – 1 | INH | 4A | | 3 | | | | | |
| DECX | | X ← (X) – 1 | INH | 5A | | 3 | | | | | |
| DEC *opr*,X | | M ← (M) – 1 | IX1 | 6A | ff | 6 | | | | | |
| DEC ,X | DEX (same as DECX) | M ← (M) – 1 | IX | 7A | | 5 | | | | | |
| EOR #*opr* | Exclusive OR A with Memory | A ← (A) ⊕ (M) | IMM | A8 | ii | 2 | – | – | △ | △ | – |
| EOR *opr* | | | DIR | B8 | dd | 3 | | | | | |
| EOR *opr* | | | EXT | C8 | hh ll | 4 | | | | | |
| EOR *opr*,X | | | IX2 | D8 | ee ff | 5 | | | | | |
| EOR *opr*,X | | | IX1 | E8 | ff | 4 | | | | | |
| EOR ,X | | | IX | F8 | | 3 | | | | | |
| INC *opr* | Increment | M ← (M) + 1 | DIR | 3C | dd | 5 | – | – | △ | △ | – |
| INCA | | A ← (A) + 1 | INH | 4C | | 3 | | | | | |
| INCX | | X ← (X) + 1 | INH | 5C | | 3 | | | | | |
| INC *opr*,X | INX (same as INCX) | M ← (M) + 1 | IX1 | 6C | ff | 6 | | | | | |
| INC ,X | | M ← (M) + 1 | IX | 7C | | 5 | | | | | |

*M68HC05 Instruction Set*

**Table 6-12.** Instruction Set Summary (Sheet 6 of 9)

| Source Form(s) | Operation | Description | Addr. Mode | Opcode | Operand(s) | Cyc. | H | I | N | Z | C |
|---|---|---|---|---|---|---|---|---|---|---|---|
| JMP opr | Jump | PC←Effective Address | DIR | BC | dd | 2 | – | – | – | – | – |
| JMP opr | | | EXT | CC | hh ll | 3 | | | | | |
| JMP opr,X | | | IX2 | DC | ee ff | 4 | | | | | |
| JMP opr,X | | | IX1 | EC | ff | 3 | | | | | |
| JMP ,X | | | IX | FC | | 2 | | | | | |
| JSR opr | Jump to Subroutine | PC←PC+n (n=1, 2, or 3) push (PCL); SP←SP–1 push (PCH); SP←SP–1 PC←Effective Address | DIR | BD | dd | 5 | – | – | – | – | – |
| JSR opr | | | EXT | CD | hh ll | 6 | | | | | |
| JSR opr,X | | | IX2 | DD | ee ff | 7 | | | | | |
| JSR opr,X | | | IX1 | ED | ff | 6 | | | | | |
| JSR ,X | | | IX | FD | | 5 | | | | | |
| LDA #opr | Load Accumulator | A ← (M) | IMM | A6 | ii | 2 | – | – | Δ | Δ | – |
| LDA opr | | | DIR | B6 | dd | 3 | | | | | |
| LDA opr | | | EXT | C6 | hh ll | 4 | | | | | |
| LDA opr,X | | | IX2 | D6 | ee ff | 5 | | | | | |
| LDA opr,X | | | IX1 | E6 | ff | 4 | | | | | |
| LDA ,X | | | IX | F6 | | 3 | | | | | |
| LDX #opr | Load Index Register | X ← (M) | IMM | AE | ii | 2 | – | – | Δ | Δ | – |
| LDX opr | | | DIR | BE | dd | 3 | | | | | |
| LDX opr | | | EXT | CE | hh ll | 4 | | | | | |
| LDX opr,X | | | IX2 | DE | ee ff | 5 | | | | | |
| LDX opr,X | | | IX1 | EE | ff | 4 | | | | | |
| LDX ,X | | | IX | FE | | 3 | | | | | |
| LSL opr | Logical Shift Left | C ← [b7 ... b0] ← 0 | DIR | 38 | dd | 5 | – | – | Δ | Δ | Δ |
| LSLA | | | INH | 48 | | 3 | | | | | |
| LSLX | | | INH | 58 | | 3 | | | | | |
| LSL opr,X | | | IX1 | 68 | ff | 6 | | | | | |
| LSL ,X | | | IX | 78 | | 5 | | | | | |

*M68HC05 Instruction Set*

**6-33**

**Table 6-12.** Instruction Set Summary (Sheet 7 of 9)

| Source Form(s) | Operation | Description | Addr. Mode | Opcode | Operand(s) | Cyc. | H | I | N | Z | C |
|---|---|---|---|---|---|---|---|---|---|---|---|
| | | | | **Machine Coding** | | | **Cond. Codes** | | | | |
| LSR opr | Logical Shift Right | $0 \rightarrow \boxed{\quad\quad} \rightarrow C$  b7  b0 | DIR | 34 | dd | 5 | - | - | 0 | △ | △ |
| LSRA | | | INH | 44 | | 3 | | | | | |
| LSRX | | | INH | 54 | | 3 | | | | | |
| LSR opr,X | | | IX1 | 64 | ff | 6 | | | | | |
| LSR ,X | | | IX | 74 | | 5 | | | | | |
| MUL | Unsigned Multiply | X:A ← (X) × (A) | INH | 42 | | 11 | 0 | - | - | - | 0 |
| NEG opr | Negate (twos complement) | M ← -(M) = $00 - (M) | DIR | 30 | dd | 5 | - | - | △ | △ | △ |
| NEGA | | A ← -(A) | INH | 40 | | 3 | | | | | |
| NEGX | | X ← -(X) | INH | 50 | | 3 | | | | | |
| NEG opr,X | | M ← -(M) | IX1 | 60 | ff | 6 | | | | | |
| NEG ,X | | M ← -(M) | IX | 70 | | 5 | | | | | |
| NOP | No Operation | | INH | 9D | | 2 | - | - | - | - | - |
| ORA #opr | Inclusive OR A with Memory | A ← (A) + (M) | IMM | AA | ii | 2 | - | - | △ | △ | - |
| ORA opr | | | DIR | BA | dd | 3 | | | | | |
| ORA opr | | | EXT | CA | hh ll | 4 | | | | | |
| ORA opr,X | | | IX2 | DA | ee ff | 5 | | | | | |
| ORA opr,X | | | IX1 | EA | ff | 4 | | | | | |
| ORA ,X | | | IX | FA | | 3 | | | | | |
| ROL opr | Rotate Left through Carry | $\boxed{C} \leftarrow \boxed{\quad\quad} \leftarrow$  b7  b0 | DIR | 39 | dd | 5 | - | - | △ | △ | △ |
| ROLA | | | INH | 49 | | 3 | | | | | |
| ROLX | | | INH | 59 | | 3 | | | | | |
| ROL opr,X | | | IX1 | 69 | ff | 6 | | | | | |
| ROL ,X | | | IX | 79 | | 5 | | | | | |
| ROR opr | Rotate Right through Carry | $\rightarrow \boxed{\quad\quad} \rightarrow \boxed{C}$  b7  b0 | DIR | 36 | dd | 5 | - | - | △ | △ | △ |
| RORA | | | INH | 46 | | 3 | | | | | |
| RORX | | | INH | 56 | | 3 | | | | | |
| ROR opr,X | | | IX1 | 66 | ff | 6 | | | | | |
| ROR ,X | | | IX | 76 | | 5 | | | | | |

*M68HC05 Instruction Set*

**Table 6-12.** Instruction Set Summary (Sheet 8 of 9)

| Source Form(s) | Operation | Description | Addr. Mode | Machine Coding Opcode | Operand(s) | Cyc. | H | I | N | Z | C |
|---|---|---|---|---|---|---|---|---|---|---|---|
| RSP | Reset Stack Pointer | SP ← $00FF | INH | 9C | | 2 | – | – | – | – | – |
| RTI | Return from Interrupt | SP=SP+1; pull (CCR)<br>SP=SP+1; pull (A)<br>SP=SP+1; pull (X)<br>SP=SP+1; pull (PCH)<br>SP=SP+1; pull (PCL) | INH | 80 | | 9 | ∆ | (from stack)<br>∆ | ∆ | ∆ | ∆ |
| RTS | Return from Subroutine | SP=SP+1; pull (PCH)<br>SP=SP+1; pull (PCL) | INH | 81 | | 6 | – | – | – | – | – |
| SBC #opr<br>SBC opr<br>SBC opr<br>SBC opr,X<br>SBC opr,X<br>SBC ,X | Subtract with Carry | A ← (A) – (M) – C | IMM<br>DIR<br>EXT<br>IX2<br>IX1<br>IX | A2<br>B2<br>C2<br>D2<br>E2<br>F2 | ii<br>dd<br>hh ll<br>ee ff<br>ff | 2<br>3<br>4<br>5<br>4<br>3 | – | – | ∆ | ∆ | ∆ |
| SEC | Set Carry Bit | C ← 1 | INH | 99 | | 2 | – | – | – | – | 1 |
| SEI | Set Interrupt Mask Bit | I ← 1 | INH | 9B | | 2 | – | 1 | – | – | – |
| STA opr<br>STA opr<br>STA opr,X<br>STA opr,X<br>STA ,X | Store A to Memory | M ← (A) | DIR<br>EXT<br>IX2<br>IX1<br>IX | B7<br>C7<br>D7<br>E7<br>F7 | dd<br>hh ll<br>ee ff<br>ff | 4<br>5<br>6<br>5<br>4 | – | – | ∆ | ∆ | – |
| STOP | Enable IRQ; Stop Oscillator | | INH | 8E | | 2 | – | 0 | – | – | – |
| STX opr<br>STX opr<br>STX opr,X<br>STX opr,X<br>STX ,X | Store X to Memory | M ← (X) | DIR<br>EXT<br>IX2<br>IX1<br>IX | BF<br>CF<br>DF<br>EF<br>FF | dd<br>hh ll<br>ee ff<br>ff | 4<br>5<br>6<br>5<br>4 | – | – | ∆ | ∆ | – |

*M68HC05 Instruction Set*

Table 6-12. Instruction Set Summary (Sheet 9 of 9)

| Source Form(s) | Operation | Description | Addr. Mode | Opcode | Operand(s) | Cyc. | H | I | N | Z | C |
|---|---|---|---|---|---|---|---|---|---|---|---|
| SUB #opr | Subtract without Carry | A ← (A) – (M) | IMM | A0 | ii | 2 | - | - | Δ | Δ | Δ |
| SUB opr | | | DIR | B0 | dd | 3 | | | | | |
| SUB opr | | | EXT | C0 | hh ll | 4 | | | | | |
| SUB opr,X | | | IX2 | D0 | ee ff | 5 | | | | | |
| SUB opr,X | | | IX1 | E0 | ff | 4 | | | | | |
| SUB ,X | | | IX | F0 | | 3 | | | | | |
| SWI | Software Interrupt | PC←PC+1; push PCL; SP=SP–1; push PCH; SP=SP–1; push X; SP=SP–1; push A; SP=SP–1; push CCR; SP=SP–1; I Bit ← 1; PCH←($xxFC) (vector); PCL←($xxFD) fetch) | INH | 83 | | 10 | - | 1 | - | - | - |
| TAX | Transfer A to X | X ← (A) | INH | 97 | | 2 | - | - | - | - | - |
| TST opr | Test for Negative or Zero | (M) – 0 | DIR | 3D | dd | 4 | - | - | Δ | Δ | - |
| TSTA | | | INH | 4D | | 3 | | | | | |
| TSTX | | | INH | 5D | | 3 | | | | | |
| TST opr,X | | | IX1 | 6D | ff | 5 | | | | | |
| TST ,X | | | IX | 7D | | 4 | | | | | |
| TXA | Transfer X to A | A ← (X) | INH | 9F | | 2 | - | - | - | - | - |
| WAIT | Wait for Interrupt | | INH | 8F | | 2 | - | 0 | - | - | - |

*M68HC05 Instruction Set*

## CPU Registers

The five CPU registers in the M68HC05 are not locations in the memory map. The *programming model* for the CPU shows the five CPU registers.

- The *accumulator* (A) is an 8-bit general purpose register.
- The *index register* (X) is an 8-bit pointer register.
- The *stack pointer* (SP) is a pointer register that is automatically decremented as data is pushed onto the stack and incremented as data is pulled off the stack.
- The *program counter* (PC) has as many bits as there are address lines. The program counter always points at the next instruction or piece of data the CPU will use.
- The *condition codes register* (CCR) contains the four arithmetic result flags, H, N, Z, and C, and the interrupt mask (disable) control bit I.

## Addressing Modes

The M68HC05 CPU has six *addressing modes* that determine how the CPU will get the operand(s) needed to complete each instruction. The M68HC05 CPU has 62 *mnemonic* instructions. There are 210 instruction *opcodes*, because each different addressing mode variation of an instruction must have a unique opcode.

- In *immediate* addressing mode, the operand for the instruction is the byte immediately after the opcode.
- In *inherent* addressing mode, the CPU needs no operands from memory. The operands, if any, are the registers or stacked data values.
- In *extended* addressing mode, the 16-bit address of the operand is located in the next two memory bytes after the instruction opcode.

- In *direct* addressing mode, the low-order eight bits of the address of the operand are located in the next byte of memory after the opcode; the high-order byte of the address is assumed to be $00. This mode is more efficient than the extended addressing mode, because the high-order address byte is not explicitly included in the program.
- In **indexed** addressing modes, the current value of the index register is added to a zero-, one-, or two-byte offset in the next zero, one, or two memory locations after the opcode, to form a pointer to the address of the operand in memory.
- *Relative* addressing mode is used for conditional branch instructions. The byte after the opcode is a signed offset value between −128 and +127. If the condition of the branch is true, the offset is added to the program counter value to get the address where the CPU will fetch the next program instruction.

## Instruction Execution

Each *opcode* tells the CPU the operation to be performed and the addressing mode to be used to address any *operands* needed to complete the instruction. The cycle-by-cycle explanations of example instructions under each addressing mode provide a view of the tiny simple steps that make up an instruction.

*M68HC05 Instruction Set*

# 7

# Programming

This chapter discusses how to plan and write computer programs. We will learn how to prepare flowcharts and write assembly language programs. A text editor or word processor is used to write computer programs. Next, a programming tool, called an assembler, is used to translate the program into a form the computer can use. Programming tools are computer programs for personal computers that help in the development of microcontroller computer programs. We will discuss assemblers, simulators, and a few other useful development tools.

# Writing a Simple Program

At this point, we will write a short program in mnemonic form and translate it into machine code. The first step will be to plan the program and document this plan with a flowchart. Next we will write instruction mnemonics for each block in the flowchart. Finally, we will use an assembler to translate our example program into the codes the computer needs to execute the program.

Our program will read the state of a switch connected to an input pin. When the switch is closed, the program will cause an LED connected to an output pin to light for about one second and then go out. The LED will not light again until the switch has been released and closed again. The length of time the switch is held closed will not affect the length of time the LED is lighted.

Although this program is very simple, it demonstrates the most common elements of any MCU application program. First, it demonstrates how a program can sense input signals such as switch closures. Second, this is an example of a program controlling an output signal. Third, the LED on-time of about one second demonstrates one way a program can be used to measure real time. Because the algorithm is somewhat complicated, it cannot be accomplished in a trivial manner with discrete components (at minimum, a one-shot IC with external timing components would be required). This example demonstrates that an MCU and a user-defined program (software) can replace complex circuits.

## Flowchart

Figure 7-1 is a *flowchart* of the example program. Flowcharts are often used as a planning tool for writing software programs because they show the function and flow of the program under development. The importance of notes, comments, and documentation for software cannot be overemphasized. **Just as you would not consider a circuit-board design complete until there is a schematic diagram, parts list, and assembly drawing, you should not consider a program complete until there is a commented listing and a comprehensive explanation of the program, such as a flowchart.**

FLOWCHART

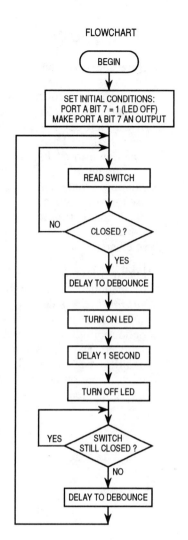

**Figure 7-1.**
Example Flowchart

# Mnemonic Source Code

Once the flowchart or plan is completed, the programmer develops a series of *assembly language* instructions to accomplish the function(s) called for in each block of the plan. The programmer is limited to selecting instructions from the instruction set for the CPU being used (in this case the M68HC05). The programmer writes instructions in a mnemonic form that is easy to understand. Figure 7-2 shows the mnemonic *source code* next to the flowchart of our example program so you can see which CPU instructions are used to accomplish each block of the flowchart. The meanings of the instruction mnemonics used in the right side of Figure 7-2 can be found in Appendix A or in Table 6-12 near the end of Chapter 6.

During development of the program instructions, it was noticed that a time delay was needed in three places. A *subroutine* was developed that generates a 50-ms delay. This subroutine is used directly in two places (for switch debouncing) and makes the one-second delay easier to produce. To keep this figure simple, the comments that would usually be included within the source program for documentation are omitted. The comments will be shown in the completed program in Listing 7-1.

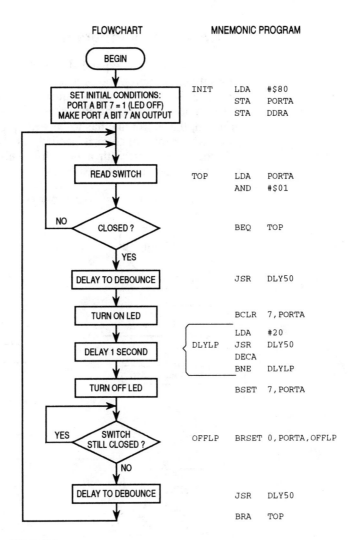

**Figure 7-2.**
Flowchart and Mnemonics

## Software Delay Program

Figure 7-3 shows an expanded flowchart of the 50-ms delay subroutine. A subroutine is a relatively small program that performs some commonly required function. Even if the function needs to be performed many times in the course of a program, the subroutine has to be written only once. At each place where this function is needed, the programmer would call the subroutine with a branch-to-subroutine (BSR) or jump-to-subroutine (JSR) instruction.

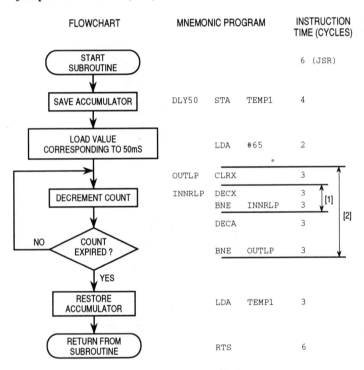

[1] - INNRLP is executed 256 times per pass through outer loop.

[2] - OUTLP is executed 65 times.

**Figure 7-3.**
Delay Routine Flowchart and Mnemonics

Before starting to execute the instructions in the subroutine, the address of the instruction that follows the JSR (or BSR) is automatically stored on the stack in temporary RAM-memory locations. When the CPU finishes executing the instructions

*Programming*

within the subroutine, a return-from-subroutine (RTS) instruction is performed as the last instruction in the subroutine. The RTS instruction causes the CPU to recover the previously saved return address. Thus, the CPU continues the program with the instruction following the JSR (or BSR) instruction that originally called the subroutine.

The delay routine of Figure 7-3 involves an inner loop (INNRLP) within another loop (OUTLP). The inner loop consists of two instructions executed 256 times before X reaches $00 and the BNE branch condition fails. This amounts to six cycles at 500 ns per cycle times 256, which equals 0.768 ms for the inner loop. The outer loop executes 65 times. The total execution time for the outer loop is 65(1,536+9) or 65(1,545)=100,425 cycles or 50.212 ms. The miscellaneous instructions in this routine other than those in the outer loop total 21 cycles. Thus, the total time required to execute the DLY50 routine is 50.223 ms, including the time required for the JSR instruction that calls DLY50.

The on-chip timer system in the MC68HC705K1 can also be used to measure time. The timer-based approach is preferred because the CPU can perform other tasks during the delay, and the delay time is not dependent on the exact number of instructions executed as it is in DLY50.

## Assembler Listing

After a complete program or subprogram is written, it must be converted from mnemonics into binary machine code that the CPU can later execute. A separate computer system, such as an IBM PC®, is used to perform this conversion to machine language. A computer program for the personal computer, called an assembler, is used. The assembler reads the mnemonic version of the program (also called the source version of the program) and produces a machine-code version in a form that can be programmed into the memory of the MCU.

The assembler also produces a composite listing showing both the original source program (mnemonics) and the object code translation. This listing is used during the debug phase of a project and as part of the documentation for the software program. Listing 7-1 shows the listing that results from

assembling the example program. Comments were added
before the program was assembled.

**Listing 7-1.**
Assembler Listing

```
         ***********************************************************
                   * Simple 68HC05 Program Example                        *
                   * Read state of switch at port A bit-0; 1=closed       *
                   * When sw. closes, light LED for about 1 sec; LED on    *
                   * when port A bit-7 = 0. Wait for sw release,          *
                   * then repeat. Debounce sw 50mS on & off               *
                   * NOTE: Timing based on instruction execution times    *
                   *   If using a simulator or crystal less than 4MHz,     *
                   *   this routine will run slower than intended          *
                   ***********************************************************
                            $BASE   10T             ;Tell assembler to use decimal
                                                    ;unless $ or % before value
0000                        PORTA   EQU     $00     ;Direct address of port A
0004                        DDRA    EQU     $04     ;Data direction control, port A
00E0                        TEMP1   EQU     $E0     ;One byte temp storage location

0200                                ORG     $0200   ;Program will start at $0200

0200  A6 80         INIT    LDA     #$80    ;Begin initialization
0202  B7 00                 STA     PORTA   ;So LED will be off
0204  B7 04                 STA     DDRA    ;Set port A bit-7 as output
                   * Rest of port A is configured as inputs

0206  B6 00         TOP     LDA     PORTA   ;Read sw at LSB of Port A
0208  A4 01                 AND     #$01    ;To test bit-0
020A  27 FA                 BEQ     TOP     ;Loop till Bit-0 = 1
020C  CD 02 23              JSR     DLY50   ;Delay about 50 mS to debounce
020F  1F 00                 BCLR    7,PORTA ;Turn on LED (bit-7 to zero)
0211  A6 14                 LDA     #20     ;Decimal 20 assembles to $14
0213  CD 02 23      DLYLP   JSR     DLY50   ;Delay 50 mS
0216  4A                    DECA            ;Loop counter for 20 loops
0217  26 FA                 BNE     DLYLP   ;20 times (20-19,19-18,...1-0)
0219  1E 00                 BSET    7,PORTA ;Turn LED back off
021B  00 00 FD      OFFLP   BRSET   0,PORTA,OFFLP  ;Loop here till sw off
021E  CD 02 23              JSR     DLY50   ;Debounce release
0221  20 E3                 BRA     TOP     ;Look for next sw closure

              ***
              * DLY50 - Subroutine to delay ~50mS
              * Save original accumulator value
              * but X will always be zero on return
              ***

0223  B7 E0         DLY50   STA     TEMP1   ;Save accumulator in RAM
0225  A6 41                 LDA     #65     ;Do outer loop 32 times
0227  5F            OUTLP   CLRX            ;X used as inner loop count
0228  5A            INNRLP  DECX            ;0-FF, FF-FE,...1-0 256 loops
0229  26 FD                 BNE     INNRLP  ;6cyc*256*500ns/cyc = 0.768ms
022B  4A                    DECA            ;65-64, 64-63,...1-0
022C  26 F9                 BNE     OUTLP   ;1545cyc*65*500ns/cyc=50.212ms
022E  B6 E0                 LDA     TEMP1   ;Recover saved Accumulator val
0230  81                    RTS             ;Return
```

Refer to Figure 7-4 for the following discussion. This figure shows some lines of the listing with reference numbers indicating the various parts of the line. The first line is an example of an assembler directive line. This line is not really part of the program. Rather, it provides information to the assembler so that the real program can be converted properly into binary machine code.

```
0000                PORTA   EQU     $00        ;Direct address of port A

0200                        ORG     $0200      ;Program will start at $0200

0206   B6 00        TOP     LDA     PORTA      ;Read sw at LSB of Port A
----   ---------    -------  ----    --------  -------------------------------
[1]      [2]          [3]    [4]      [5]       [6]->
```

**Figure 7-4.**
Explanation of Assembler Listing

EQU, short for equate, is used to give a specific memory location or binary number a name that can then be used in other program instructions. In this case, the EQU directive is used to assign the name PORTA to the value $00, which is the address of the port A register in the MC68HC705K1. It is easier for a programmer to remember the mnemonic name, PORTA, rather than the anonymous numeric value $00. When the assembler encounters one of these names, it is automatically replaced by its corresponding binary value, in much the same way that instruction mnemonics are replaced by binary instruction codes.

The second line shown in Figure 7-4 is another assembler directive. The mnemonic ORG, which is short for originate, tells the assembler where the program will start (the address of the start of the first instruction following the ORG directive line). More than one ORG directive may be used in a program to tell the assembler to put different parts of the program in specific places in memory. Refer to the memory map of the MCU to select an appropriate memory location where a program should start.

In this assembler listing, the first two fields, [1] and [2], are generated by the assembler. The last four fields, [3], [4], [5], and [6], are from the original source program written by the programmer. Field [3] is a label (TOP), which can be referred to in other instructions. In our example program, the last instruction was "BRA TOP", which simply means the CPU will continue execution with the instruction that is labeled "TOP".

When the programmer is writing a program, the addresses where instructions will be located are not typically known. Worse yet, in branch instructions, rather than using the address of a destination, the CPU uses an offset (difference) between the current PC value and the destination address. Fortunately, the programmer does not have to worry about these problems because the assembler takes care of these details through a system of labels. This system of labels is a convenient way for the programmer to identify specific points in the program (without knowing their exact addresses). The assembler can later convert these mnemonic labels into specific memory addresses and even calculate offsets for branch instructions so that the CPU can use them.

Field [4] is the instruction field. The LDA mnemonic is short for load accumulator. Since there are six variations (different opcodes) of the load accumulator instruction, additional information is required before the assembler can choose the correct binary opcode for the CPU to use during execution of the program. Field [5] is the operand field, providing information about the specific memory location or value to be operated on by the instruction. The assembler uses both the instruction mnemonic and the operand specified in the source program to determine the specific opcode for the instruction.

The different ways of specifying the value to be operated on are called addressing modes (a more complete discussion of addressing modes was presented in Chapter 6). The syntax of the operand field is slightly different for each addressing mode in order that the assembler can determine the correct intended addressing mode from the syntax of the operand. In this case, the operand [5] is PORTA, which the assembler automatically converts to $00 (recall the EQU directive). The assembler interprets $00 as a direct addressing mode address between $0000 and $00FF, thus selecting the opcode $B6, which is the direct addressing mode variation of the LDA instruction. If PORTA had been preceded by a # symbol, that syntax would have been interpreted by the assembler as an immediate addressing mode value, and the opcode $A6 would have been chosen instead of $B6.

Field [6] is called the comment field and is not used by the assembler to translate the program into machine code. Rather, the comment field is used by the programmer to document the program. Although the CPU does not use this information during program execution, a good programmer knows that it is one of the most important parts of a good program. The comment [6] for this line of the program says ";Read sw at LSB of port A." This comment tells someone who is reading the listing why port A is being read, **which is essential for understanding how the program works**. The semicolon indicates that the rest of the line should be treated as a comment (not all assemblers require this semicolon). An entire line can be made into a comment line by using an asterisk (*) as the first character in the line. In addition to good comments in the listing, it is also important to document programs with a flowchart or other detailed information, explaining the overall flow and operation of the program.

## Object Code File

We learned in chapter 5 that the computer expects the program to be a series of 8-bit values in memory. So far, our program still looks as if it was written for people. The version the computer needs to load into its memory is called an *object code file*. For Motorola microcontrollers, the most common form of object code file is the *S-record* file. The assembler can be directed to optionally produce a listing file and/or an object code file.

An S-record file is an ASCII text file that can be viewed by a text editor or word processor. You should not try to edit these files because their structure and content are critical to their proper operation. Each line of an S-record file is a *record*. Each record begins with a capitol letter S followed by a code number from 0 to 9. The only code numbers that are important to us are S0, S1, and S9. S0 is an optional header record that may contain the name of the file for the benefit of humans that need to maintain these files. S1 records are the main data records. An S9 record marks the end of the S-record file. For the work we are doing with 8-bit microcontrollers, the information in the S9 record is not important, but an S9 record is required at the end of our S-record files. Figure 7-5 shows the syntax of an S1 record.

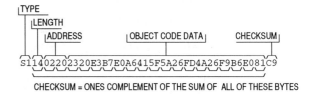

CHECKSUM = ONES COMPLEMENT OF THE SUM OF ALL OF THESE BYTES

**Figure 7-5.**
Syntax of an S1 Record

All of the numbers in an S-record file are in hexadecimal. The type field is S0, S1, or S9 for the S-record files we will use. The length field is the number of pairs of hexadecimal digits in the record, excluding the type and length fields. The address field is the 16-bit address where the first data byte will be stored in memory. Each pair of hexadecimal digits in the machine code data field represents an 8-bit data value to be stored in successive locations in memory. The *checksum* field is an 8-bit value that represents the ones complement of the sum of all bytes in the S-record, except the type and checksum fields. This checksum is used during loading of the S-record file to verify that the data is complete and correct for each record.

Figure 7-6 is the S-record file that results from assembling the example program of Listing 7-1. The two bytes of machine code data that are bold are the same two bytes that were highlighted in Figure 5-2 and the text that follows Figure 5-2. These bytes were located by looking in the listing and finding that the address where this instruction started was $0223. In the S-record file, we found the S1 record with the address $0220. Moving to the right we found the data $23 for address $0220, $20 for address $0221, $E3 for address $0222, and finally the bytes we wanted for address $0223 and $0224.

```
S1230200A680B700B704B600A40127FACD02231F00A614CD02234A26FA1E000000FDCD02B5
S11402202320E3B7E0A6415F5A26FD4A26F9B6E081C9
S9030000FC
```

**Figure 7-6.**
S-Record File for Example Program

# Assembler Directives

In this section we will discuss six of the most important assembler directives. Assemblers from different vendors differ in the number and kind of assembler directives supported. You should always refer to the documentation for the assembler you are using.

## Originate (ORG)

This directive is used to set the location counter for the assembler. The location counter keeps track of the address where the next byte of machine code will be stored in memory. In our example program, there was an ORG directive to set the start of our program to $0200.

As the assembler translates program statements into machine code instructions and data, the location counter is advanced to point at the next available memory location.

Every program has at least one ORG directive to establish the starting place in memory for the program. Most complete programs will also have a second ORG directive near the end of the program to set the location counter to the address where the reset and interrupt vectors are located ($03F8 to $03FF in the MC68HC705K1). **The reset vector must always be specified. It is good practice to also specify interrupt vectors, even if you do not expect to use interrupts.**

## Equate (EQU)

This directive is used to associate a binary value with a label. The value may be either an 8-bit value or a 16-bit address value. This directive does not generate any object code.

During the assembly process, the assembler must keep a cross-reference list where it stores the binary equivalent of each label. When a label appears in the source program, the assembler looks in this cross reference table to find the binary equivalent. Each EQU directive generates an entry in this cross-reference table.

An assembler reads the source program twice. On the first pass, the assembler just counts bytes of object code and internally builds the cross-reference table. On the second pass, the assembler generates the listing file and/or the S-record object file. This two-pass arrangement allows the programmer to reference labels that are defined later in the program.

EQU directives should appear near the beginning of a program, before their labels are used by other program statements. If the assembler encounters a label before it is defined, it has no choice but to assume the worst case of a 16-bit address value. This would cause the extended addressing mode to be used in places where the more efficient direct addressing mode could have been used. In other cases, the indexed 16-bit offset addressing mode may be used where a more efficient indexed (no offset or 8-bit offset) instruction could have been used.

In the example program, there were two EQU directives to equate the labels PORTA and DDRA to their direct page addresses. Another use for EQU directives is to identify a bit position with a label like this.

```
LED     EQU     %10000000   ;LED is connected to bit-7
  "       "        "          "
  "       "        "          "
INIT    LDA     #LED        ;There's a 1 in LED bit position
        STA     PORTA       ;So LED will be off
        STA     DDRA        ;So LED pin is an output
```

The % symbol indicates the value that follows is expressed in binary. If we moved the LED to a different pin during development, we would need to change only the EQU statement and reassemble the program.

## Form Constant Byte (FCB)

The arguments for this directive are labels or numbers, separated by commas, that can be converted into single bytes of data. Each byte specified in an FCB directive generates a byte of machine code in the object code file. FCB directives define constants in a program.

## Form Double Byte (FDB)

The arguments for this directive are labels or numbers, separated by commas, that can be converted into 16-bit data values. Each argument specified in an FDB directive generates two bytes of machine code in the object code file.

The following lines from an assembly listing demonstrate ORG directives and FDB directives.

```
 "       "   "       "         "         "         "
 "       "   "       "         "         "         "
0200                 ORG       $0200     ;Beginning of EPROM in 705K1

0200  B6  00  START   LDA      PORTA     ;Read sw at LSB of port A
 "       "   "       "         "         "         "
 "       "   "       "         "         "         "
031F  80      UNUSED  RTI                ;Return from unexpected int
 "       "   "       "         "         "         "
 "       "   "       "         "         "         "
03F8                 ORG       $03F8     ;Start of vector area

03F8  03  1F  TIMVEC  FDB      UNUSED    ;An unused vector
03FA  03  1F  IRQVEC  FDB      $031F     ;Argument can be a hex value
03FC  03  1F  SWIVEC  FDB      UNUSED    ;An unused vector
03FE  02  00  RESETV  FDB      START     ;Go to START on reset
```

## Reserve Memory Byte (RMB)

This directive sets aside space in RAM for program variables. The RMB directive does not generate any object code, but it normally generates an entry in the assembler's internal cross-reference table.

In the example program (Listing 7-1), the RAM variable TEMP1 was assigned with an EQU directive. Another way to assign this variable would have been like this:

```
 "       "   "       "         "         "         "
00E0                 ORG       $00E0     ;Beginning of RAM in 705K1

00E0          TEMP1   RMB      1         ;One byte temp storage location
 "       "   "       "         "         "
```

This is the preferred way to assign RAM storage, because it is common to add and delete variables in the course of developing a program. If you use EQU directives, you might have to change several statements after removing a single variable. With RMB directives, the assembler assigns addresses as they are needed.

## Set Default Number Base to Decimal

Some assemblers, such as the P & E Microcomputer Systems IASM assembler, assume that any value that is not specifically marked otherwise should be interpreted as a hexadecimal value. The idea is to simplify entry of numeric information by eliminating the need for a $ symbol before each value. If you want the assembler to assume that unmarked values are decimal numbers, use the $BASE directive:

```
"      "  "     "        "         "           "
....          $BASE   10T                ;Set default # base to decimal
000A          TEN     EQU   #10          ;Decimal 10 not $10=16
"      "  "     "        "         "           "
```

This directive is slightly different from the others described in this chapter. The $BASE directive starts in the leftmost column of the source program and is included near the start of each example program in this textbook. If you are using an assembler that does not require this directive, you can delete it or add an asterisk (*) at the start of the line to "comment the line out." When you comment a line out of the program, you change the whole line into a comment. Comments do not affect assembly of a program.

# Instruction Set Dexterity

As in most engineering fields, there is more than one sequence of instructions that can perform any task. A good way to learn a new instruction set is to see how many different ways you can solve some small programming problem. I call this "instruction set dexterity".

Figure 7-7 shows four different ways to check for closure of a switch connected to port A bit-0. Two of these ways were used in the example program of Listing 7-1. Although all of the sequences accomplish the same basic task, there are subtle differences. Usually, these differences are not significant, but sometimes they can save execution time or program memory space. In a small microcontroller, memory space can be an important consideration.

```
0000                    PORTA   EQU     $00         ;Direct address of port A

0200                            ORG     $0200       ;Program will start at $0200

0200  B6 00     [ 3]  TOP1      LDA     PORTA       ;Read sw at LSB of Port A
0202  A4 01     [ 2]            AND     #$01        ;To test bit-0
0204  27 FA     [ 3]            BEQ     TOP1        ;Loop till Bit-0 = 1

0206  01 00 FD  [ 5]  TOP2      BRCLR   0,PORTA,TOP2  ;Loop here till sw ON

0209  B6 00     [ 3]  TOP3      LDA     PORTA       ;Read sw at LSB of Port A
020B  44        [ 3]            LSRA                ;Bit-0 shifts to carry
020C  24 FB     [ 3]            BCC     TOP3        ;Loop till switch ON

020E  A6 01     [ 2]            LDA     #$01        ;1 in LSB
0210  B5 00     [ 3]  TOP4      BIT     PORTA       ;To test sw at bit-0
0212  27 FC     [ 3]            BEQ     TOP4        ;Loop till switch ON
```

**Figure 7-7.**
Four Ways to Check a Switch

The numbers in brackets are the number of CPU cycles required for the instruction on that line of the program. The TOP1 sequence takes six bytes of program space and eight cycles. The accumulator is $01 when the program falls through the BEQ statement. The TOP2 sequence takes only three bytes and five cycles, and the accumulator is not disturbed. (This is probably the best sequence in most cases.) The TOP3 sequence takes one less byte than the TOP1 sequence but also takes 1 extra cycle to execute. After the TOP3 sequence, the accumulator still holds the other 7 bits from the port A read, although they have been shifted one position to the right. The last sequence takes 6 bytes and a total of 8 cycles, but the loop itself is only 6 cycles. By working through exercises like this, you will improve your instruction set dexterity. This will be very helpful when you need to reduce a program by a few bytes to fit it into the available memory space.

# Application Development

A very small development system for the MC68HC705K1 is offered by Motorola (M68HC705KICS). This system includes an in-circuit simulator (software and hardware circuit board). The circuit board plugs into a parallel I/O port on a personal computer. A connector and cable allow the in-circuit simulator to be plugged into an application system to take the place of the microcontroller that will eventually be used. A socket is also provided that allows an EPROM or OTP version of the MC68HC705K1 to be programmed from the personal computer.

A *simulator* is a program for a personal computer that helps during program development and debugging. This tool simulates the actions of a real microcontroller, but has some important advantages. In a simulator, you have complete control over when and if the simulated CPU should advance to the next instruction. You can also look at and change registers or memory locations before going to the next instruction.

Simulators do not run at real-time speed. Since the personal computer is *simulating* MCU actions with software programs, each MCU instruction takes much longer to execute than it would in a real MCU. For many MCU programs, this speed reduction is not noticeable. As slow as a simulator can be, it is still very fast in human terms. Some MCU programs generate time delays with software loops (like the DLY50 routine in Listing 7-1). The 50 millisecond delay of DLY50 might take tens of seconds on some personal computers. To make the simulation run faster, you can temporarily replace the loop count value (65) with a much smaller number (say 2). Remember to put the original number back before programming the finished program into the EPROM of a real MCU.

An *in-circuit simulator* is a simulator that can be connected to a user system in place of the microcontroller. An ordinary simulator normally only takes input information from the personal computer and displays outputs and results on the personal computer display. An in-circuit simulator goes beyond this to emulate the input and output interfaces of the real microcontroller.

Program development is easier with a simulator than with a real MCU. It is easier to make program changes and try them out in the simulator than to program an EPROM device and try it out. With the real MCU, you can see only the input and output pins. You cannot easily stop a program between instructions. With the simulator, you can execute a single instruction at a time and look at registers and memory contents at every step. This makes it easier to see which instructions failed to perform as intended. A simulator can also inform you if the program attempts to use the value of a variable before it has been initialized.

An *in-circuit emulator* is a real-time development tool. The emulator is built around an actual MCU so it can execute program instructions exactly as they will be executed in the finished application. An emulator has RAM memory where the ROM or EPROM memory will be located in the final MCU. This allows you to quickly load programs into the emulator and to change these programs during development.

Extra circuitry in the emulator allows you to set *breakpoints* in the program under development. When the program reaches one of these breakpoint addresses, the program under development is temporarily stopped and a development *monitor program* takes control. This monitor program allows you to look at or change CPU registers, memory locations, or control registers. An emulator typically has less visibility of internal MCU actions than a simulator, but it can run at full real-time speed. An emulator cannot normally stop clocks to internal peripheral systems like a timer, when control switches from the application program to the monitor program. A simulator can stop such clocks.

# Chapter 7 Review

The process of writing a program begins with a plan. A flowchart can be used to document the plan. Mnemonic source-code statements are then written for each block of the flowchart. Mnemonic source-code statements can include any of the instructions from the instruction set of the microcontroller. The next step is to combine all of the program instructions with assembler directives to get a text source file.

Assembler directives are program statements that give instructions to the assembler rather than to the CPU of the microcontroller. These instructions tell the assembler things like where to locate instructions in the memory of the microcontroller. Assembler directives can also inform the assembler of the binary meaning of a mnemonic label. Six directives were discussed:

ORG — Originate directives set the starting address for the object code that follows.

EQU — Equate directives associate a label with a binary number or address.

FCB — Form constant byte directives introduce 8-bit constant data values into a program.

FDB — Form double byte directives introduce 16-bit data or address constants into a program.

RMB — Reserve memory byte(s) directives assign labels (belonging to program variables) to RAM addresses.

$BASE 10T — Change default number base to decimal.

After the complete source program is written, it is processed by an assembler to produce a listing file and an S-record object file. The listing file is part of the documentation of the program. The S-record object file can be loaded into the simulator or it can be programmed into a microcontroller.

A conditional loop can produce a timed delay. The delay is dependent on the execution time of the instructions in the loop. A subroutine such as this delay routine can be used many times in a program by calling it with JSR or BSR instructions.

Instruction set dexterity is the ability to solve a programming problem in several different ways with different sequences of instructions. Since each sequence takes a different number of program bytes and a different number of CPU cycles to execute, you can select a sequence that is best for each situation.

A simulator is an application development tool that runs on a personal computer and simulates the behavior of a microcontroller (though not at real-time speed). An in-circuit simulator takes this idea further to also simulate the I/O interfaces of the microcontroller. The in-circuit simulator can be plugged into an application circuit in place of the microcontroller. A simulator makes application development easier. It allows instructions to be executed one at a time. It also provides visibility into the contents of registers and memory and allows changes before executing a new instruction.

An emulator is built around a real MCU so it can run at the full speed of the final MCU. Emulators use RAM instead of ROM or EPROM, so the program under development can be modified easily during development.

# The Paced Loop

This chapter presents a general-purpose software structure that may be used as a framework for many microcontroller applications. Major system tasks are written as subroutines. These subroutines are organized into a loop so that each is called once per pass through the loop. At the top of the loop, there is a small routine that paces the loop so it is executed at regular intervals. A software clock is maintained as the first task in the loop. This clock can be an input for the other task subroutines to decide what the routine should do on each pass through the major loop.

In addition to the loop structure itself, this chapter discusses system initialization issues and software setup details, so you can go directly to the routines that deal with your specific applications.

# System Equates

It is inconvenient to use binary bit patterns and addresses in program instructions. Equate (EQU) directives assign mnemonic names to register addresses and bit positions. These names can then be used in program instructions instead of the binary numbers. This makes the program easier to write and to read. When an application program is developed with an in-circuit simulator, the mnemonic names can be used in the debug displays instead of the binary addresses.

## Register Equates for MC68HC705K1

The manufacturer's recommended names for registers and control bits are included in the paced loop program framework of Listing 8-1 (page 8-14). This allows you to write program instructions using names that make sense to people instead of obscure binary numbers and addresses.

Each register is equated to its direct-page binary address with an EQU directive. Each control bit is defined in two ways. First, an EQU directive equates the bit name to a number between 7 and 0, corresponding to the bit number where each bit is located in a control register. Second, most control bits are equated to a binary bit pattern such as 0010 0000 ($20), which can be used as a bit mask to identify the location of the bit in a register. Since you cannot equate the same name to two different binary values, the second equate uses a period after the bit name. To get a bit name's bit number (7 to 0), use the name; to get a mask indicating the bit position, use the name followed by a period. This convention is used in the paced loop framework, but it is not necessarily a standard that is recommended by Motorola or the assembler companies.

In the M68HC05 instruction set, the bit manipulation instructions are of the form...

```
xxxx 14 08        ----- BSET   bit#,dd   ;Set bit in location dd
```

*Bit#* is a number between 7 and 0 that identifies the bit within the register at location *dd* that is to be changed or tested.

In other cases, you may want to build up a mask with several bits set, and then write this composite value to a register location. For example, suppose you want to set RTIFR, RTIE, and RT1 bits in the TCSR register. You could use the following instructions:

```
xxxx A6 16          LDA  #{RTIFR.+RTIE.+RT1.}  ;Form mask
xxxx B7 08          STA  TCSR   ;Write mask to TCSR register
```

The # symbol means immediate addressing mode. The expression (RTIFR.+RTIE.+RT1.) is the Boolean OR of three bit-position masks. The assembler evaluates the Boolean expression during program assembly and substitutes the answer (a single 8-bit binary value) into the assembled program. The following program statements would produce exactly the same results, but they are not as easy to read:

```
xxxx A6 16          LDA  #%00010110 ;Form mask
xxxx B7 08          STA  $08        ;Write mask to TCSR
```

## Application System Equates

There will usually be some application-specific equate directives in a program to define the signals connected to I/O pins. These EQU directives should be placed after the standard MCU equate directives and before the main program starts. The paced loop framework program was developed with a particular small development PC board in mind. This system has a switch connected to port A bit 0 and an LED connected to port A bit 7, so these connections were defined with EQU directives.

The switch is not used in the paced loop framework program of Listing 8-1, but it does no harm to include the related EQU directives. EQU directives do not generate any object code that takes up memory space in the final computer system.

# Vector Setup

**All MCU programs should set up the reset and interrupt vectors!** Vectors specify the address where the CPU will start processing instructions when a reset or interrupt occurs. Reset and each interrupt source expects to find their associated vector in a specific pair of memory locations. For example, the reset vector is at the highest two locations in memory ($03FE and $03FF in the MC68HC705K1). If you do not place values in these locations, the CPU will take whatever binary values it finds there and treat them as if they were a two-byte address you stored there.

## Reset Vector

The usual way to define a vector is with an FDB directive:

```
03FE 02 00    RESETV    FDB    START    ;Beginning of program on reset
```

During assembly, the assembler evaluates the label START into a two-byte address and stores this address in the next two available memory locations of the program. The columns at the left of the listing line show that the address $0200 was stored at $03FE and $03FF ($02 @ $03FE and $00 @ $03FF).

RESETV is an optional label on this program line. Although it is not used for reference by other statements in this particular program, it was included to identify this FDB directive line as the statement that defines the reset vector.

The reset vector was set up to point at the label START. The in-circuit simulator system that Motorola offers as a low-cost development tool uses this information to set up the simulator screen. When a program is loaded into the simulator, the simulator looks for the address in the reset vector of the loaded program. If one is found, the simulator selects that program instruction and displays it in the source program window of the simulator. The simulator's PC is also set to this address. If there is no reset vector, the simulator displays a warning message that says that the reset vector was not initialized. You could still debug the program, but it would not work if it were programmed into an EPROM MCU because the program would not start up at reset.

## Unused Interrupts

For interrupts that are used, the vectors can be defined just as the reset vector was defined (with an FDB directive). In the paced loop framework program, the timer interrupt is used for real time interrupts (RTIs). The external interrupt and the SWI interrupt are not used.

It is a good idea to set up the unused interrupt vectors just in case one of these interrupts is unexpectedly requested. This is

*The Paced Loop*

not to say that unexpected interrupts can occur in a working computer system. Rather, it says that when a programmer is first starting out, programming mistakes could result in unintended interrupt sources being enabled and triggered.

The following listing lines show how interrupt and reset vectors were set up in the paced loop framework program:

```
          ***********************************************************
          * RTIF interrupt service routine
          ***********************************************************
0245 3A E0  RTICNT  DEC    RTIFs      ;On each RTIF
  "   "  "     "      "      "          "
  "   "  "     "      "      "          "
0251 80     AnRTI   RTI               ;Return from RTIF interrupt

0251        UNUSED  EQU    AnRTI      ;Use RTI at AnRTI for unused
                                      ;interrupts to just return


          ***********************************************************
          * Interrupt & reset vectors
          ***********************************************************
03F8                ORG    $03F8      ;Start of vector area

03F8 02 45  TIMVEC  FDB    RTICNT     ;Count RTIFs 3/TIC
03FA 02 51  IRQVEC  FDB    UNUSED     ;Change if vector used
03FC 02 51  SWIVEC  FDB    UNUSED     ;Change if vector used
03FE 02 00  RESETV  FDB    START      ;Beginning of program on reset
```

The first lines in this partial listing show the first and last lines of the timer interrupt service routine. The line…

```
0251 80     AnRTI   RTI               ;Return from RTIF interrupt
```

shows a return from interrupt (RTI) instruction with the label "AnRTI". The next line equates the label "UNUSED" to the address of the RTI instruction at AnRTI. Further down in the listing, the unused interrupt vectors for external interrupts and SWI interrupts are set up to point at this RTI instruction. During assembly, the assembler encounters the label "UNUSED" and finds it should be equal to "AnRTI," which is, in turn, equal to the binary address of the RTI instruction ($0251).

If an SWI interrupt were unexpectedly encountered, the CPU would save the CPU registers on the stack (temporary RAM) and load the program counter with the address $0251 from the SWI vector. The CPU would then load the instruction RTI from address $0251. The RTI instruction would tell the CPU to recover the saved CPU registers (including the program counter) from the stack. The recovered program counter value would determine what the CPU did next.

An alternative way to respond to unexpected interrupts would be to reset the stack pointer (with an RSP instruction) and then jump to the same address as if a reset had occurred. This approach makes the pessimistic assumption that if an unexpected interrupt occurs, there may be other serious problems. By resetting the stack pointer and starting all over, you are more likely to correct whatever caused the unexpected interrupt.

While debugging a program on a simulator, there is another possible way to handle unused interrupts:

```
 "     "    "        "      "      "          "
0251            BADINT  BRA    BADINT    ;Infinite loop to here
 "     "    "        "      "      "          "
 "     "    "        "      "      "          "
03FA  02  51    VECTOR  FDB    BADINT    ;Hang on unexpected int
 "     "    "        "      "      "          "
```

In this scheme, an unexpected interrupt will cause the CPU to vector to BADINT. The instruction at BADINT is an infinite loop back to BADINT, so the system will hang there. You can stop the simulator and check the CPU register values on the stack to see what the program was doing when it got the unexpected interrupt.

# RAM Variables

Program variables change value during the course of executing the program. These values cannot be specified before the program is written and programmed into the MCU. The CPU must use program instructions to initialize and modify these values. When the program is written, space is reserved for variables in the RAM of the MCU, using reserve memory byte(s) (RMB) directives.

First, you would put an originate (ORG) directive to set the assembler's location counter to the address of the start of RAM in the MCU ($00E0 in the MC68HC705K1). Each variable or group of variables would be set up with an RMB directive. The RMB line is identified by the name of the variable. The assembler assigns the name (label) to the next available address. After each new variable or group of variables is assigned, the location counter is advanced to point at the next free memory location.

As the program in Listing 8-1 shows, some programmers feel it is good practice to clear all RAM locations as one of the first initialization steps after any reset. While you are debugging a system, it is useful to have a known set of starting conditions. If the entire RAM is cleared at the start of a program, it is easy to tell if any locations have been written.

# Paced Loop

The paced loop is a general-purpose software structure that is suitable for a wide variety of MCU applications. The main idea is to break the overall application into a series of tasks, such as keeping track of time, reading system inputs, and updating system outputs. Each task is written as a subroutine. A main loop is constructed out of jump to subroutine (JSR) instructions for each task. At the top of the loop, there is a software pacemaker. When the pacemaker triggers, the list of task subroutines is executed once and a branch instruction takes you to the top of the loop to wait for the next pacemaker trigger.

Figure 8-1 shows a flowchart for the main paced loop. The top block is a loop that waits for the pacemaker trigger (every 100 milliseconds). The next few blocks have to do with maintaining the TIC counter. The version of this program in Listing 8-1 has two simple main tasks: TIME and BLINK. You would remove one or both of these routines and substitute your own tasks. The only limitation on the number of main tasks is that they must all finish quickly enough so no pacemaker triggers are lost. The last block in the flowchart is just a branch back to the top of the loop to wait for the next pacemaker trigger.

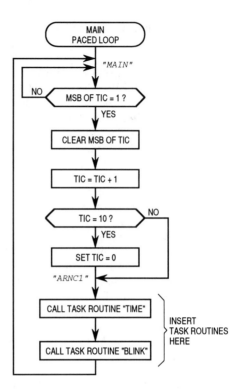

**Figure 8-1.**
Flowchart of Main Paced Loop

## Loop Trigger

In the paced loop program of Listing 8-1, the pacemaker is based on the on-chip real-time interrupt (RTI). This RTI is set to generate an interrupt to the CPU every 32.8 milliseconds. The flowchart in Figure 8-2 shows what happens at each RTI interrupt. This interrupt activity can be thought of as taking place asynchronously with respect to the main program. The most significant bit of the TIC variable is used as a flag to tell the main program when it is time to increment TIC and execute one pass through the paced loop.

*The Paced Loop*

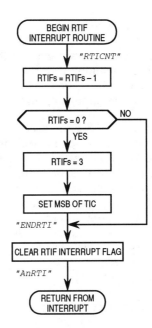

**Figure 8-2.**
Flowchart of RTI Interrupt Service Routine

The RAM variable "RTIFs" is used to count three real time interrupts before setting the MSB of TIC. The main program will be watching TIC to see when the MSB becomes set.

Every 32.8 ms, the RTIF flag will get set, triggering a timer interrupt request. One of the duties of an interrupt service routine is to clear the flag that caused the interrupt before returning from the interrupt. If RTIF is not cleared before the return, a new interrupt request is generated immediately instead of waiting for the 32.8 ms trigger.

## Loop System Clock

The variable "TIC" is the most basic clock for the pacemaker. TIC counts from zero to 10. As TIC is incremented from nine to 10, the program recognizes this and resets TIC to zero. Except within the pacemaker itself, TIC appears to count from zero to nine. TIC is equal to zero on every tenth trigger of the pacemaker.

The first task subroutine in the main loop is called "TIME." This routine maintains a slower clock, called "TOC." TOC is incremented each time the paced loop executes and TIC is zero (i.e., every tenth pass through the paced loop). TOC is set up as a software counter that counts from zero through 59. The remaining task routines after TIME can use the current values of TIC and TOC to decide what needs to be done on this pass through the paced loop.

In Listing 8-1 the pace is keyed to the RTI interrupt, which does not happen to be an integer submultiple of one second. Three RTI periods equal 98.4 milliseconds. This is pretty close to 0.1 second, but not close enough to be used like a wristwatch. You could get accurate real time if you modified the paced loop program to use a different trigger source such as *zero crossings* of the ac line (60Hz). Although the ac line is not as accurate as a crystal over short periods of time, it is very accurate over long periods of time. (Most clocks that plug into the wall use the ac line timing as the basis for keeping time.)

## Your Programs

There are very few restrictions on the task subroutines. Each task subroutine should do everything it needs to do as quickly as it can, and then execute a return from subroutine (RTS). The total time required to execute one pass through all of the task subroutines must be less than two pacemaker triggers (we will explain this in greater detail in a little while). The important point is that a task subroutine should not wait for the occurrence of some external event, like a switch to be pressed. This would defeat the time-keeping aspects of the paced loop.

The paced loop can automatically provide for switch debouncing. Switches are notorious for bouncing between the closed and opened conditions as they are pressed and released. It is not at all unusual for a switch to bounce for 50 milliseconds or more as it is pressed. A microcontroller can execute instructions so fast that a single press of a switch might look like several presses to a program, unless steps are taken to account for switch bounce. There are hardware methods for debouncing switches, but they require extra components and increase the cost of a product.

Software can also be used to debounce a switch. The example program in Figure 7-2 used a simple software delay program to debounce a switch, but this routine should not be used directly in the paced loop structure because it takes too much time. In a paced loop, you can debounce a switch by reading it on consecutive passes through the paced loop. The first time you see the switch pressed, you can write a special value to a variable to indicate that a switch was tentatively pressed (you would not consider this switch as pressed yet). On the next pass through the paced loop, you would either mark the switch as really pressed, or clear the mark to indicate that it was a false detection. Similarly, when the switch is eventually released, you can mark it as tentatively released, and on the next pass mark it as really released.

## Timing Considerations

Ideally, you should finish all of the task subroutines in the paced loop before the next pacemaker trigger arrives. If a single pass through the loop takes longer than the pacemaker trigger period, the flag that indicates it is time to start the next pass through the main loop will already be set when you get back to the top of the loop. Nothing bad happens unless you get so far behind that a new pacemaker trigger comes before the previous one has been recognized. The paced loop remains valid unless any two consecutive passes take more than two pacemaker trigger periods.

A little bit of planning can assure that no two consecutive passes through the loop take longer than two pacemaker periods. Especially long task subroutines can be scheduled to execute during a particular paced loop pass when very little other activity is scheduled. A simple check of one of the time variables, such as TIC or TOC, can be used to decide whether or not to perform a particularly slow routine. If there were several things that needed to be done once per second, one could be scheduled for the TIC=0 pass, another could be scheduled for the TIC=2 pass, and so on.

## Stack Considerations

Small microcontrollers like the MC68HC705K1 have only small amounts of RAM for the stack and program variables. Interrupts take five bytes of stack RAM and each subroutine call takes two bytes on the stack. If a subroutine called another subroutine, and an interrupt was requested before the second subroutine was finished, the stack would use 2+2+5=9 RAM bytes of the available 32. If the stack gets too deep, there is a danger that RAM variables could get overwritten with stack data. To avoid these problems, you should calculate the worst-case depth to which your stack can ever get. The sum of all system variables plus the worst-case stack depth must be less than or equal to the 32 available RAM locations in the MC68HC705K1.

Fortunately, an interrupt causes the interrupt mask (I) bit in the condition code register to be set in response to any interrupt. This blocks additional interrupts until the I bit is cleared (normally upon return from the interrupt).

# An Application-Ready Framework

The paced loop program of Listing 8-1 can be used as the basis for your own applications. This framework provides the following main parts:

- Equate statements for all MC68HC705K1 register and bit names
- Application-specific equate statements
- Program variables section
- Initialization section (START)
- Pacemaker for main loop based on RTI interrupts
- Calls to task subroutines
- Two simple examples of task subroutines (TIME and BLINK)
- An interrupt service routine (for RTIF interrupts)
- Vector definition section.

The pacemaker in this particular paced loop program triggers a pass through the main loop about once every 100 milliseconds (actually 98.4 ms). This can easily be changed to some other number of real time interrupts, and the RTI rate can be changed. For applications that need real time, the pacemaker can be modified to work from interrupts generated at zero crossings of the ac power line.

Additional RMB directives should be added to the program variables section. Additional EQU statements can be added just above the program variables section, to add application-specific equates.

In its present form, the paced loop has only two simple task subroutines: TIME and BLINK. The TIME task just maintains a zero to 59 count (TOC), which could be useful for measuring or generating longer time periods. The BLINK task is just a dummy routine to demonstrate how a task can use the time variable TOC to control a system action. In this case, the action is to turn on an LED when TOC is even, and turn it off when TOC is odd. To use the framework program for your own application, you should remove the BLINK task and replace it with your own tasks.

The RTI interrupt service routine serves as an example of an interrupt handler, and counts real-time interrupts to set the pacemaker rate.

**Listing 8-1.**
Paced Loop Framework Program  (sheet 1 of 6)

```
                $BASE     10T                      ;Set decimal as default # base
                ********************************************************
                * Equates for MC68HC705K1 MCU
                * Use bit names without a dot in BSET..BRCLR
                * Use bit name followed by a dot in expressions such as
                *   #ELAT.+EPGM. to form a bit mask
                ********************************************************
0000            PORTA     EQU     $00              ;I/O port A
0007            PA7       EQU     7                ;Bit #7 of port A
0006            PA6       EQU     6                ;Bit #6 of port A
0005            PA5       EQU     5                ;Bit #5 of port A
0004            PA4       EQU     4                ;Bit #4 of port A
0003            PA3       EQU     3                ;Bit #3 of port A
0002            PA2       EQU     2                ;Bit #2 of port A
0001            PA1       EQU     1                ;Bit #1 of port A
0000            PA0       EQU     0                ;Bit #0 of port A
0080            PA7.      EQU     $80              ;Bit position PA7
0040            PA6.      EQU     $40              ;Bit position PA6
0020            PA5.      EQU     $20              ;Bit position PA5
0010            PA4.      EQU     $10              ;Bit position PA4
0008            PA3.      EQU     $08              ;Bit position PA3
0004            PA2.      EQU     $04              ;Bit position PA2
0002            PA1.      EQU     $02              ;Bit position PA1
0001            PA0.      EQU     $01              ;Bit position PA0

0001            PORTB     EQU     $01              ;I/O port B
0007            PB7       EQU     7                ;Bit #7 of port B
0006            PB6       EQU     6                ;Bit #6 of port B
0080            PB7.      EQU     $80              ;Bit position PB7
0040            PB6.      EQU     $40              ;Bit position PB6

0004            DDRA      EQU     $04              ;Data direction for port A
0007            DDRA7     EQU     7                ;Bit #7 of port A DDR
0006            DDRA6     EQU     6                ;Bit #6 of port A DDR
0005            DDRA5     EQU     5                ;Bit #5 of port A DDR
0004            DDRA4     EQU     4                ;Bit #4 of port A DDR
0003            DDRA3     EQU     3                ;Bit #3 of port A DDR
0002            DDRA2     EQU     2                ;Bit #2 of port A DDR
0001            DDRA1     EQU     1                ;Bit #1 of port A DDR
0000            DDRA0     EQU     0                ;Bit #0 of port A DDR
0080            DDRA7.    EQU     $80              ;Bit position DDRA7
0040            DDRA6.    EQU     $40              ;Bit position DDRA6
0020            DDRA5.    EQU     $20              ;Bit position DDRA5
0010            DDRA4.    EQU     $10              ;Bit position DDRA4
0008            DDRA3.    EQU     $08              ;Bit position DDRA3
0004            DDRA2.    EQU     $04              ;Bit position DDRA2
0002            DDRA1.    EQU     $02              ;Bit position DDRA1
0001            DDRA0.    EQU     $01              ;Bit position DDRA0

0005            DDRB      EQU     $05              ;Data direction for port B
0007            DDRB7     EQU     7                ;Bit #7 of port B DDR
0006            DDRB6     EQU     6                ;Bit #6 of port B DDR
0080            DDRB7.    EQU     $80              ;Bit position DDRB7
0040            DDRB6.    EQU     $40              ;Bit position DDRB6
```

**Listing 8-1.**
Paced Loop Framework Program (sheet 2 of 6)

```
0008          TCSR      EQU      $08        ;Timer control & status reg
0007          TOF       EQU      7          ;Timer overflow flag
0006          RTIF      EQU      6          ;Real time interrupt flag
0005          TOIE      EQU      5          ;TOF interrupt enable
0004          RTIE      EQU      4          ;RTI interrupt enable
0003          TOFR      EQU      3          ;TOF flag reset
0002          RTIFR     EQU      2          ;RTIF flag reset
0001          RT1       EQU      1          ;RTI rate select bit 1
0000          RT0       EQU      0          ;RTI rate select bit 0
0080          TOF.      EQU      $80        ;Bit position TOF
0040          RTIF.     EQU      $40        ;Bit position RTIF
0020          TOIE.     EQU      $20        ;Bit position TOIE
0010          RTIE.     EQU      $10        ;Bit position RTIE
0008          TOFR.     EQU      $08        ;Bit position TOFR
0004          RTIFR.    EQU      $04        ;Bit position RTIFR
0002          RT1.      EQU      $02        ;Bit position RT1
0001          RT0.      EQU      $01        ;Bit position RT0

0009          TCR       EQU      $09        ;Timer counter register

000A          ISCR      EQU      $0A        ;IRQ status & control reg
0007          IRQE      EQU      7          ;IRQ edge/edge-level
0003          IRQF      EQU      3          ;External interrupt flag
0001          IRQR      EQU      1          ;IRQF flag reset

000E          PEBSR     EQU      $0E        ;PEPROM bit select register
0007          PEB7      EQU      7          ;Select PEPROM bit 7
0006          PEB6      EQU      6          ;Select PEPROM bit 6
0005          PEB5      EQU      5          ;Select PEPROM bit 5
0004          PEB4      EQU      4          ;Select PEPROM bit 4
0003          PEB3      EQU      3          ;Select PEPROM bit 3
0002          PEB2      EQU      2          ;Select PEPROM bit 2
0001          PEB1      EQU      1          ;Select PEPROM bit 1
0000          PEB0      EQU      0          ;Select PEPROM bit 0
0080          PEB7.     EQU      $80        ;Bit position PEB7
0040          PEB6.     EQU      $40        ;Bit position PEB6
0020          PEB5.     EQU      $20        ;Bit position PEB5
0010          PEB4.     EQU      $10        ;Bit position PEB4
0008          PEB3.     EQU      $08        ;Bit position PEB3
0004          PEB2.     EQU      $04        ;Bit position PEB2
0002          PEB1.     EQU      $02        ;Bit position PEB1
0001          PEB0.     EQU      $01        ;Bit position PEB0

000F          PESCR     EQU      $0F        ;PEPROM status & control reg
0007          PEDATA    EQU      7          ;PEPROM data
0005          PEPGM     EQU      5          ;PEPROM program control
0000          PEPRZF    EQU      0          ;PEPROM row zero flag
0080          PEDATA.   EQU      $80        ;Bit position PEDATA
0020          PEPGM.    EQU      $20        ;Bit position PEPGM
0001          PEPRZF.   EQU      $01        ;Bit position PEPRZF
```

**Listing 8-1.**
Paced Loop Framework Program (sheet 3 of 6)

```
0010          PDRA      EQU    $10      ;Pulldown register for port A
0007          PDIA7     EQU    7        ;Pulldown inhibit for PA7
0006          PDIA6     EQU    6        ;Pulldown inhibit for PA6
0005          PDIA5     EQU    5        ;Pulldown inhibit for PA5
0004          PDIA4     EQU    4        ;Pulldown inhibit for PA4
0003          PDIA3     EQU    3        ;Pulldown inhibit for PA3
0002          PDIA2     EQU    2        ;Pulldown inhibit for PA2
0001          PDIA1     EQU    1        ;Pulldown inhibit for PA1
0000          PDIA0     EQU    0        ;Pulldown inhibit for PA0
0080          PDIA7.    EQU    $80      ;Bit position PDIA7
0040          PDIA6.    EQU    $40      ;Bit position PDIA6
0020          PDIA5.    EQU    $20      ;Bit position PDIA5
0010          PDIA4.    EQU    $10      ;Bit position PDIA4
0008          PDIA3.    EQU    $08      ;Bit position PDIA3
0004          PDIA2.    EQU    $04      ;Bit position PDIA2
0002          PDIA1.    EQU    $02      ;Bit position PDIA1
0001          PDIA0.    EQU    $01      ;Bit position PDIA0

0011          PDRB      EQU    $11      ;Pulldown register for port B
0007          PDIB7     EQU    7        ;Pulldown inhibit for PB7
0006          PDIB6     EQU    6        ;Pulldown inhibit for PB6
0080          PDIB7.    EQU    $80      ;Bit position PDIB7
0040          PDIB6.    EQU    $40      ;Bit position PDIB6

0017          MOR       EQU    $17      ;Mask option register
0007          SWPDI     EQU    7        ;Software pulldown inhibit
0006          PIN3      EQU    6        ;3-pin RC oscillator
0005          RC        EQU    5        ;RC oscillator
0004          SWAIT     EQU    4        ;STOP coversion to wait
0003          LVRE      EQU    3        ;Low voltage reset enable
0002          PIRQ      EQU    2        ;Port A IRQ enable
0001          LEVEL     EQU    1        ;Edge & level/ edge-only
0000          COPEN     EQU    0        ;COP watchdog enable
0080          SWPDI.    EQU    $80      ;Bit position SWPDI
0040          PIN3.     EQU    $40      ;Bit position PIN3
0020          RC.       EQU    $20      ;Bit position RC
0010          SWAIT.    EQU    $10      ;Bit position SWAIT
0008          LVRE.     EQU    $08      ;Bit position LVRE
0004          PIRQ.     EQU    $04      ;Bit position PIRQ
0002          LEVEL.    EQU    $02      ;Bit position LEVEL
0001          COPEN.    EQU    $01      ;Bit position COPEN

0018          EPROG     EQU    $18      ;EPROM programming register
0002          ELAT      EQU    2        ;EPROM latch control
0001          MPGM      EQU    1        ;MOR programming control
0000          EPGM      EQU    0        ;EPROM program control
0004          ELAT.     EQU    $04      ;Bit position ELAT
0002          MPGM.     EQU    $02      ;Bit position MPGM
0001          EPGM.     EQU    $01      ;Bit position EPGM

03F0          COPR      EQU    $03F0    ;COP watchdog reset register
0000          COPC      EQU    0        ;COP watchdog clear
0001          COPC.     EQU    $01      ;Bit position COPC
```

**Listing 8-1.**
Paced Loop Framework Program  (sheet 4 of 6)

```
                      * Memory area equates
00E0                  RAMStart  EQU   $00E0     ;Start of on-chip RAM
0200                  ROMStart  EQU   $0200     ;Start of on-chip ROM
03EF                  ROMEnd    EQU   $03EF     ;End of on-chip ROM
03F8                  Vectors   EQU   $03F8     ;Reset/interrupt vector area

                      * Application specific equates
0007                  LED       EQU   PA7       ;LED ON when PA7 is low (0)
0080                  LED.      EQU   PA7.      ;LED bit position
0000                  SW        EQU   PA0       ;Switch on PA0, closed=hi (1)
0001                  SW.       EQU   PA0.      ;Switch bit position

                      ********************************************************
                      * Put program variables here (use RMBs)
                      ********************************************************
00E0                            ORG   $00E0     ;Start of 705K1 RAM

00E0                  RTIFs     RMB   1         ;3 RTIFs/TIC (3-0)
00E1                  TIC       RMB   1         ;10 TICs make 1 TOC (10-0)
                                                ;MSB=1 means RTIFs rolled over
00E2                  TOC       RMB   1         ;1 TOC=10*96.24ms= about 1 sec

                      ********************************************************
                      * Program area starts here
                      ********************************************************
0200                            ORG   $0200     ;Start of 705K1 EPROM

                      * First initialize any control registers and variables

0200 A6 80            START     LDA   #LED.     ;Configure and turn off LED
0202 B7 00                      STA   PORTA     ;Turns off LED
0204 B7 04                      STA   DDRA      ;Makes LED pin an output
0206 A6 16                      LDA   #{RTIFR.+RTIE.+RT1.}
0208 B7 08                      STA   TCSR      ;To clear and enable RTIF
                                                ;and set RTI rate for 32.8 ms
020A A6 03                      LDA   #3        ;RTIFs counts 3->0
020C B7 E0                      STA   RTIFs     ;Reset TOFS count
020E 3F E1                      CLR   TIC       ;Initial value for TIC
0210 3F E2                      CLR   TOC       ;Initial value for TOC
```

Listing 8-1.
Paced Loop Framework Program (sheet 5 of 6)

```
                   *********************************************************
                   * MAIN - Beginning of main program loop
                   *        Loop is executed once every 100ms (98.4ms)
                   *        A pass through all major task routines takes
                   *        less than 100mS and then time is wasted until
                   *        MSB of TIC set (every 3 RTIFs = 98.4ms).
                   *        At each RTIF interrupt, RTIF cleared & RTIFs
                   *        gets decremented (3-0). When RTIFs=0, MSB of
                   *        TIC gets set and RTIFs is set back to 3.
                   *        (3*32.8/RTIF = 98.4ms).
                   *
                   *        The variable TIC keeps track of 100mS periods
                   *        When TIC increments from 9 to 10 it is cleared
                   *        to 0 and TOC is incremented.
                   *********************************************************
0212 0F E1 FD  MAIN     BRCLR   7,TIC,MAIN  ;Loop here till TIC edge
0215 B6 E1              LDA     TIC         ;Get current TIC value
0217 A4 0F              AND     #$0F        ;Clears MSB
0219 4C                 INCA                ;TIC=TIC+1
021A B7 E1              STA     TIC         ;Update TIC
021C A1 0A              CMP     #10         ;10th TIC ?
021E 26 02              BNE     ARNC1       ;If not, skip next clear
0220 3F E1              CLR     TIC         ;Clear TIC on 10th
0222           ARNC1    EQU     *           ;
                   * End of synchronization to 100mS TIC; Run main tasks
                   *   & branch back to MAIN within 100mS.  Sync OK as long
                   *   as no 2 consecutive passes take more than 196.8mS

0222 CD 02 2A           JSR     TIME        ;Update TOCs

0225 CD 02 39           JSR     BLINK       ;Blink LED

                   * Other main tasks would go here

0228 20 E8              BRA     MAIN        ;Back to Top for next TIC

                   ** END of Main Loop *********************************

                   *********************************************************
                   * TIME - Update TOCs
                   *   If TIC = 0, increment 0->59
                   *   If TIC not = 0, just skip whole routine
                   *********************************************************
022A           TIME     EQU     *           ;Update TOCs
022A 3D E1              TST     TIC         ;Check for TIC=zero
022C 26 0A              BNE     XTIME       ;If not; just exit
022E 3C E2              INC     TOC         ;TOC=TOC+1
0230 A6 3C              LDA     #60
0232 B1 E2              CMP     TOC         ;Did TOC -> 60 ?
0234 26 02              BNE     XTIME       ;If not; just exit
0236 3F E2              CLR     TOC         ;TOCs rollover
0238 81        XTIME    RTS                 ;Return from TIME
```

**Listing 8-1.**
Paced Loop Framework Program  (sheet 6 of 6)

```
              *****************************************************
              * BLINK - Update LED
              *  If TOC is even, light LED
              *    else turn off LED
              *****************************************************
0239          BLINK     EQU    *          ;Update LED
0239 B6 E2              LDA    TOC         ;If even, LSB will be zero
023B 44                 LSRA              ;Shift LSB to carry
023C 25 04              BCS    LEDOFF      ;If not, turn off LED
023E 1E 00              BSET   LED,PORTA   ;Turn on LED
0240 20 02              BRA    XBLINK      ;Then exit
0242 1F 00   LEDOFF     BCLR   LED,PORTA   ;Turn off LED
0244 81      XBLINK     RTS               ;Return from BLINK


              *****************************************************
              * RTIF interrupt service routine
              *****************************************************
0245 3A E0   RTICNT     DEC    RTIFs       ;On each RTIF decrement RTIFs
0247 26 06              BNE    ENDRTI      ;Done if RTIFs not 0
0249 A6 03              LDA    #3          ;RTIFs counts 3->0
024B B7 E0              STA    RTIFs       ;Reset TOFS count
024D 1E E1              BSET   7,TIC       ;Set MSB as a flag to MAIN
024F 14 08   ENDRTI     BSET   RTIFR,TCSR  ;Clear RTIF flag
0251 80      AnRTI      RTI               ;Return from RTIF interrupt

0251         UNUSED     EQU    AnRTI       ;Use RTI at AnRTI for unused
                                          ;interrupts to just return


              *****************************************************
              * Interrupt & reset vectors
              *****************************************************
03F8                    ORG    $03F8       ;Start of vector area

03F8 02 45   TIMVEC     FDB    RTICNT      ;Count RTIFs 3/TIC
03FA 02 51   IRQVEC     FDB    UNUSED      ;Change if vector used
03FC 02 51   SWIVEC     FDB    UNUSED      ;Change if vector used
03FE 02 00   RESETV     FDB    START       ;Beginning of program on reset
```

*The Paced Loop*                                                    **8-19**

An equate (EQU) directive associates a label with a binary value. The binary value may be an address or a numeric constant.

There are two different ways to equate a control bit, depending upon how the label will be used. For bit set, clear, and branch instructions, you want the equate to associate the label with a number between seven and zero. For building logical masks, you want the label to be equated to a bit mask, where the bit that is set is in the same bit position as the control bit.

Reset and interrupt vectors should be initialized with form double-byte (FDB) directives. Even if an interrupt source is not going to be used, it is a good idea to initialize the vector in case an unexpected request is generated.

Space is reserved in RAM for program variables, using reserve memory byte (RMB) directives.

The paced loop software structure is a good general purpose programming structure. A loop structure is established with a pacemaker at the top of the loop. The pacemaker triggers and causes the other instructions in the loop to be executed at regular time intervals (such as every 100 milliseconds). Tasks for an application are written as subroutines. A list of jump to subroutine (JSR) instructions in the main paced loop cause each task subroutine to be executed exactly once per pacemaker trigger.

The routines in the main loop should be designed so that the combined execution time of all routines in the loop is less than the pacemaker trigger period. An individual pass through the loop can take longer than the pacemaker trigger, provided the next pass is shorter. Loop synchronization is maintained as long as no two consecutive passes through the main loop take longer than twice the pacemaker period.

In the smallest microcontrollers, the number of RAM locations available is very small, so it is important to be aware of stack requirements. An interrupt requires five bytes of stack RAM; a subroutine call requires two bytes (in an M68HC05).

# 9

# On-Chip Peripheral Systems

To solve real-world problems, a microcontroller must have more than just a powerful CPU, a program, and data memory resources. In addition, it must contain hardware allowing the CPU to access information from the outside world. Once the CPU gathers information and processes the data, it must also be able to effect change on some portion of the outside world. These hardware devices, called peripherals, are the CPU's windows to the outside.

On-chip peripherals extend the capability of a microcontroller. An MCU with on-chip peripherals can do more than one with only general-purpose I/O ports. Peripherals serve specialized needs and reduce the processing load on the CPU.

The most basic form of peripheral available on microcontrollers is the general-purpose I/O port. The MC68HC705K1 has 10 general-purpose I/O pins that are arranged as a single 8-bit port and a single 2-bit port. Each of the I/O pins can be used as either an input or an output. The function of each pin is determined by setting or clearing corresponding bits in a data direction register (DDR) during the initialization stage of a program. Each output pin may be driven to either a logic 1 or a logic 0 by using CPU instructions to set or clear the corresponding bit in the port data register. Also, the logic state of each input pin may be viewed by the CPU by using program instructions.

On-chip peripherals provide an interface to the outside world from the CPU. Peripherals augment the CPU's capabilities by performing tasks at which the CPU is not good. Most microcontroller peripherals perform very specific functions or tasks. For instance, a peripheral may be capable of performing frequency and pulse-width measurements or it may generate output wave forms. Because most peripherals do not have any intelligence of their own, they require some "assistance" from the CPU. To prevent peripherals from requiring constant attention from the CPU, they often perform their functions in an interrupt-driven manner. A peripheral requests service from the CPU only when it requires an additional piece of data to perform its job or when a peripheral has a piece of information that the CPU requires to do its job.

Peripherals can be extremely powerful and can perform complex functions without any CPU intervention, once they are set up. However, because of the cost sensitivity of most M68HC05 family members, the peripherals used on M68HC05 parts require a fair amount of CPU intervention.

## Types of Peripherals

With the exception of general-purpose I/O ports, most peripherals perform specific tasks. These tasks can be very diverse and may range from time measurement and calculation to communication with other microcontrollers or external peripherals. The following paragraphs contain a general description of some types of peripherals found on M68HC05 microcontrollers.

## Timers

Though a wide variety of timers exist on the many members of the M68HC05 family, their basic functions relate to the measurement or generation of time-based events. Timers usually measure time relative to the internal clock of the microcontroller, although some may be clocked from an external source. With the number of parts available in the M68HC05 family, the capabilities of the timers on each part can vary greatly. The most sophisticated timer module of the MC68HC05Bx family can simultaneously generate two PWM outputs, measure the pulse width of two external signals, *and* generate two additional output pulse trains. The simplest timer of the MC68HC05Jx and MC68HC05Kx families generates only two periodic interrupts -- one at a fixed rate and one at a selectable rate.

Many more-sophisticated timer modules exist on Motorola's higher-power processors. For instance, the MC68332 and MC68HC16Y1 contain a time processing unit (TPU) that is a microcode-programmable time processor with its own ALU. The TPU was designed especially for internal combustion engine control and can run an engine at steady state with no CPU intervention.

## Serial Ports

Some M68HC05 family members contain peripherals that allow the CPU to communicate bit-serially with external devices. Using a bit-serial format instead of a bit-parallel format requires fewer I/O pins to perform the communication function. Two basic types of serial ports exist on M68HC05 family: the serial communications interface (SCI) and the serial peripheral interface (SPI).

The SCI port is a universal asynchronous receiver/transmitter (UART) that communicates asynchronously with other devices. This type of serial port requires the simplest hardware interface. Only two pins are required for bidirectional data transfers. Data is transmitted out of the MCU on one pin and received by the MCU on the other pin. Each piece of data transmitted or received by the SCI has a start bit, several data bits, and a stop bit. The start and stop bits synchronize the two communicating devices. This type of serial interface is used most often when a microcontroller must communicate over fairly long distances. With EIA-232 level-translators connected to the transmit and receive pins, the SCI can communicate with personal computers or other larger computers.

As the name implies, the SPI port is primarily used to communicate with inexpensive external peripherals. Because the SPI communicates synchronously with other devices, bidirectional data transfers require at least three MCU pins. In addition to one pin each for transmitted and received data, the third pin provides the synchronization clock for the communicating devices. This style of serial interface is usually used to communicate with peripheral devices on the same board as the MCU. Standard SPI peripherals are available from many manufacturers. A-to-D (analog-to-digital) converters, display drivers, EEPROM, and shift registers are just a few examples of available SPI peripherals.

## Analog-to-Digital Converters

As mentioned in Chapter 1, many signals that exist in the real world are not directly compatible with an MCU's I/O pins. In fact, many signals are continuously varying analog signals that cannot be directly translated into a logic 1 or 0 that the microcontroller can use. Some members of the M68HC05 family include an analog-to-digital (A-to-D) converter that can convert the voltage level of analog signals into a binary number that the MCU can use.

## Digital-to-Analog Converters

A digital-to-analog (D-to-A) converter performs just the opposite function of an A-to-D converter. It allows the MCU to convert a digital number into a proportional analog voltage or current that can control various output devices in a system. Later in this chapter we will be developing a small application showing how a D-to-A converter may be implemented using an on-chip timer and a software program.

## EEPROM

Since EEPROM is a type of memory, most would not consider it a peripheral. The contents of an EEPROM can be altered as a program is running. It is nonvolatile memory that is electrically erasable, so it is certainly in a different class from RAM, ROM, or EPROM. Several M68HC05 family members contain EEPROM memory on the same chip as the MCU. As mentioned previously, EEPROM may even be added to a system as an external SPI peripheral.

# Controlling Peripherals

The control and status information for peripherals appears to the CPU as data bits in a memory location. Using this type of arrangement for peripheral control and status registers is known as *memory mapped I/O*. There is a great advantage to having peripherals appear as memory locations. Any CPU instruction that can operate on a memory location can be used to control or check the status of a peripheral. This type of I/O architecture is especially advantageous with the M68HC05 family because of the CPU's bit-manipulation instructions. This group of instructions gives a programmer the ability to individually set, clear, or test the state of any bit in the peripheral control registers (at addresses $0000 to $00FF).

Depending upon the type and complexity of a peripheral, its associated control and status registers may occupy one or several locations in the microcontroller's memory map. For instance, a general-purpose I/O port occupies two memory locations in a microcontroller's memory map. One byte location, called the data direction register (DDR), controls the function of each I/O pin. The other byte location, the port data register, reads the state of input pins or asserts a logic level on an output pin. A complex peripheral, such as the timer in the MC68HC705C8, occupies 10 byte locations in that MCU's memory map.

In the next section we will take a detailed look at the timer in the MC68HC705K1. While this 15-stage multifunction timer is very simple compared to many other timer systems, it can perform somewhat sophisticated timing functions. A complete example will be discussed, showing how this timer system can be used to generate an accurate low-frequency PWM signal.

# The MC68HC705K1 Timer

Figure 9-1 shows a block diagram of the MC68HC705K1's 15-stage multifunction timer. The timer consists of three connected sections, each performing separate timing functions.

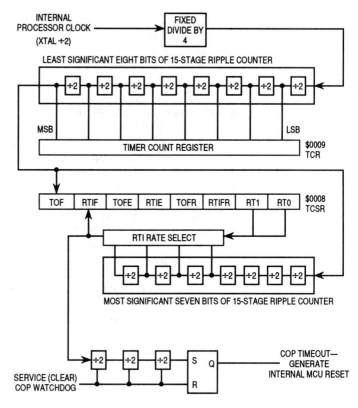

**Figure 9-1.**
15-Stage Multifunction Timer Block Diagram

The timing chain begins with the microcontroller's internal bus-rate clock, the E-clock. The E-clock is derived by dividing the crystal frequency by two. The E-clock is used to drive a fixed divide-by-four prescaler. In turn, the output of the prescaler clocks an 8-bit ripple counter. The value of this counter may be read anytime by the CPU at memory location $09, the timer counter register (TCR). The counter value may not be altered by the CPU. This may seem like a simple timer.

*On-Chip Peripheral Systems*

However, it is very useful in many applications. When the 8-bit ripple counter overflows from $FF to $00, a timer overflow flag (TOF) status bit in the timer control and status register (TCSR) is set to a one. The state of this status flag may be tested at any time by any of several CPU instructions. Optionally, if the timer overflow interrupt enable (TOIE) bit in the timer control and status register is set, the ripple counter overflow will generate a CPU interrupt. Therefore, the timer overflow function allows a potential interrupt to be generated. The timer overflows every 1,024 E-clock cycles ($\div 4$ prescaler followed by an 8-bit $\div 256$ ripple counter).

Besides providing a potential periodic interrupt, the output of the 8-bit ripple counter drives the input of an additional 7-bit ripple counter. The output from any of the last four bits of this counter may be used to generate an additional periodic interrupt. One of four rates may be selected by using a 1-of-4 selector controlled by two bits, RT1 and RT0, in the timer control and status register. Table 9-1 shows the four real-time interrupt rates available when operating the microcontroller at an E-clock frequency of 2.0 MHz.

**Table 9-1.**
RTI and COP Timer Rates (E-clock = 2.0 MHz)

| RT1 | RT0 | RTI Rate | Minimum COP Reset Period |
|-----|-----|----------|--------------------------|
| 0 | 0 | 8.2 ms | 57.3 ms |
| 0 | 1 | 16.4 ms | 114.7 ms |
| 1 | 0 | 32.8 ms | 229.4 ms |
| 1 | 1 | 65.5 ms | 458.8 ms |

The final stage of the multifunction timer system has a 3-bit counter that forms the computer-operating-properly (COP) watchdog system. The COP system is meant to protect against software failures. When enabled, a COP reset sequence must be performed before the time-out period expires, so that the COP does not time out and initiate an MCU reset. To prevent the COP from timing out and generating an MCU reset, bit 0 at memory location $03F0 (COPR) must be written to zero before the COP reset period has expired. Because the input of the COP watchdog timer is clocked by the output of the real-time interrupt circuit, changing the RTI rate will affect the minimum COP reset period. Table 9-1 shows the four COP reset periods available for corresponding RTI rates.

## A Timer Example

In this section, we will develop software that uses both the real-time interrupt and the timer overflow interrupt to produce a low-frequency pulse width modulated (PWM) signal on a general-purpose I/O pin. PWM signals are useful for a variety of control functions. They can control the speed of a motor or easily be converted to a dc level to drive an analog output device or to form part of an A-to-D converter.

A PWM signal, as the name implies, has a fixed frequency but varies the width of the on and off times. Figure 9-2 shows three PWM signals with different duty cycles. For each signal, the waveform period T1 is constant but the *on* time varies (the period of time shown by T2). Duty cycle is usually expressed as a percentage (the ratio of T2 to T1).

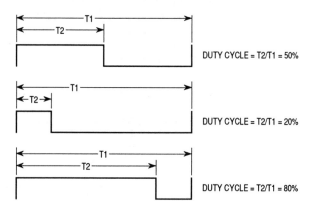

**Figure 9-2.**
PWM Wave Forms With Various Duty Cycles

To generate an accurate PWM signal, two timing references are required. One timing reference sets the constant frequency (period) of the PWM signal, while the second determines the amount of time that the PWM output remains high (on time). The basic strategy for the PWM software we will develop is as follows: A real-time interrupt (RTIF) will generate the PWM period, and the timer overflow (TOF) will determine the PWM high time. The rest of this chapter is a detailed development of this basic idea into a working application.

*On-Chip Peripheral Systems*

Begin by taking a closer look at the MC68HC705K1's timer. Figure 9-3 shows the timer redrawn to emphasize the portion in which we are interested. Conceptually, the eight counter stages surrounded by the gray box form the *timer* that we will use to generate our PWM signal.

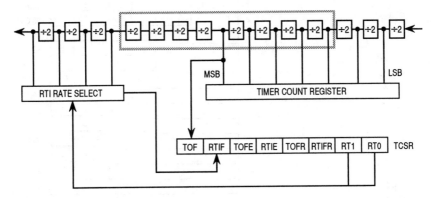

**Figure 9-3.**
Portion of the MC68HC705K1 Timer

Examination of Figure 9-3 shows four counter stages between the timer overflow interrupt output and the first input to the RTI rate select multiplexer. This indicates that timer overflow interrupts will occur at a rate 16 times faster than the fastest selectable real-time interrupt. Using the RTI to generate the base frequency of a PWM signal and the TOF interrupt to determine the duty cycle, we would be able to generate a PWM output with 16 discrete duty cycles (including 100 percent) as shown in Figure 9-4. The numbers down the left hand side of the figure indicate the number of TOF interrupts that will occur before the PWM output is set low. The numbers down the right hand side of the figure indicate the duty cycle of the waveform. The alert reader will note that there is no TOF interrupt count associated with the 100 percent duty cycle waveform. As will be shown later, this is a special case that must be tested in the RTI interrupt routine.

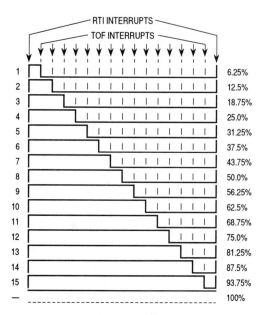

| | |
|---|---|
| 1 | 6.25% |
| 2 | 12.5% |
| 3 | 18.75% |
| 4 | 25.0% |
| 5 | 31.25% |
| 6 | 37.5% |
| 7 | 43.75% |
| 8 | 50.0% |
| 9 | 56.25% |
| 10 | 62.5% |
| 11 | 68.75% |
| 12 | 75.0% |
| 13 | 81.25% |
| 14 | 87.5% |
| 15 | 93.75% |
| — | 100% |

**Figure 9-4.**
PWM With 16 Discrete Duty Cycle Outputs

While the software to implement the illustrated PWM output is very simple, having only 16 choices for pulse width limits the usefulness of this PWM to a small number of applications (where accurate control is not necessary). For example, if a motor speed control system were built using this PWM, the target speed could only be controlled to ±6.25% (assuming that motor speed is directly proportional to the average applied voltage). For most motor speed control applications, a 12.5% variation in rotation speed would be unacceptable.

Obviously, much finer control of the PWM duty cycle is desired. One approach might be to use a slower RTI rate, which would result in a greater number of TOF interrupts for each RTI. For some applications this may be acceptable. However, for many applications the resulting frequency of the PWM waveform would be too low to be of practical use. Table 9-2 shows the four available RTI rates and the corresponding PWM frequency, the number of TOF interrupts between RTIs, and the minimum variation in duty cycle that is possible.

*On-Chip Peripheral Systems*

**Table 9-2.**
PWM Characteristics for Various RTI Rates

| RTI Rate | PWM Frequency | TOF Interrupts | Minimum Duty Cycle |
|----------|---------------|----------------|--------------------|
| 8.2 ms   | 122 Hz        | 16             | 6.25%              |
| 16.4 ms  | 61.0 Hz       | 32             | 3.125%             |
| 32.8 ms  | 30.5 Hz       | 64             | 1.56%              |
| 65.5 ms  | 15.3 Hz       | 128            | 0.78%              |

Table 9-2 seems to suggest that we are stuck trading off PWM frequency for duty cycle accuracy. However, the following software program can deliver much better results than expected.

Reexamining the portion of the timer in Figure 9-3 surrounded by the gray box shows 8 bits of the 15-bit timer chain. Four of the bits are accessible to the CPU as the upper four bits of the TCR. The other four bits form a divide-by-16 counter chain whose value is not directly accessible. However, by counting the number of TOF interrupts that occur after each RTI, we can always know the state of these four counter bits. By using an 8-bit number to represent the PWM duty cycle, we can achieve a duty cycle accuracy of 1÷255 or 0.4 percent.

To get this level of control with the MC68HC705K1 timer, we cannot use an 8-bit duty cycle value directly. The 8-bit number must be separated into two components. One component will represent the value of the inaccessible four bits of the 'counter' (the number of TOF interrupts that occur after each RTI). The other component will represent the value of the upper four bits of the TCR (the lower four bits of our counter that are directly accessible to the CPU).

To make these two components easy for the software to use, the upper four bits of the desired PWM duty cycle must be placed in the lower four bits of a variable we will call PWMCoarse. This value will determine the TOF interrupt during which the PWM output should be set low. The lower four bits of the desired PWM duty cycle will be placed in the upper four bits of a variable we will call PWMFine. This value is used within the TOF interrupt to determine precisely when, during the TOF interrupt, the PWM output should be set low. By comparing the value in PWMFine to the upper four bits of the TCR, we can effectively divide each TOF interrupt into 16 separate time intervals as shown in Figure 9-5.

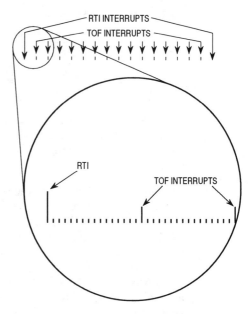

**Figure 9-5.**
Each TOF Interrupt Sliced Into 16 Separate Time Intervals

Now that we have described the theory involved in generating an accurate PWM wave form using the MC68HC05K1's timer, the next step is to write the software. We will begin by generating flowcharts to describe the actions necessary to produce the PWM waveform and finish by translating the flowcharts into M68HC05 assembly language.

The flowcharts in Figures 9-6, 9-7, and 9-8 describe the PWM software. The flowchart in Figure 9-6, although very simple, is included for completeness and clarity. Because the MC68HC05K1 contains only one timer interrupt vector, a small routine must determine whether a timer interrupt was caused by a TOF or RTIF interrupt, and then branch to the appropriate service routine.

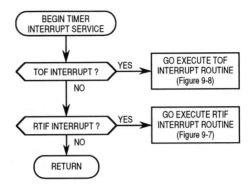

**Figure 9-6.**
Timer Interrupt Service Routine

As shown in Figure 9-7, the RTIF interrupt routine checks for two special conditions, zero percent and 100 percent duty cycle. It then sets up the PWMFine and PWMCoarse variables for use by the TOF interrupt service routine. If a zero percent duty cycle is desired, the PWM output is set low and the RTIF interrupt service routine returns immediately. If a 100 percent duty cycle is desired, the PWM output is set high and the RTIF interrupt service routine will return immediately. If a duty cycle between zero percent and 100 percent is desired, the variable DesiredPWM is split into the two components: PWMFine and PWMCoarse. If the resulting value of PWMCoarse is zero, the program will jump to the second part of the TOF interrupt routine, which continually compares the value in PWMFine to the upper four bits of the TCR. If the value of PWMCoarse is not zero, TOF interrupts are enabled and the RTIF interrupt routine returns.

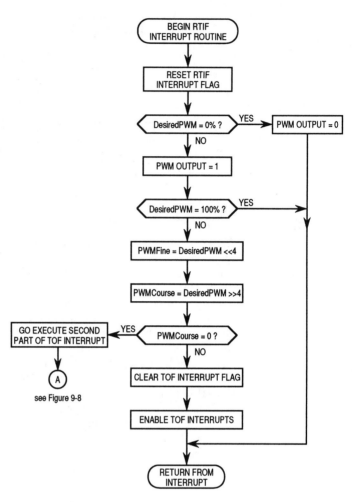

**Figure 9-7.**
Real Time Interrupt Routine Flowchart

The flowchart in Figure 9-8 describes the actions required for the TOF interrupt routine. The first action is to decrement the value of PWMCoarse. When PWMCoarse becomes zero, it means that the value in the upper four bits of our counter is equal to the upper four bits of DesiredPWM. Next, we continually compare the upper four bits of the TCR with the value of PWMFine (which is the lower four bits of DesiredPWM). When these two values match, the PWM output is set low, the TOF interrupt is reset and disabled, and the TOF interrupt returns.

*On-Chip Peripheral Systems*

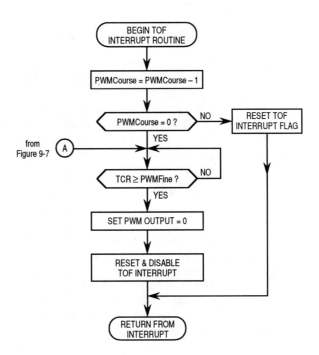

**Figure 9-8.**
Timer Overflow Interrupt Flowchart

Listing 9-1 shows the assembly language listing for the three routines described by the flowcharts in Figures 9-6, 9-7, and 9-8. The translation of the flowcharts into assembly language is fairly straightforward. The possible exception is the assembly code in the RTIF interrupt routine that splits the DesiredPWM variable into the PWMCoarse and PWMFine components. This routine works by using a combination of shift left and rotate left instructions that operate on the A and X registers. The LSLA instruction shifts the most significant bit of the A register into the carry and a zero into the least significant bit of A. The ROLX instruction places the carry (from the previous LSLA instruction) into the least significant bit of the X register. After the execution of four of these instruction pairs, the four most significant bits of the A register (DesiredPWM) will end up in the least significant four bits of the X register (PWMCoarse). The least significant four bits of the A register will end up in the most significant four bits of the A register (PWMFine).

## Using The PWM Software

In normal circumstances, the PWM software of Listing 9-1 would be used as a part of a larger program. The value of DesiredPWM would be generated by some other part of the main program. To demonstrate the PWM software, the value of DesiredPWM was arbitrarily set to $80 ($128_{10}$) by program instructions. If a simulator or emulator is used to study this program, you can change the value of DesiredPWM and observe the effect.

The PWM program is interrupt driven. This means that the timer generates interrupt requests for the CPU to stop processing the main program and respond to the interrupt request. Since the demonstration version of this program in Listing 9-1 has no other main program to perform, a "branch-to-here" instruction was included after the clear interrupt mask (CLI) instruction. This instruction is an infinite loop. Timer interrupts will cause the CPU to periodically leave this infinite loop to respond to the timer requests, then return to executing the infinite loop.

**Listing 9-1.**
PWM Program Listing (Sheet 1 of 2)

```
                    ;Equates for all 705K1 registers included but not shown
                    ; in this listing
                    ;
00FF                Percent100 EQU    $FF      ;DesiredPWM value for 100% duty
0007                PWM        EQU    PA7       ;PWM output on port A bit 7

00E0                           ORG    RAMStart

00E0                DesiredPWM RMB    1         ;Desired PWM duty cycle...
                    ; expressed as the numerator of DesiredPWM/255.
                    ; 0 = continuous low      255 = continuous high.

00E1                PWMCoarse  RMB    1         ;Number of TOF interrupts...
                    ; before we start to compare PWMFine to value in the TCR.

00E2                PWMFine    RMB    1         ;When TCR matches PWMFine,...
                    ;                          ; the PWM is set low.
                    ; PWMFine is derived from the lower 4 bits of DesiredPWM.
                    ; These 4 bits are placed in the upper 4 bits of PWMFine.

00E3                VarEnd     EQU    *

                    ;************************************************************
                    ;
0200                           ORG    ROMStart
                    ;
0200                Start      EQU    *
0200 9C                        RSP              ;Reset the stack pointer
0201 3F 00                     CLR    PORTA     ;Set Port A outputs to all 0's
0203 A6 FF                     LDA    #$FF      ;Make all Port A's pins outputs
0205 B7 04                     STA    DDRA
             ;                          Clear out all of RAM
0207 AE E0                     LDX    #RAMStart ;Point to the start of RAM
0209 7F             ClrLoop    CLR    0,X       ;Clear a byte
020A 5C                        INCX             ;Point to the next location
                                                ;Cleared the last location?
020B 26 FC                     BNE    ClrLoop   ;No, Continue to clear RAM

020D A6 80                     LDA    #$80      ;Corresponds to 50% (128/255)
020F B7 E0                     STA    DesiredPWM ;Establish a PWM duty cycle
0211 A6 1C                     LDA    #$1C      ;Clear timer ints...
0213 B7 08                     STA    TCSR      ;and enable RTIF interrupt
0215 9A                        CLI              ;Enable interrupts
0216 20 FE                     BRA    *         ;Infinite loop, PWM uses ints

                    ;************************************************************
                    ;RTI sets period. @2MHz & RT1:RT0 = 0:0, period = 8.192ms
                    ;or about 122 Hz
0218                TimerInt   EQU    *
0218 0E 08 04                  BRSET  TOF,TCSR,TOFInt     ;TOF interrupt?
021B 0C 08 12                  BRSET  RTIF,TCSR,RTIInt    ;RTI interrupt?
021E 80                        RTI
```

**Listing 9-1.**
PWM Program Listing (Sheet 2 of 2)

```
                ;*************************************************************
                ;TOF interrupt response - Decrement PWMCoarse, when 0...
                ;Compare PWMFine to TCR. When TCR passes PWMFine clear
                ;PWM output pin and disable further TOF. RTI re-enables.
                ;
021F            TOFInt    EQU    *
021F 3A E1                DEC    PWMCoarse  ;Is PWMCoarse=0?
0221 26 0A                BNE    ExitTOF    ;No. Clear TOF and return
0223 B6 E2      TOFInt1   LDA    PWMFine    ;To compare to upper 4 of TCR
0225 B1 09      CmpMore   CMPA   TCR
0227 22 FC                BHI    CmpMore    ;Loop till PWMFine <= TCR
0229 1F 00                BCLR   PWM,PortA  ;Set the PWM output low (0V)
022B 1B 08                BCLR   TOIE,TCSR  ;Disable the TOF Interrupt
022D 16 08      ExitTOF   BSET   TOFR,TCSR  ;Reset the TOF Interrupt Flag
022F 80                   RTI               ;Return to the main program


                ;*************************************************************
                ;RTIF interrupt response - Set PWM out pin high, and
                ;enable TOF. Make PWMCoarse & PWMFine from DesiredPWM
                ;
0230            RTIInt    EQU    *
0230 14 08                BSET   RTIFR,TCSR ;Clear the RT Interrupt Flag
0232 B6 E0                LDA    DesiredPWM ;Get desired PWM level. =0?
0234 27 19                BEQ    RTIInt2    ;Yes. Leave PWM output low
0236 1E 00                BSET   PWM,PORTA  ;No. Set PWM output high
0238 A1 FF                CMPA   #Percent100 ;Desired PWM level 100%?
023A 27 13                BEQ    RTIInt2    ;Yes. Leave PWM output high
023C 5F                   CLRX              ;No. Put upper 4 bits of
023D 48                   LSLA              ;DesiredPWM into lower 4 bits
023E 59                   ROLX              ;of A and the lower 4 bits of
023F 48                   LSLA              ;DesiredPWM into the upper
0240 59                   ROLX              ;4 bits of X.
0241 48                   LSLA
0242 59                   ROLX
0243 48                   LSLA
0244 59                   ROLX
0245 B7 E2                STA    PWMFine    ;Save result into PWMFine.
0247 BF E1      RTIInt1   STX    PWMCoarse  ;Save result into PWMCoarse.
0249 27 D8                BEQ    TOFInt1    ;If PWMCoarse=0, go to 2nd
                                            ;half of the TOF routine
024B 16 08                BSET   TOFR,TCSR  ;Clear Timer Overflow Flag
024D 1A 08                BSET   TOIE,TCSR  ;re-enable the TOF interrupt
024F 80         RTIInt2   RTI               ;return from RTIF interrupt


03F8                      ORG    Vectors    ;interrupt/reset vectors.

03F8 02 18                FDB    TimerInt   ;timer interrupt routine.
03FA 02 00                FDB    Start      ;IRQ vector (not used)
03FC 02 00                FDB    Start      ;SWI vector (not used)
03FE 02 00                FDB    Start      ;Reset vector.
```

# A Practical Motor Control Example

In this section we will develop a practical application by expanding some of the software developed in this book. The example will add some external hardware to the MC68HC705K1 so that we can observe the effects of our software on the world outside the microcontroller. We will use a slightly modified version of the PWM routine that was developed in this chapter to control the speed of a small permanent-magnet direct current (DC) motor. In addition, we will use the concepts developed in Chapter 7 that allow the CPU to read the state of switches connected to the MCU's general-purpose I/O pins.

## Theory

DC motors are often the best choice for variable-speed motor applications. Brush DC motors are the easiest to control electronically. Electronic control of brushless DC, Stepper, AC induction, and switched reluctance motors all require more-complex control circuits in addition to more power-switching devices. Small, low-cost brush DC motors are available off-the-shelf for many low-volume applications where custom designs would be too expensive. The reliability of brush motors is adequate for most applications. However, the brushes will eventually wear out and need to be replaced.

To vary the speed of a brush DC motor, we must vary the voltage that is applied to the motor. There are several approaches that can be used to accomplish this. We will examine several of the methods, explaining the major advantages and disadvantages of each.

The first and most obvious approach to varying the voltage applied to a motor might be to place a variable resistor in series with the motor and the power source, as shown in Figure 9-9. While this approach is very simple, it has some serious disadvantages. First, the resistor's power dissipation capabilities must be matched to the power requirements of the motor. For very small fractional-horsepower DC motors, the size of the variable resistor will be quite modest. However, as the size of the motor increases, the motor's power requirement increases and the size and cost of the variable resistor will increase.

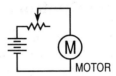

**Figure 9-9**
Motor Speed Controlled by a Variable Resistor

The second major disadvantage of this type of speed control is the inability to automatically adjust the speed of the motor to compensate for varying loads. This is a primary disadvantage for applications that require precise speed control under varying mechanical loads.

An electronic variation of the variable resistor form of speed control is shown in Figure 9-10. In this arrangement we have replaced the variable resistor with a transistor. Here, the transistor is operated in its linear mode. When a transistor operates in this mode, it essentially behaves as an electrically controlled variable resistor. By applying a proportional analog control signal to the transistor, the 'resistivity' of the transistor can be varied, which will in turn vary the speed of the motor. By using a transistor to control the speed of the motor in this manner, the magnitude of the control signal is reduced to much lower voltage and current levels that can be readily generated by electronic circuitry.

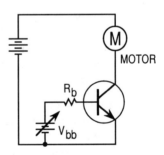

**Figure 9-10.**
Motor Speed Controlled by a Transistor

Unfortunately, using a transistor in its linear mode still retains a major disadvantage of using a variable resistor. Like a variable resistor, a power transistor operating in its linear region will have to dissipate large amounts of power under varying speed and load conditions. Even though power

*On-Chip Peripheral Systems*

transistors capable of handling high power levels are widely available at relatively modest prices, the power dissipated by the transistor will usually require a large heat sink to prevent the device from destroying itself.

In addition to being operated as a linear device, transistors may also be operated as electronic switches. By applying the proper control signal to a transistor, the device will either be turned *on* or turned *off*. As shown in Figure 9-11, when the transistor is turned on, it will essentially behave as a mechanical switch allowing electric current to pass through it and its load virtually unimpeded. When turned off, no current passes through the transistor or its load. Because the transistor dissipates very little power when it is fully turned on or *saturated*, the device operates in an efficient manner.

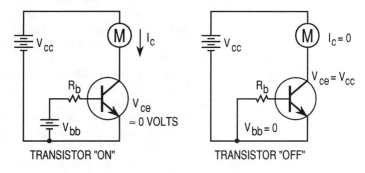

**Figure 9-11.**
Transistor Used as an Electronic Switch

It would seem that, when using a transistor to control the speed of a DC motor, we are stuck using the device in its inefficient linear mode if we want a motor to operate at something other than full speed. Fortunately, there is an alternative method of controlling the speed of a DC motor using a transistor. By using the transistor as an electronically controlled switch and applying a PWM control signal of sufficient frequency, we can control the speed of the motor. To help understand how turning a motor fully on and then fully off can control its speed, consider the PWM waveforms in Figure 9-12.

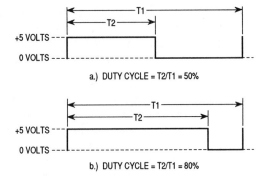

**Figure 9-12.**
PWM Waveforms with 50 and 80 Percent Duty Cycles

Figure 9-12a shows a single cycle of a 50 percent duty cycle PWM waveform that is at 5 volts during the first half of its period and at 0 volts during the second half. If we integrate (or average) the voltage of the PWM waveform in Figure 9-12a over its period, T1, the average DC voltage is 50 percent of 5 volts or 2.5 volts. Correspondingly, the average DC voltage of the PWM waveform in Figure 9-12b, which has a duty cycle of 80 percent, is 80 percent of 5 volts or 4.5 volts. By using a PWM signal to switch a motor on and off in this manner, it will produce the same effect as applying a continuous or average DC voltage at varying levels to the motor. The frequency of the PWM signal must be sufficiently high so that the rotational inertia of the motor integrates the on/off pulses and causes the motor to run smoothly.

## Motor Control Circuit

As mentioned earlier, we will be using a slightly modified version of our PWM routine to control the speed of a small motor. However, before discussing the software involved, we need to take a look at the hardware components required to drive the motor.

Figure 9-13 is a schematic diagram of the power section of our motor control circuit. There are a number of differences between this schematic and the conceptual ones used in Figures 9-10 and 9-11. We will describe these differences in the following paragraphs.

The most noticeable difference is the schematic symbol for the power transistor that will be used as an electronic switch. This device is a power MOSFET. Unlike the bipolar transistor shown in Figures 9-10 and 9-11, this special type of transistor is controlled by the magnitude of a voltage applied to its gate. Additionally, this particular power MOSFET, the MTP3055EL, may be completely saturated with only 5 volts applied to its gate. These two characteristics allow this device to be controlled directly by a microcontroller's output pin for many applications.

Because the input impedance of a power MOSFET is very high (greater than 40 megohms), a 10KΩ resistor is placed between the MOSFET gate and ground to prevent erratic operation of the motor should the connection between the microcontroller and the gate ever become cut. The 15 volt zener diode is placed in parallel with the resistor to protect the gate of the MOSFET from possible damage from high voltage transients that may be generated in the system. The 1N4001 diode in parallel with the motor is used to snub the inductive kick of the motor each time the MOSFET is turned off. The 0.1µf capacitor in parallel with the motor is used to reduce the electrical noise generated by the motor's brushes.

For further information on designing with power MOSFETs, it is suggested that the reader study the Theory and Applications section of the *Motorola Power MOSFET Transistor Data Book* (DL153).

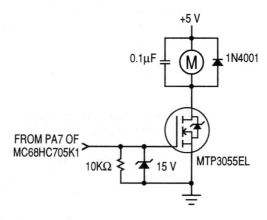

**Figure 9-13.**
Power Section of the Motor Speed Control Circuit

Figure 9-14 is a schematic diagram of the microprocessor section of the circuit that we will be using in this example. In addition to generating a PWM output, the MC68HC705K1 is reading three momentary pushbutton switches connected to its I/O pins. As the schematic shows, a single switch turns the motor on and off while two switches set the speed of the motor.

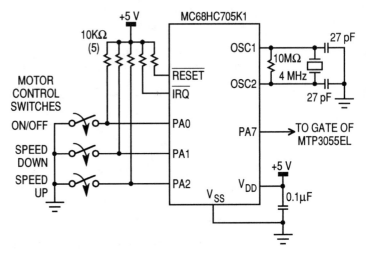

**Figure 9-14.**
Microcontroller Section of the Motor Speed Control Circuit

One side of each switch is connected to circuit ground, while the other side of the switch is connected to an I/O pin on the MC68HC705K1 microcontroller. Each of the input pins on the microcontroller is "pulled up" through a 10KΩ resistor to +5 volts. These 10KΩ pullup resistors keep each of the three input pins at a logic 1 when the pushbutton switches are not pressed.

In this example circuit, the switch controls will operate in the following manner. The motor on/off switch operates as an alternate-action control. Each time the switch is pushed and released, the motor will alternately be turned on or off. When the motor is turned on, its speed will be set to the speed it was going the last time the motor was on.

The speed up and speed down switches increase or decrease motor speed, respectively. To increase or decrease the speed

*On-Chip Peripheral Systems*

of the motor, the respective switch must be pressed and held. The motor speed PWM will be increased or decreased at a rate of approximately 0.4 percent every 24ms. This "ramp" rate will allow the motor speed to be adjusted across its entire speed range in approximately 6 seconds.

## Motor Control Software

Figure 9-15 shows a flowchart that describes the new RTI interrupt software. The only functional change to the PWM routine developed earlier in this chapter is the addition of one instruction at the beginning of the RTI interrupt service routine. This instruction decrements the variable RTIDlyCnt. This variable is used by the three routines that read the input switches to develop a switch debounce delay.

As mentioned in chapter 7, there are usually many ways to perform a specific task using the microcontroller's instruction set. To demonstrate this, one part of the revised RTI interrupt routine has been implemented in a slightly different manner. Remember, looking at listing 9-1, that we had to split the variable DesiredPWM into two parts, PWMFine and PWMCoarse. To do this we used a combination of shifts and rotates to place the upper four bits of the A accumulator (DesiredPWM) into the lower four bits of the X register (PWMCoarse) and the lower four bits of A into the upper four bits of A (PWMFine). This method required nine bytes of program memory and 26 CPU cycles. By using the alternative approach in listing 9-2, we can get the same result in only three bytes of program memory and 13 CPU cycles.

The RTIInt routine in listing 9-2 demonstrates the alternative approach. The original nine-byte instruction sequence has been replaced with two instructions, LDX #16 and MUL. The MUL instruction multiplies the value in the accumulator by the value in the index register and places the result in X:A (concatenation of X and A). Multiplying a binary number by 16 is equivalent to shifting the value left by four positions. Just as in the original implementation, the upper four bits of DesiredPWM are now in the lower four bits of the X register (PWMCourse) and the lower four bits of the A register have been moved into the upper four bits of A (PWMFine).

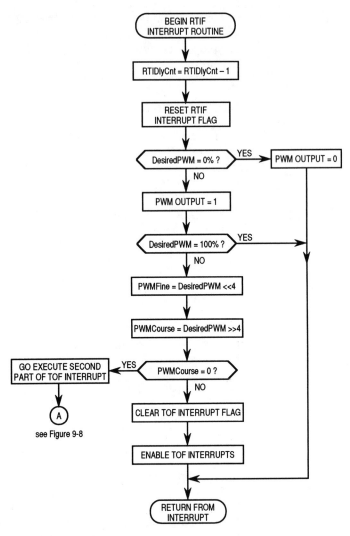

**Figure 9-15.**
Revised RTI Routine Flowchart

The flowchart in Figure 9-16 describes the main loop routine of our motor control module. This module checks the state of each of the three input switches. If any one of the three switches is pressed, a routine that handles the actions for that switch is called. If there are no switches pressed, the main loop is repeated.

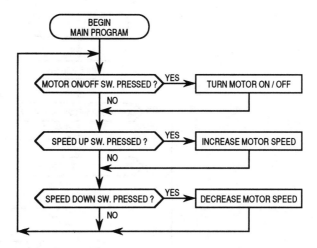

**Figure 9-16.**
Flowchart for Main Program Loop

Figures 9-17, 9-18, and 9-19 are flowcharts for the three routines that handle the actions of the three input switches. Each of these routines begins with the execution of a 50 mS switch debounce routine. As described in Chapter 7, this delay is required because the mechanical bounce produced by the closure of a switch is seen by the microcontroller as multiple switch closures during the first several milliseconds after the switch is pressed. This small section of code stores the value DebounceDly into the variable RTIDlyCnt and then waits until the value is decremented to zero by the RTI interrupt service routine. When the value reaches zero, the switch is again checked to be sure a valid switch closure occurred. The value used for the delay constant (DebounceT) will produce a minimum delay of approximately 50 milliseconds.

The flowchart in Figure 9-17 describes the MotorOnOff routine. It is responsible for handling the actions of the alternate action switch that turns the motor on and off. After the switch debounce delay, this routine waits until the on/off switch is released before it performs the rest of its task and returns to the main loop. Otherwise, the main loop would detect another switch closure as soon as the MotorOnOff program finished and returned to the main program loop.

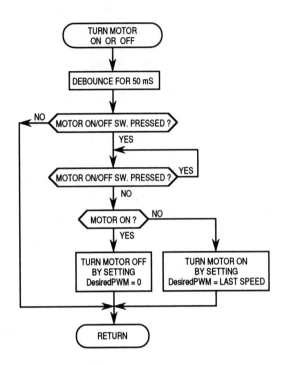

**Figure 9-17.**
Flowchart for Motor On/Off Routine

The routines described by the flowcharts in Figures 9-18 and 9-19 operate in essentially the same manner. First, each of these routines checks to see if the motor is currently turned on. If the motor is off, the routine returns to the main program loop. Each routine then loops continuously as long as its associated switch remains pressed. Each time through the loop, the MotorPWM and DesiredPWM variables are incremented or decremented to increase or decrease the duty cycle of the PWM output. To keep the speed of the motor from increasing or decreasing too rapidly when a switch is pressed, a delay of approixmately 25 ms is inserted each time through the loop. This 25 ms delay allows the motor to be adjusted across its entire speed range in approximately six seconds.

*On-Chip Peripheral Systems*

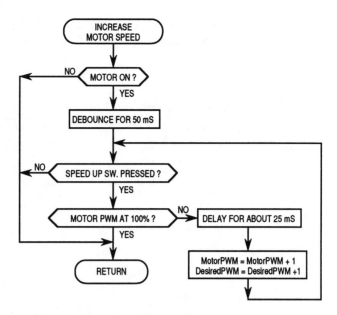

**Figure 9-18.**
Flowchart for Motor Speed-Up Routine

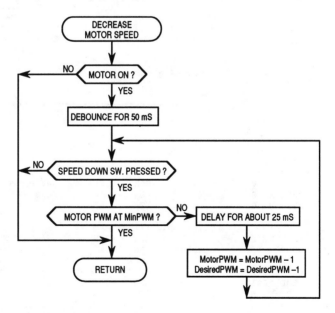

**Figure 9-19.**
Flowchart for Motor Speed-Down Routine

Listing 9-2 contains the assembly language listing for the routines described by the flowcharts in Figures 9-8 and 9-15 through 9-19.

**Listing 9-2.**
Speed Control Program Listing (Sheet 1 of 4)

```
                          ;Equates for all 705K1 are included but not shown

00FF                      Percent100 EQU  $FF      ;DesiredPWM value for 100% duty
0003                      RampTime   EQU  3        ;Speed up/down ramp constant
0007                      DebounceT  EQU  7        ;Switch debounce constant
0010                      MinPWM     EQU  $10      ;Minimum PWM value.
0007                      PWM        EQU  PA7      ;Port A bit 7 is PWM output
0000                      MotorOnOff EQU  PA0      ;Sw. for the Motor On/Off
0001                      SpeedUp    EQU  PA1      ;Sw. for raising the speed
0002                      SpeedDn    EQU  PA2      ;Sw. for lowering the speed

00E0                                 ORG  RAMStart

00E0                      DesiredPWM RMB  1        ;Desired PWM/255 = duty cycle
                                                   ;   0 = continuous low
                                                   ; 255 = continuous high

00E1                      PWMCoarse  RMB  1        ;Number of TOFs before...
                                                   ; start watching PWMFine vs TCR
00E2                      PWMFine    RMB  1        ;When TCR matches PWMFine,...
                                                   ; set PWM output low

00E3                      MotorPWM   RMB  1        ;Last PWM/speed while motor.on
00E4                      RTIDlyCnt  RMB  1        ;Decremented on each RTI...
                                                   ; used to debounce switches

00E5                      MotorOnFlg RMB  1        ;1 = PWM out is on / 0 = off
00E6                      VarEnd     EQU  *

                          ;**************************************************************
0200                                 ORG  ROMStart

0200                      Start      EQU  *

0200 9C                              RSP           ;Reset stack pointer in case...
                                                   ; we got here from an error
0201 3F 00                           CLR  PortA    ;Set up Port A outs to all 0's
0203 A6 80                           LDA  #$80     ;Make PA7 an output
0205 B7 04                           STA  DDRA

                          ;Clear out all of RAM
0207 AE E0                           LDX  #RAMStart ;Point to the start of RAM
0209 7F                   ClrLoop    CLR  0,x      ;Clear a byte.
020A 5C                              INCX          ;Point to the next loc./ done?
020B 26 FC                           BNE  ClrLoop  ;No; continue to clear RAM
020D A6 1C                           LDA  #$1C     ;Enable TOF & RTI interrupts
020F B7 08                           STA  TSCR
0211 A6 10                           LDA  #MinPWM  ;Initialize PWM to min speed
0213 B7 E3                           STA  MotorPWM
0215 9A                              CLI           ;Enable interrupts
```

**Listing 9-2.**
Speed Control Program Listing (Sheet 2 of 4)

```
              ;**********************************************************
              ;Main program loop. Read motor control switches. If a
              ; switch is pressed, BSR to perform the requested action.
              ; Loop continuously looking for switch closures.
              ;
0216 00 00 02 Main       BRSET MotorOnOff,PortA,Main1 ;On/Off pressed?
0219 AD 0C               BSR   DoOnOff       ;If yes, go to DoOnOff
021B 02 00 02 Main1      BRSET SpeedUp,PortA,Main2  ;Speed Up pressed?
021E AD 25               BSR   DoSpeedUp     ;If yes, go to DoSpeedUp
0220 04 00 F3 Main2      BRSET SpeedDn,PortA,Main   ;Speed Down ?
0223 AD 44               BSR   DoSpeedDn     ;If yes, go to DoSpeedDown
0225 20 EF               BRA   Main          ;Repeat loop continuously

              ;**********************************************************
              ;DoOnOff handles the closure of the Motor On/Off switch
              ; Debounces switch and waits for release.
              ;
0227          DoOnOff    EQU   *
0227 A6 07               LDA   #DebounceT    ;DebounceT * RTI time = 50mS
0229 B7 E4               STA   RTIDlyCnt     ;Initialize software counter
022B 3D E4    DoOnOff1   TST   RTIDlyCnt     ;RTI interrupt decrements it
022D 26 FC               BNE   DoOnOff1      ;Loop till RTIDlyCnt = 0
022F 00 00 12            BRSET MotorOnOff,PortA,DoOnOff3 ;Then check sw
                                             ;If open, not a good press
0232 01 00 FD            BRCLR MotorOnOff,PortA,*  ;Wait for sw release
0235 3D E5               TST   MotorOnFlg    ;Motor already on?
0237 26 07               BNE   DoOnOff2      ;Yes, turn the motor off.
0239 3C E5               INC   MotorOnFlg    ;No, Set 'MotorOn' flag
023B B6 E3               LDA   MotorPWM      ;And get last motor speed
023D B7 E0               STA   DesiredPWM    ;Turns on the PWM output
023F 81                  RTS                 ;Return (1 of 2)
0240 3F E0    DoOnOff2   CLR   DesiredPWM    ;Turns the PWM output off
0242 3F E5               CLR   MotorOnFlg    ;Clear 'MotorOn' flag
0244 81       DoOnOff3   RTS                 ;Return (2 of 2)
              ;**********************************************************
              ;DoSpeedUp handles the closure of the Speed Up switch
              ; Debounces sw then increments duty cycle till release
              ; Duty cycle incremented approx every 24 ms.
              ; Adj across full speed range in approx 6 seconds
              ;
0245          DoSpeedUp  EQU   *
0245 3D E5               TST   MotorOnFlg    ;Motor currently on?
0247 26 01               BNE   DoSpeedUp2    ;Yes, branch
0249 81       DoSpeedUp1 RTS                 ;No, sws don't work if off
024A A6 07    DoSpeedUp2 LDA   #DebounceT    ;Debounce delay approx 50 ms
024C B7 E4               STA   RTIDlyCnt     ;Initialize software counter
024E 3D E4    DoSpeedUp3 TST   RTIDlyCnt     ;RTI interrupt decrements it
0250 26 FC               BNE   DoSpeedUp3    ;Loop till RTIDlyCnt = 0
0252 02 00 F4 DoSpeedUp4 BRSET SpeedUp,PortA,DoSpeedUp1 ;RTS if sw off
0255 B6 E3               LDA   MotorPWM      ;Sw pressed, do speed up
0257 A1 FF               CMPA  #Percent100   ;Already full on?
0259 27 EE               BEQ   DoSpeedUp1    ;If yes just return
025B A6 03               LDA   #RampTime     ;No, get ramp time delay
                                             ;(3 * 8.2Ms = 24.6)
025D B7 E4               STA   RTIDlyCnt     ;Store to software counter
```

**Listing 9-2.**
Speed Control Program Listing (Sheet 3 of 4)

```
025F 3D E4     DoSpeedUp5 TST    RTIDlyCnt     ;Ramp time delay expired?
0261 26 FC                BNE    DoSpeedUp5    ;No, continue to wait
0263 3C E3                INC    MotorPWM      ;Yes, increase motor speed
0265 3C E0                INC    DesiredPWM    ;Adv the desired PWM value
0267 20 E9                BRA    DoSpeedUp4    ;Loop for sw still pressed


               ;**********************************************************
               ;DoSpeedDn handles the closure of the Speed Down switch
               ; Debounces sw then increments duty cycle till release
               ; Duty cycle incremented approx every 24 ms.
               ; Adj across full speed range in approx 6 seconds
               ;
0269           DoSpeedDn  EQU    *
0269 3D E5                TST    MotorOnFlg    ;Motor currently on?
026B 26 01                BNE    DoSpeedDn2    ;Yes, branch
026D 81        DoSpeedDn1 RTS                  ;No, sws don't work if off
026E A6 07     DoSpeedDn2 LDA    #DebounceT    ;Debounce delay approx 50 ms
0270 B7 E4                STA    RTIDlyCnt     ;Initialize software counter
0272 3D E4     DoSpeedDn3 TST    RTIDlyCnt     ;RTI interrupt decrements it
0274 26 FC                BNE    DoSpeedDn3    ;Loop till RTIDlyCnt = 0
0276 02 00 F4  DoSpeedDn4 BRSET  SpeedUp,PortA,DoSpeedDn1 ;RTS if sw off
0279 B6 E3                LDA    MotorPWM      ;Sw pressed, do speed up
027B A1 10                CMPA   #MinPWM       ;Already at minimum speed?
027D 27 EE                BEQ    DoSpeedDn1    ;If yes just return
027F A6 03                LDA    #RampTime     ;No, get ramp time delay
                                               ;(3 * 8.2Ms = 24.6)
0281 B7 E4                STA    RTIDlyCnt     ;Store to software counter
0283 3D E4     DoSpeedDn5 TST    RTIDlyCnt     ;Ramp time delay expired?
0285 26 FC                BNE    DoSpeedDn5    ;No, continue to wait
0287 3A E3                DEC    MotorPWM      ;Yes, decrease motor speed
0289 3A E0                DEC    DesiredPWM    ;Reduce desired PWM value
028B 20 E9                BRA    DoSpeedDn4    ;Loop for sw still pressed


               ;**********************************************************
               ;Since RTI and TOF interrupts share 1 vector, TimerInt is
               ;used to decide which source was requesting service.
               ;TOFInt and RTIInt service routines are used together to
               ;generate a PWM signal.
               ;
028D           TimerInt   EQU    *
028D 0E 08 04             BRSET  TOF,TSCR,TOFInt        ;TOF interrupt?
0290 0C 08 12             BRSET  RTIF,TSCR,RTIInt       ;RTI interrupt?
0293 80                   RTI          ;Shouldn't get here (defensive code)
```

**Listing 9-2.**
Speed Control Program Listing (Sheet 4 of 4)

```
              ;*********************************************************
              ;TOF interrupt response - Decrement PWMCoarse, when 0...
              ;Compare PWMFine to TCR. When TCR passes PWMFine clear
              ;PWM output pin and disable further TOF. RTI re-enables.
              ;
0294          TOFInt    EQU    *
0294 3A E1              DEC    PWMCoarse   ;Is PWMCoarse=0?
0296 26 0A              BNE    ExitTOF     ;No. Clear TOF and return
0298 B6 E2    TOFInt1   LDA    PWMFine     ;To compare to upper 4 of TCR
029A B1 09    CmpMore   CMPA   TCR
029C 22 FC              BHI    CmpMore     ;Loop till PWMFine <= TCR
029E 1F 00              BCLR   PWM,PortA   ;Set the PWM output low (0V)
02A0 1B 08              BCLR   TOIE,TSCR   ;Disable the TOF Interrupt
02A2 16 08    ExitTOF   BSET   TOFR,TSCR   ;Reset the TOF Interrupt Flag
02A4 80                 RTI                ;Return to the main program


              ;*********************************************************
              ;RTIF interrupt response - Set PWM out pin high, and
              ;enable TOF. Make PWMCoarse & PWMFine from DesiredPWM
              ;
02A5          RTIInt    EQU    *
02A5 3A E4              DEC    RTIDlyCnt   ;RTIDlyCnt = RTIDlyCnt - 1.
02A7 14 08              BSET   RTIFR,TSCR  ;Clear the RT Interrupt Flag
02A9 B6 E0              LDA    DesiredPWM  ;Get desired PWM level = 0?
02AB 26 03              BNE    RTIInt2     ;No,. Go set the output high
02AD 1F 00              BCLR   PWM,PortA   ;Make out low, duty is 0%
02AF 80                 RTI                ;Return from interrupt

02B0 1E 00    RTIInt2   BSET   PWM,PortA   ;PWM output high, duty > 0%
02B2 A1 FF              CMPA   #Percent100 ;Is desired PWM duty = 100%?
02B4 27 0D              BEQ    RTIInt3     ;Yes, Output always high
02B6 AE 10              LDX    #16         ;No, Put upper 4-bits of
02B8 42                 MUL                ;DesiredPWM in low 4-bits of
                                           ;X & low 4-bits of DesiredPWM
                                           ;in upper 4-bits of A.
02B9 B7 E2              STA    PWMFine     ;Save result into PWMFine
02BB BF E1              STX    PWMCoarse   ;Save result into PWMCoarse
02BD 27 D9              BEQ    TOFInt1     ;If PWMCoarse=0, go to 2nd
                                           ;half of TOF routine
02BF 16 08              BSET   TOFR,TSCR   ;Clear Timer Overflow Flag
02C1 1A 08              BSET   TOIE,TSCR   ;re-enable the TOF interrupt
02C3 80       RTIInt3   RTI                ;Return from RTIF interrupt


              ;*********************************************************
03F8                    ORG    Vectors     ;Interrupt & reset vectors

03F8 02 8D              FDB    TimerInt    ;Timer interrupt routine
03FA 02 00              FDB    Start       ;External IRQ (not used)
03FC 02 00              FDB    Start       ;SWI vector (not used)
03FE 02 00              FDB    Start       ;Reset vector
```

# Chapter 9 Review

> A *peripheral* is a specialized piece of computer hardware that allows the CPU to gather information about, and affect change on, the system of which a microcontroller is part.

General-purpose I/O ports may be programmed to act as either inputs or outputs. When a port pin is configured to act as an input, the CPU may read the logic level that is present on the port pin. When configured as an output, the CPU may set the port pin's output level to a logic 1 or logic 0.

Although all microcontrollers contain some general-purpose I/O ports as peripherals, they also contain additional peripherals that perform more specific tasks.

## Other Kinds Of Peripherals

**Timers** - Timers are peripherals that measure or generate time-related events in a microcontroller system. Timers are capable of performing frequency measurements or generating variable-width pulse trains. Timers can be sophisticated or simple.

**Serial Ports** - Sometimes microcontrollers need to communicate with specialized external peripherals or with another computer system. The communication is usually performed bit-serially (one bit of information at a time). The two most common types of serial ports are the Serial Communications Interface (SCI) and the Serial Peripheral Interface (SPI). The SCI communicates asynchronously with other devices and is usually used to exchange data between two computer systems. The SPI communicates synchronously with other devices and is usually used to control peripheral devices that are external to the microcontroller.

*On-Chip Peripheral Systems*

**Analog-to-Digital Converters** - Many signals that exist outside the microcontroller are continuously varying analog signals. An Analog-to-Digital (A-to-D) converter is a peripheral that converts these signals into a binary number that the microcontroller can use.

**Digital-to-Analog Converters** - A digital-to-analog (D-to-A) converter performs the opposite function of an A-to-D converter. It allows the microcontroller to convert a digital number into a proportional analog voltage or current that can control various output devices in a microcontroller system.

**EEPROM** - Although EEPROM is a type of nonvolatile memory, it is considered by many to be a peripheral. EEPROM is unique because its contents may be erased and rewritten under program control. Some EEPROM devices are external components that are connected to SPI ports.

# Combining Hardware and Software

The motor speed control example described at the end of this chapter shows how hardware circuitry and software programs work together to solve practical problems. The microcontroller performs timing and control logic tasks, while an external power driver and simple switches complete the system.

# M68HC05 Instruction Set Details

This appendix contains complete detailed information for all M68HC05 instructions. The instructions are arranged in alphabetical order with the instruction mnemonic set in larger type for easy reference.

The nomenclature listed below is used in the instruction description sheets throughout this appendix.

## Operators

( ) = Contents of register or memory location shown inside parentheses

← = Is loaded with (read: "gets")

↑ = Is pulled from stack

↓ = Is pushed onto stack

• = Boolean AND

+ = Arithmetic addition (except where used as inclusive-OR in Boolean formula)

⊕ = Boolean exclusive-OR

× = Multiply

: = Concatenate

− = Negate (twos complement)

## CPU Registers

ACCA = Accumulator

CCR = Condition Code register

X = Index register

PC = Program Counter

PCH = Program Counter, Higher-order (most significant) eight bits

PCL = Program Counter, Lower-order (least significant) eight bits

SP = Stack Pointer

## Memory and Addressing

M = A memory location or absolute data, depending on addressing mode

Rel = Relative offset (i.e., the twos-complement number stored in the last byte of machine code corresponding to a branch instruction)

## Condition Code Register (CCR) bits

H = Half carry, bit 4

I = Interrupt mask, bit 3

N = Negative indicator, bit 2

C = Carry/borrow, bit 1

Z = Zero indicator, bit 0

## Bit status BEFORE execution

$\text{An} = $ Bit n of ACCA (n = 7, 6, 5, ... 0)

$\text{Xn} = $ Bit n of X (n = 7, 6, 5, ... 0)

$\text{Mn} = $ Bit n of M (n = 7, 6, 5, ... 0)

## Bit status AFTER execution

$\text{Rn} = $ bit n of the result (n = 7, 6, 5, ... 0)

## CCR activity figure notation

$- = $ Bit not affected

$0 = $ Bit forced to zero

$1 = $ Bit forced to one

$\Delta = $ Bit set or cleared according to results of operation

## Machine coding notation

dd = Low-order eight bits of a direct address $0000 - $00FF (high byte assumed to be $00)

ee = Upper eight bits of 16-bit offset

ff = Lower eight bits of 16-bit offset or eight-bit offset

ii = One byte of immediate data

hh = High-order byte of 16-bit extended address

ll = Low-order byte of 16-bit extended address

rr = Relative offset

## Source form notation

*opr* = Operand (one or two bytes, depending on address mode)

*rel* = Relative offset used in branch and bit manipulation instructions

,X = Indexed addressing mode

## Address modes

INH = Inherent

IMM = Immediate

DIR = Direct

EXT = Extended

IX = Indexed — No offset

IX1 = Indexed — Eight-bit offset

IX2 = Indexed — 16-bit offset

REL = Relative

# ADC

**Add with Carry**

# ADC

**Operation:**     ACCA ← (ACCA) + (M) + (C)

**Description:**    Adds the contents of the C bit to the sum of the contents of ACCA and M and places the result in ACCA.

## Condition Codes and Boolean Formulae:

| | | | H | I | N | Z | C |
|---|---|---|---|---|---|---|---|
| 1 | 1 | 1 | Δ | – | Δ | Δ | Δ |

H:   A3•M3 + M3•$\overline{R3}$ + $\overline{R3}$•A3
     Set if there was a carry from bit 3; cleared otherwise.

N:   R7
     Set if MSB of result is one; cleared otherwise.

Z:   $\overline{R7}$•$\overline{R6}$•$\overline{R5}$•$\overline{R4}$•$\overline{R3}$•$\overline{R2}$•$\overline{R1}$•$\overline{R0}$
     Set if the result is $00; cleared otherwise.

C:   A7•M7 + M7•$\overline{R7}$ + $\overline{R7}$•A7
     Set if there was a carry from the MSB of the result; cleared otherwise.

## Source Forms, Addressing Modes, Machine Code, and Cycles:

| Source Forms | Addr Mode | Machine Code | | HCMOS Cycles |
|---|---|---|---|---|
| | | Opcode | Operand(s) | |
| ADC  #opr | IMM | A9 | ii | 2 |
| ADC  opr | DIR | B9 | dd | 3 |
| ADC  opr | EXT | C9 | hh  ll | 4 |
| ADC  ,X | IX | F9 | | 3 |
| ADC  opr,X | IX1 | E9 | ff | 4 |
| ADC  opr,X | IX2 | D9 | ee  ff | 5 |

# ADD

## Add without Carry

# ADD

**Operation:**     $ACCA \leftarrow (ACCA) + (M)$

**Description:**    Adds the contents of M to the contents of ACCA and places the result in ACCA.

## Condition Codes and Boolean Formulae:

| | | | H | I | N | Z | C |
|---|---|---|---|---|---|---|---|
| 1 | 1 | 1 | Δ | – | Δ | Δ | Δ |

H:  A3•M3 + M3•$\overline{R3}$ + $\overline{R3}$•A3
    Set if there was a carry from bit 3; cleared otherwise.

N:  R7
    Set if MSB of result is one; cleared otherwise.

Z:  $\overline{R7}$•$\overline{R6}$•$\overline{R5}$•$\overline{R4}$•$\overline{R3}$•$\overline{R2}$•$\overline{R1}$•$\overline{R0}$
    Set if the result is $00; cleared otherwise.

C:  A7•M7 + M7•$\overline{R7}$ + $\overline{R7}$•A7
    Set if there was a carry from the MSB of the result; cleared otherwise.

## Source Forms, Addressing Modes, Machine Code, and Cycles:

| Source Forms | Addr Mode | Machine Code | | HCMOS Cycles |
|---|---|---|---|---|
| | | Opcode | Operand(s) | |
| ADD    #opr | IMM | AB | ii | 2 |
| ADD    opr | DIR | BB | dd | 3 |
| ADD    opr | EXT | CB | hh    ll | 4 |
| ADD    ,X | IX | FB | | 3 |
| ADD    opr,X | IX1 | EB | ff | 4 |
| ADD    opr,X | IX2 | DB | ee    ff | 5 |

# AND

**Logical AND**

# AND

**Operation:**    $ACCA \leftarrow (ACCA) \cdot (M)$

**Description:**    Performs the logical AND between the contents of ACCA and the contents of M and places the result in ACCA. (Each bit of ACCA after the operation will be the logical AND of the corresponding bits of M and of ACCA before the operation.)

## Condition Codes and Boolean Formulae:

| | | | H | I | N | Z | C |
|---|---|---|---|---|---|---|---|
| 1 | 1 | 1 | – | – | Δ | Δ | – |

N: R7
   Set if MSB of result is one; cleared otherwise.

Z: $\overline{R7 \cdot R6 \cdot R5 \cdot R4 \cdot R3 \cdot R2 \cdot R1 \cdot R0}$
   Set if the result is $00; cleared otherwise.

## Source Forms, Addressing Modes, Machine Code, and Cycles:

| Source Forms | Addr Mode | Machine Code Opcode | Operand(s) | HCMOS Cycles |
|---|---|---|---|---|
| AND    #opr | IMM | A4 | ii | 2 |
| AND    opr | DIR | B4 | dd | 3 |
| AND    opr | EXT | C4 | hh    ll | 4 |
| AND    ,X | IX | F4 | | 3 |
| AND    opr,X | IX1 | E4 | ff | 4 |
| AND    opr,X | IX2 | D4 | ee    ff | 5 |

*M68HC05 Instruction Set Details*

# ASL

### Arithmetic Shift Left
### (Same as LSL)

# ASL

**Operation:**

$$\boxed{C} \leftarrow \boxed{b7 -- \quad -- b0} \leftarrow 0$$

**Description:** Shifts all bits of the ACCA, X, or M one place to the left. Bit 0 is loaded with a zero. The C bit in the CCR is loaded from the most significant bit of ACCA, X, or M.

## Condition Codes and Boolean Formulae:

|   |   |   | H | I | N | Z | C |
|---|---|---|---|---|---|---|---|
| 1 | 1 | 1 | – | – | Δ | Δ | Δ |

N: R7
Set if MSB of result is one; cleared otherwise.

Z: $\overline{R7} \cdot \overline{R6} \cdot \overline{R5} \cdot \overline{R4} \cdot \overline{R3} \cdot \overline{R2} \cdot \overline{R1} \cdot \overline{R0}$
Set if the result is $00; cleared otherwise.

C: b7
Set if, before the shift, the MSB of the shifted value was set; cleared otherwise.

## Source Forms, Addressing Modes, Machine Code, and Cycles:

| Source Forms | Addr Mode | Machine Code Opcode | Operand(s) | HCMOS Cycles |
|---|---|---|---|---|
| ASLA | INH (A) | 48 |  | 3 |
| ASLX | INH (X) | 58 |  | 3 |
| ASL  opr | DIR | 38 | dd | 5 |
| ASL  ,X | IX | 78 |  | 5 |
| ASL  opr,X | IX1 | 68 | ff | 6 |

# ASR                    Arithmetic Shift Right                    ASR

**Operation:**

**Description:**    Shifts all bits of ACCA, X, or M one place to the right. Bit 7 is held constant. Bit 0 is loaded into the C bit of the CCR. This operation effectively divides a twos complement value by two without changing its sign. The carry bit can be used to round the result.

## Condition Codes and Boolean Formulae:

|   |   |   | H | I | N | Z | C |
|---|---|---|---|---|---|---|---|
| 1 | 1 | 1 | – | – | Δ | Δ | Λ |

N: R7
Set if MSB of result is one; cleared otherwise.

Z: $\overline{R7} \cdot \overline{R6} \cdot \overline{R5} \cdot \overline{R4} \cdot \overline{R3} \cdot \overline{R2} \cdot \overline{R1} \cdot \overline{R0}$
Set if the result is $00; cleared otherwise.

C: b0
Set if, before the shift, the LSB of the shifted value was set; cleared otherwise.

## Source Forms, Addressing Modes, Machine Code, and Cycles:

| Source Forms | Addr Mode | Machine Code | | HCMOS Cycles |
|---|---|---|---|---|
| | | Opcode | Operand(s) | |
| ASRA | INH (A) | 47 | | 3 |
| ASRX | INH (X) | 57 | | 3 |
| ASR    *opr* | DIR | 37 | dd | 5 |
| ASR    ,X | IX | 77 | | 5 |
| ASR    *opr*,X | IX1 | 67 | ff | 6 |

# BCC

**Branch if Carry Clear**

**(Same as BHS)**

# BCC

**Operation:** $\quad$ PC $\leftarrow$ (PC) + \$0002 + Rel $\qquad$ if (C) = 0

**Description:** Tests the state of the C bit in the CCR and causes a branch if C is clear. See BRA instruction for further details of the execution of the branch.

## Condition Codes and Boolean Formulae:

| | | | H | I | N | Z | C |
|---|---|---|---|---|---|---|---|
| 1 | 1 | 1 | – | – | – | – | – |

## Source Forms, Addressing Modes, Machine Code, and Cycles:

| Source Forms | Addr Mode | Machine Code | | HCMOS Cycles |
|---|---|---|---|---|
| | | Opcode | Operand(s) | |
| BCC  *rel* | REL | 24 | rr | 3 |

The following is a summary of all branch instructions.

| Branch | | | | Opposite Branch | | | Type |
|---|---|---|---|---|---|---|---|
| Test | Boolean | Mnemonic | Opcode | Test | Mnemonic | Opcode | |
| r > m | C + Z = 0 | BHI | 22 | r ≤ m | BLS | 23 | Unsigned |
| r ≥ m | C = 0 | BHS (BCC) | 24 | r < m | BLO (BCS) | 25 | Unsigned |
| r = m | Z = 1 | BEQ | 27 | r ≠ m | BNE | 26 | Unsigned |
| r ≤ m | C + Z = 1 | BLS | 23 | r > m | BHI | 22 | Unsigned |
| r < m | C = 1 | BLO (BCS) | 25 | r ≥ m | BHS (BCC) | 24 | Unsigned |
| Carry | C = 1 | BCS | 25 | No Carry | BCC | 24 | Simple |
| r = \$00 | Z = 1 | BEQ | 27 | r ≠ \$00 | BNE | 26 | Simple |
| Negative | N = 1 | BMI | 2B | Plus | BPL | 2A | Simple |
| I Mask | I = 1 | BMS | 2D | I Mask = 0 | BMC | 2C | Simple |
| H-Bit | H = 1 | BHCS | 29 | H = 0 | BHCC | 28 | Simple |
| IRQ High | - | BIH | 2F | IRQ Low | BIL | 2E | Simple |
| Always | - | BRA | 20 | Never | BRN | 21 | Uncond. |

r = register (ACCA or X)  m = memory operand

# BCLR n            Clear Bit in Memory            BCLR n

**Operation:**       Mn ← 0

**Description:**     Clear bit n (n = 7, 6, 5, ... 0) in location M. All other bits in M
                     are unaffected. M can be any RAM or I/O register address in
                     the $0000 to $00FF area of memory (i.e., direct addressing
                     mode is used to specify the address of the operand).

## Condition Codes and Boolean Formulae:

|   |   |   | H | I | N | Z | C |
|---|---|---|---|---|---|---|---|
| 1 | 1 | 1 | – | – | – | – | – |

## Source Forms, Addressing Modes, Machine Code, and Cycles:

| Source Forms | Addr Mode | Machine Code | | HCMOS Cycles |
|---|---|---|---|---|
|  |  | Opcode | Operand(s) |  |
| BCLR   0,*opr* | DIR b0 | 11 | dd | 5 |
| BCLR   1,*opr* | DIR b1 | 13 | dd | 5 |
| BCLR   2,*opr* | DIR b2 | 15 | dd | 5 |
| BCLR   3,*opr* | DIR b3 | 17 | dd | 5 |
| BCLR   4,*opr* | DIR b4 | 19 | dd | 5 |
| BCLR   5,*opr* | DIR b5 | 1B | dd | 5 |
| BCLR   6,*opr* | DIR b6 | 1D | dd | 5 |
| BCLR   7,*opr* | DIR b7 | 1F | dd | 5 |

# BCS

### Branch if Carry Set
### (Same as BLO)

# BCS

**Operation:**     $PC \leftarrow (PC) + \$0002 + Rel \qquad$ if $(C) = 1$

**Description:**    Tests the state of the C bit in the CCR and causes a branch if C is set. See BRA instruction for further details of the execution of the branch.

## Condition Codes and Boolean Formulae:

|   |   |   | H | I | N | Z | C |
|---|---|---|---|---|---|---|---|
| 1 | 1 | 1 | – | – | – | – | – |

## Source Forms, Addressing Modes, Machine Code, and Cycles:

| Source Forms | Addr Mode | Machine Code | | HCMOS Cycles |
|---|---|---|---|---|
| | | Opcode | Operand(s) | |
| BCS   *rel* | REL | 25 | rr | 3 |

The following is a summary of all branch instructions.

| Branch | | | | Opposite Branch | | | Type |
|---|---|---|---|---|---|---|---|
| Test | Boolean | Mnemonic | Opcode | Test | Mnemonic | Opcode | |
| r > m | C + Z = 0 | BHI | 22 | r ≤ m | BLS | 23 | Unsigned |
| r ≥ m | C = 0 | BHS (BCC) | 24 | r < m | BLO (BCS) | 25 | Unsigned |
| r = m | Z = 1 | BEQ | 27 | r ≠ m | BNE | 26 | Unsigned |
| r ≤ m | C + Z = 1 | BLS | 23 | r > m | BHI | 22 | Unsigned |
| r < m | C = 1 | BLO (BCS) | 25 | r ≥ m | BHS (BCC) | 24 | Unsigned |
| Carry | C = 1 | BCS | 25 | No Carry | BCC | 24 | Simple |
| r = $00 | Z = 1 | BEQ | 27 | r ≠ $00 | BNE | 26 | Simple |
| Negative | N = 1 | BMI | 2B | Plus | BPL | 2A | Simple |
| I Mask | I = 1 | BMS | 2D | I Mask = 0 | BMC | 2C | Simple |
| H-Bit | H = 1 | BHCS | 29 | H = 0 | BHCC | 28 | Simple |
| $\overline{\text{IRQ}}$ High | - | BIH | 2F | $\overline{\text{IRQ}}$ Low | BIL | 2E | Simple |
| Always | - | BRA | 20 | Never | BRN | 21 | Uncond. |

r = register (ACCA or X)   m = memory operand

# BEQ

### Branch if Equal

# BEQ

**Operation:**  $PC \leftarrow (PC) + \$0002 + Rel$    if $(Z) = 1$

**Description:** Tests the state of the Z bit in the CCR and causes a branch if Z is set. After a CMP or SUB instruction, BEQ will cause a branch if the arguments were equal. See BRA instruction for further details of the execution of the branch.

## Condition Codes and Boolean Formulae:

| | | | H | I | N | Z | C |
|---|---|---|---|---|---|---|---|
| 1 | 1 | 1 | – | – | – | – | – |

## Source Forms, Addressing Modes, Machine Code, and Cycles:

| Source Forms | Addr Mode | Machine Code Opcode | Operand(s) | HCMOS Cycles |
|---|---|---|---|---|
| BEQ  *rel* | REL | 27 | rr | 3 |

The following is a summary of all branch instructions.

| Branch | | | | Opposite Branch | | | Type |
|---|---|---|---|---|---|---|---|
| Test | Boolean | Mnemonic | Opcode | Test | Mnemonic | Opcode | |
| r > m | C + Z = 0 | BHI | 22 | r ≤ m | BLS | 23 | Unsigned |
| r ≥ m | C = 0 | BHS (BCC) | 24 | r < m | BLO (BCS) | 25 | Unsigned |
| r = m | Z = 1 | BEQ | 27 | r ≠ m | BNE | 26 | Unsigned |
| r ≤ m | C + Z = 1 | BLS | 23 | r > m | BHI | 22 | Unsigned |
| r < m | C = 1 | BLO (BCS) | 25 | r ≥ m | BHS (BCC) | 24 | Unsigned |
| Carry | C = 1 | BCS | 25 | No Carry | BCC | 24 | Simple |
| r = $00 | Z = 1 | BEQ | 27 | r ≠ $00 | BNE | 26 | Simple |
| Negative | N = 1 | BMI | 2B | Plus | BPL | 2A | Simple |
| I Mask | I = 1 | BMS | 2D | I Mask = 0 | BMC | 2C | Simple |
| H-Bit | H = 1 | BHCS | 29 | H = 0 | BHCC | 28 | Simple |
| IRQ High | - | BIH | 2F | IRQ Low | BIL | 2E | Simple |
| Always | - | BRA | 20 | Never | BRN | 21 | Uncond. |

r = register (ACCA or X)  m = memory operand

*M68HC05 Instruction Set Details*

# BHCC        Branch if Half Carry Clear        BHCC

**Operation:**        PC ← (PC) + $0002 + Rel        if (H) = 0

**Description:**        Tests the state of the H bit in the CCR and causes a branch if H is clear. This instruction is used in algorithms involving BCD numbers. See BRA instruction for further details of the execution of the branch.

## Condition Codes and Boolean Formulae:

| | | | H | I | N | Z | C |
|---|---|---|---|---|---|---|---|
| 1 | 1 | 1 | – | – | – | – | – |

## Source Forms, Addressing Modes, Machine Code, and Cycles:

| Source Forms | Addr Mode | Machine Code Opcode | Operand(s) | HCMOS Cycles |
|---|---|---|---|---|
| BHCC  *rel* | REL | 28 | rr | 3 |

The following is a summary of all branch instructions.

| Branch | | | | Opposite Branch | | | Type |
|---|---|---|---|---|---|---|---|
| Test | Boolean | Mnemonic | Opcode | Test | Mnemonic | Opcode | |
| r > m | C + Z = 0 | BHI | 22 | r ≤ m | BLS | 23 | Unsigned |
| r ≥ m | C = 0 | BHS (BCC) | 24 | r < m | BLO (BCS) | 25 | Unsigned |
| r = m | Z = 1 | BEQ | 27 | r ≠ m | BNE | 26 | Unsigned |
| r ≤ m | C + Z = 1 | BLS | 23 | r > m | BHI | 22 | Unsigned |
| r < m | C = 1 | BLO (BCS) | 25 | r ≥ m | BHS (BCC) | 24 | Unsigned |
| Carry | C = 1 | BCS | 25 | No Carry | BCC | 24 | Simple |
| r = $00 | Z = 1 | BEQ | 27 | r ≠ $00 | BNE | 26 | Simple |
| Negative | N = 1 | BMI | 2B | Plus | BPL | 2A | Simple |
| I Mask | I = 1 | BMS | 2D | I Mask = 0 | BMC | 2C | Simple |
| H-Bit | H = 1 | BHCS | 29 | H = 0 | BHCC | 28 | Simple |
| IRQ High | - | BIH | 2F | IRQ Low | BIL | 2E | Simple |
| Always | - | BRA | 20 | Never | BRN | 21 | Uncond. |

r = register (ACCA or X)  m = memory operand

# BHCS

**Branch if Half Carry Set**

# BHCS

**Operation:**      PC ← (PC) + $0002 + Rel     if (H) = 1

**Description:**     Tests the state of the H bit in the CCR and causes a branch if H is set. This instruction is used in algorithms involving BCD numbers. See BRA instruction for further details of the execution of the branch.

## Condition Codes and Boolean Formulae:

| | | | H | I | N | Z | C |
|---|---|---|---|---|---|---|---|
| 1 | 1 | 1 | – | – | – | – | – |

## Source Forms, Addressing Modes, Machine Code, and Cycles:

| Source Forms | Addr Mode | Machine Code Opcode | Operand(s) | HCMOS Cycles |
|---|---|---|---|---|
| BHCS *rel* | REL | 29 | rr | 3 |

The following is a summary of all branch instructions.

| Branch | | | | Opposite Branch | | | Type |
|---|---|---|---|---|---|---|---|
| Test | Boolean | Mnemonic | Opcode | Test | Mnemonic | Opcode | |
| r > m | C + Z = 0 | BHI | 22 | r ≤ m | BLS | 23 | Unsigned |
| r ≥ m | C = 0 | BHS (BCC) | 24 | r < m | BLO (BCS) | 25 | Unsigned |
| r = m | Z = 1 | BEQ | 27 | r ≠ m | BNE | 26 | Unsigned |
| r ≤ m | C + Z = 1 | BLS | 23 | r > m | BHI | 22 | Unsigned |
| r < m | C = 1 | BLO (BCS) | 25 | r ≥ m | BHS (BCC) | 24 | Unsigned |
| Carry | C = 1 | BCS | 25 | No Carry | BCC | 24 | Simple |
| r = $00 | Z = 1 | BEQ | 27 | r ≠ $00 | BNE | 26 | Simple |
| Negative | N = 1 | BMI | 2B | Plus | BPL | 2A | Simple |
| I Mask | I = 1 | BMS | 2D | I Mask = 0 | BMC | 2C | Simple |
| H-Bit | H = 1 | BHCS | 29 | H = 0 | BHCC | 28 | Simple |
| IRQ High | - | BIH | 2F | IRQ Low | BIL | 2E | Simple |
| Always | - | BRA | 20 | Never | BRN | 21 | Uncond. |

r = register (ACCA or X)   m = memory operand

# BHI        Branch if Higher        BHI

**Operation:**      $PC \leftarrow (PC) + \$0002 + Rel$     if $(C) + (Z) = 0$

i.e., if $(ACCA) > (M)$     (unsigned binary numbers)

**Description:**      Causes a branch if both C and Z are cleared. If the BHI instruction is executed immediately after execution of a CMP or SUB instruction, the branch will occur if the unsigned binary number in ACCA was greater than the unsigned binary number in M. See BRA instruction for further details of the execution of the branch.

## Condition Codes and Boolean Formulae:

| | | | H | I | N | Z | C |
|---|---|---|---|---|---|---|---|
| 1 | 1 | 1 | – | – | – | – | – |

## Source Forms, Addressing Modes, Machine Code, and Cycles:

| Source Forms | Addr Mode | Machine Code Opcode | Operand(s) | HCMOS Cycles |
|---|---|---|---|---|
| BHI *rel* | REL | 22 | rr | 3 |

The following is a summary of all branch instructions.

| Branch | | | | Opposite Branch | | | Type |
|---|---|---|---|---|---|---|---|
| Test | Boolean | Mnemonic | Opcode | Test | Mnemonic | Opcode | |
| r > m | C + Z = 0 | BHI | 22 | r ≤ m | BLS | 23 | Unsigned |
| r ≥ m | C = 0 | BHS (BCC) | 24 | r < m | BLO (BCS) | 25 | Unsigned |
| r = m | Z = 1 | BEQ | 27 | r ≠ m | BNE | 26 | Unsigned |
| r ≤ m | C + Z = 1 | BLS | 23 | r > m | BHI | 22 | Unsigned |
| r < m | C = 1 | BLO (BCS) | 25 | r ≥ m | BHS (BCC) | 24 | Unsigned |
| Carry | C = 1 | BCS | 25 | No Carry | BCC | 24 | Simple |
| r = $00 | Z = 1 | BEQ | 27 | r ≠ $00 | BNE | 26 | Simple |
| Negative | N = 1 | BMI | 2B | Plus | BPL | 2A | Simple |
| I Mask | I = 1 | BMS | 2D | I Mask = 0 | BMC | 2C | Simple |
| H-Bit | H = 1 | BHCS | 29 | H = 0 | BHCC | 28 | Simple |
| IRQ High | - | BIH | 2F | IRQ Low | BIL | 2E | Simple |
| Always | - | BRA | 20 | Never | BRN | 21 | Uncond. |

r = register (ACCA or X)   m = memory operand

# BHS

### Branch if Higher or Same
### (Same as BCC)

# BHS

**Operation:**

$PC \leftarrow (PC) + \$0002 + Rel$     if $(C) = 0$

i.e., if $(ACCA) \geq (M)$     (unsigned binary numbers)

**Description:**

If the BHS instruction is executed immediately after execution of a CMP or SUB instruction, the branch will occur if the unsigned binary number in ACCA was greater than or equal to the unsigned binary number in M. See BRA instruction for further details of the execution of the branch.

## Condition Codes and Boolean Formulae:

| | | | H | I | N | Z | C |
|---|---|---|---|---|---|---|---|
| 1 | 1 | 1 | – | – | – | – | – |

## Source Forms, Addressing Modes, Machine Code, and Cycles:

| Source Forms | Addr Mode | Machine Code Opcode | Operand(s) | HCMOS Cycles |
|---|---|---|---|---|
| BHS *rel* | REL | 24 | rr | 3 |

The following is a summary of all branch instructions.

| Branch | | | | Opposite Branch | | | Type |
|---|---|---|---|---|---|---|---|
| Test | Boolean | Mnemonic | Opcode | Test | Mnemonic | Opcode | |
| r > m | C + Z = 0 | BHI | 22 | r ≤ m | BLS | 23 | Unsigned |
| r ≥ m | C = 0 | BHS (BCC) | 24 | r < m | BLO (BCS) | 25 | Unsigned |
| r = m | Z = 1 | BEQ | 27 | r ≠ m | BNE | 26 | Unsigned |
| r ≤ m | C + Z = 1 | BLS | 23 | r > m | BHI | 22 | Unsigned |
| r < m | C = 1 | BLO (BCS) | 25 | r ≥ m | BHS (BCC) | 24 | Unsigned |
| Carry | C = 1 | BCS | 25 | No Carry | BCC | 24 | Simple |
| r = $00 | Z = 1 | BEQ | 27 | r ≠ $00 | BNE | 26 | Simple |
| Negative | N = 1 | BMI | 2B | Plus | BPL | 2A | Simple |
| I Mask | I = 1 | BMS | 2D | I Mask = 0 | BMC | 2C | Simple |
| H-Bit | H = 1 | BHCS | 29 | H = 0 | BHCC | 28 | Simple |
| IRQ High | - | BIH | 2F | IRQ Low | BIL | 2E | Simple |
| Always | - | BRA | 20 | Never | BRN | 21 | Uncond. |

r = register (ACCA or X)   m = memory operand

# BIH          Branch if Interrupt Pin is High          BIH

**Operation:**          $PC \leftarrow (PC) + \$0002 + Rel$     if $\overline{IRQ} = 1$

**Description:**          Tests the state of the external interrupt pin and causes a branch if the pin is high. See BRA instruction for further details of the execution of the branch.

## Condition Codes and Boolean Formulae:

|   |   |   | H | I | N | Z | C |
|---|---|---|---|---|---|---|---|
| 1 | 1 | 1 | – | – | – | – | – |

## Source Forms, Addressing Modes, Machine Code, and Cycles:

| Source Forms | Addr Mode | Machine Code | | HCMOS Cycles |
|---|---|---|---|---|
| | | Opcode | Operand(s) | |
| BIH  *rel* | REL | 2F | rr | 3 |

The following is a summary of all branch instructions.

| Branch | | | | Opposite Branch | | | Type |
|---|---|---|---|---|---|---|---|
| Test | Boolean | Mnemonic | Opcode | Test | Mnemonic | Opcode | |
| r > m | C + Z = 0 | BHI | 22 | r ≤ m | BLS | 23 | Unsigned |
| r ≥ m | C = 0 | BHS (BCC) | 24 | r < m | BLO (BCS) | 25 | Unsigned |
| r = m | Z = 1 | BEQ | 27 | r ≠ m | BNE | 26 | Unsigned |
| r ≤ m | C + Z = 1 | BLS | 23 | r > m | BHI | 22 | Unsigned |
| r < m | C = 1 | BLO (BCS) | 25 | r ≥ m | BHS (BCC) | 24 | Unsigned |
| Carry | C = 1 | BCS | 25 | No Carry | BCC | 24 | Simple |
| r = $00 | Z = 1 | BEQ | 27 | r ≠ $00 | BNE | 26 | Simple |
| Negative | N = 1 | BMI | 2B | Plus | BPL | 2A | Simple |
| I Mask | I = 1 | BMS | 2D | I Mask = 0 | BMC | 2C | Simple |
| H-Bit | H = 1 | BHCS | 29 | H = 0 | BHCC | 28 | Simple |
| $\overline{IRQ}$ High | - | BIH | 2F | $\overline{IRQ}$ Low | BIL | 2E | Simple |
| Always | - | BRA | 20 | Never | BRN | 21 | Uncond. |

r = register (ACCA or X)   m = memory operand

**Operation:**     $PC \leftarrow (PC) + \$0002 + Rel$     if $\overline{IRQ} = 0$

**Description:**     Tests the state of the external interrupt pin and causes a branch if the pin is low. See BRA instruction for further details of the execution of the branch.

## Condition Codes and Boolean Formulae:

| | | H | I | N | Z | C |
|---|---|---|---|---|---|---|
| 1 | 1 | 1 | – | – | – | – | – |

## Source Forms, Addressing Modes, Machine Code, and Cycles:

| Source Forms | Addr Mode | Machine Code Opcode | Operand(s) | HCMOS Cycles |
|---|---|---|---|---|
| BIL *rel* | REL | 2E | rr | 3 |

The following is a summary of all branch instructions.

| Branch | | | | Opposite Branch | | | Type |
|---|---|---|---|---|---|---|---|
| Test | Boolean | Mnemonic | Opcode | Test | Mnemonic | Opcode | |
| r > m | C + Z = 0 | BHI | 22 | r ≤ m | BLS | 23 | Unsigned |
| r ≥ m | C = 0 | BHS (BCC) | 24 | r < m | BLO (BCS) | 25 | Unsigned |
| r = m | Z = 1 | BEQ | 27 | r ≠ m | BNE | 26 | Unsigned |
| r ≤ m | C + Z = 1 | BLS | 23 | r > m | BHI | 22 | Unsigned |
| r < m | C = 1 | BLO (BCS) | 25 | r ≥ m | BHS (BCC) | 24 | Unsigned |
| Carry | C = 1 | BCS | 25 | No Carry | BCC | 24 | Simple |
| r = $00 | Z = 1 | BEQ | 27 | r ≠ $00 | BNE | 26 | Simple |
| Negative | N = 1 | BMI | 2B | Plus | BPL | 2A | Simple |
| I Mask | I = 1 | BMS | 2D | I Mask = 0 | BMC | 2C | Simple |
| H-Bit | H = 1 | BHCS | 29 | H = 0 | BHCC | 28 | Simple |
| $\overline{IRQ}$ High | - | BIH | 2F | $\overline{IRQ}$ Low | BIL | 2E | Simple |
| Always | - | BRA | 20 | Never | BRN | 21 | Uncond. |

r = register (ACCA or X)   m = memory operand

# BIT

**Bit Test Memory with Accumulator**

# BIT

**Operation:**     (ACCA) • (M)

**Description:**    Performs the logical AND comparison of the contents of ACCA and the contents of M, and modifies the condition codes accordingly. Neither the contents of ACCA or M are altered. (Each bit of the result of the AND would be the logical AND of the corresponding bits of ACCA and M.)

## Condition Codes and Boolean Formulae:

| | | | H | I | N | Z | C |
|---|---|---|---|---|---|---|---|
| 1 | 1 | 1 | – | – | Δ | Δ | – |

N: R7
   Set if MSB of result is one; cleared otherwise.

Z: $\overline{R7 \cdot R6 \cdot R5 \cdot R4 \cdot R3 \cdot R2 \cdot R1 \cdot R0}$
   Set if the result is $00; cleared otherwise.

## Source Forms, Addressing Modes, Machine Code, and Cycles:

| Source Forms | Addr Mode | Machine Code Opcode | Operand(s) | HCMOS Cycles |
|---|---|---|---|---|
| BIT  #*opr* | IMM | A5 | ii | 2 |
| BIT  *opr* | DIR | B5 | dd | 3 |
| BIT  *opr* | EXT | C5 | hh    ll | 4 |
| BIT  ,X | IX | F5 | | 3 |
| BIT  *opr*,X | IX1 | E5 | ff | 4 |
| BIT  *opr*,X | IX2 | D5 | ee    ff | 5 |

# BLO

### Branch if Lower
### (Same as BCS)

# BLO

**Operation:** $PC \leftarrow (PC) + \$0002 + Rel$     if $(C) = 1$

i.e.; if $(ACCA) < (M)$     (unsigned binary numbers)

**Description:** If the BLO instruction is executed immediately after execution of a CMP or SUB instruction, the branch will occur if the unsigned binary number in ACCA was less than the unsigned binary number in M. See BRA instruction for further details of the execution of the branch.

## Condition Codes and Boolean Formulae:

| | | | H | I | N | Z | C |
|---|---|---|---|---|---|---|---|
| 1 | 1 | 1 | – | – | – | – | – |

## Source Forms, Addressing Modes, Machine Code, and Cycles:

| Source Forms | Addr Mode | Machine Code Opcode | Operand(s) | HCMOS Cycles |
|---|---|---|---|---|
| BLO  *rel* | REL | 25 | rr | 3 |

The following is a summary of all branch instructions.

| Branch | | | | Opposite Branch | | | Type |
|---|---|---|---|---|---|---|---|
| Test | Boolean | Mnemonic | Opcode | Test | Mnemonic | Opcode | |
| r > m | C + Z = 0 | BHI | 22 | r ≤ m | BLS | 23 | Unsigned |
| r ≥ m | C = 0 | BHS (BCC) | 24 | r < m | BLO (BCS) | 25 | Unsigned |
| r = m | Z = 1 | BEQ | 27 | r ≠ m | BNE | 26 | Unsigned |
| r ≤ m | C + Z = 1 | BLS | 23 | r > m | BHI | 22 | Unsigned |
| r < m | C = 1 | BLO (BCS) | 25 | r ≥ m | BHS (BCC) | 24 | Unsigned |
| Carry | C = 1 | BCS | 25 | No Carry | BCC | 24 | Simple |
| r = $00 | Z = 1 | BEQ | 27 | r ≠ $00 | BNE | 26 | Simple |
| Negative | N = 1 | BMI | 2B | Plus | BPL | 2A | Simple |
| I Mask | I = 1 | BMS | 2D | I Mask = 0 | BMC | 2C | Simple |
| H-Bit | H = 1 | BHCS | 29 | H = 0 | BHCC | 28 | Simple |
| $\overline{\text{IRQ}}$ High | - | BIH | 2F | $\overline{\text{IRQ}}$ Low | BIL | 2E | Simple |
| Always | - | BRA | 20 | Never | BRN | 21 | Uncond. |

r = register (ACCA or X)  m = memory operand

# BLS      Branch if Lower or Same      BLS

**Operation:**     $PC \leftarrow (PC) + \$0002 + Rel$     if $[(C) + (Z)] = 1$

i.e.; if $(ACCA) \leq (M)$     (unsigned binary numbers)

**Description:**     Causes a branch if either C or Z is set. If the BLS instruction is executed immediately after execution of a CMP or SUB instruction, the branch will occur if the unsigned binary number in ACCA was less than or equal to the unsigned binary number in M. See BRA instruction for further details of the execution of the branch.

## Condition Codes and Boolean Formulae:

|   |   |   | H | I | N | Z | C |
|---|---|---|---|---|---|---|---|
| 1 | 1 | 1 | – | – | – | – | – |

## Source Forms, Addressing Modes, Machine Code, and Cycles:

| Source Forms | Addr Mode | Machine Code Opcode | Operand(s) | HCMOS Cycles |
|---|---|---|---|---|
| BLS *rel* | REL | 23 | rr | 3 |

The following is a summary of all branch instructions.

| Branch | | | | Opposite Branch | | | Type |
|---|---|---|---|---|---|---|---|
| Test | Boolean | Mnemonic | Opcode | Test | Mnemonic | Opcode | |
| r > m | C + Z = 0 | BHI | 22 | r ≤ m | BLS | 23 | Unsigned |
| r ≥ m | C = 0 | BHS (BCC) | 24 | r < m | BLO (BCS) | 25 | Unsigned |
| r = m | Z = 1 | BEQ | 27 | r ≠ m | BNE | 26 | Unsigned |
| r ≤ m | C + Z = 1 | BLS | 23 | r > m | BHI | 22 | Unsigned |
| r < m | C = 1 | BLO (BCS) | 25 | r ≥ m | BHS (BCC) | 24 | Unsigned |
| Carry | C = 1 | BCS | 25 | No Carry | BCC | 24 | Simple |
| r = $00 | Z = 1 | BEQ | 27 | r ≠ $00 | BNE | 26 | Simple |
| Negative | N = 1 | BMI | 2B | Plus | BPL | 2A | Simple |
| I Mask | I = 1 | BMS | 2D | I Mask = 0 | BMC | 2C | Simple |
| H-Bit | H = 1 | BHCS | 29 | H = 0 | BHCC | 28 | Simple |
| IRQ High | - | BIH | 2F | IRQ Low | BIL | 2E | Simple |
| Always | - | BRA | 20 | Never | BRN | 21 | Uncond. |

r = register (ACCA or X)  m = memory operand

# BMC　　Branch if Interrupt Mask is Clear　　BMC

**Operation:**　　$PC \leftarrow (PC) + \$0002 + Rel$　　if $I = 0$

**Description:**　　Tests the state of the I bit in the CCR and causes a branch if I is clear (i.e., if interrupts are enabled). See BRA instruction for further details of the execution of the branch.

## Condition Codes and Boolean Formulae:

| | | | H | I | N | Z | C |
|---|---|---|---|---|---|---|---|
| 1 | 1 | 1 | – | – | – | – | – |

## Source Forms, Addressing Modes, Machine Code, and Cycles:

| Source Forms | Addr Mode | Machine Code Opcode | Operand(s) | HCMOS Cycles |
|---|---|---|---|---|
| BMC　*rel* | REL | 2C | rr | 3 |

The following is a summary of all branch instructions.

| Branch | | | | Opposite Branch | | | Type |
|---|---|---|---|---|---|---|---|
| **Test** | **Boolean** | **Mnemonic** | **Opcode** | **Test** | **Mnemonic** | **Opcode** | |
| r > m | C + Z = 0 | BHI | 22 | r ≤ m | BLS | 23 | Unsigned |
| r ≥ m | C = 0 | BHS (BCC) | 24 | r < m | BLO (BCS) | 25 | Unsigned |
| r = m | Z = 1 | BEQ | 27 | r ≠ m | BNE | 26 | Unsigned |
| r ≤ m | C + Z = 1 | BLS | 23 | r > m | BHI | 22 | Unsigned |
| r < m | C = 1 | BLO (BCS) | 25 | r ≥ m | BHS (BCC) | 24 | Unsigned |
| Carry | C = 1 | BCS | 25 | No Carry | BCC | 24 | Simple |
| r = $00 | Z = 1 | BEQ | 27 | r ≠ $00 | BNE | 26 | Simple |
| Negative | N = 1 | BMI | 2B | Plus | BPL | 2A | Simple |
| I Mask | I = 1 | BMS | 2D | I Mask = 0 | BMC | 2C | Simple |
| H-Bit | H = 1 | BHCS | 29 | H = 0 | BHCC | 28 | Simple |
| $\overline{\text{IRQ}}$ High | - | BIH | 2F | $\overline{\text{IRQ}}$ Low | BIL | 2E | Simple |
| Always | - | BRA | 20 | Never | BRN | 21 | Uncond. |

r = register (ACCA or X)　m = memory operand

# BMI    Branch if Minus    BMI

**Operation:** $PC \leftarrow (PC) + \$0002 + Rel$    if $(N) = 1$

**Description:** Tests the state of the N bit in the CCR and causes a branch if N is set. See BRA instruction for further details of the execution of the branch.

## Condition Codes and Boolean Formulae:

| | | | H | I | N | Z | C |
|---|---|---|---|---|---|---|---|
| 1 | 1 | 1 | – | – | – | – | – |

## Source Forms, Addressing Modes, Machine Code, and Cycles:

| Source Forms | Addr Mode | Machine Code Opcode | Operand(s) | HCMOS Cycles |
|---|---|---|---|---|
| BMI   *rel* | REL | 2B | rr | 3 |

The following is a summary of all branch instructions.

| Branch | | | | Opposite Branch | | | Type |
|---|---|---|---|---|---|---|---|
| **Test** | **Boolean** | **Mnemonic** | **Opcode** | **Test** | **Mnemonic** | **Opcode** | |
| r > m | C + Z = 0 | BHI | 22 | r ≤ m | BLS | 23 | Unsigned |
| r ≥ m | C = 0 | BHS (BCC) | 24 | r < m | BLO (BCS) | 25 | Unsigned |
| r = m | Z = 1 | BEQ | 27 | r ≠ m | BNE | 26 | Unsigned |
| r ≤ m | C + Z = 1 | BLS | 23 | r > m | BHI | 22 | Unsigned |
| r < m | C = 1 | BLO (BCS) | 25 | r ≥ m | BHS (BCC) | 24 | Unsigned |
| Carry | C = 1 | BCS | 25 | No Carry | BCC | 24 | Simple |
| r = $00 | Z = 1 | BEQ | 27 | r ≠ $00 | BNE | 26 | Simple |
| Negative | N = 1 | BMI | 2B | Plus | BPL | 2A | Simple |
| I Mask | I = 1 | BMS | 2D | I Mask = 0 | BMC | 2C | Simple |
| H-Bit | H = 1 | BHCS | 29 | H = 0 | BHCC | 28 | Simple |
| IRQ High | - | BIH | 2F | IRQ Low | BIL | 2E | Simple |
| Always | - | BRA | 20 | Never | BRN | 21 | Uncond. |

r = register (ACCA or X)   m = memory operand

# BMS

### Branch if Interrupt Mask is Set

# BMS

**Operation:**  $PC \leftarrow (PC) + \$0002 + Rel$   if I = 1

**Description:** Tests the state of the I bit in the CCR and causes a branch if I is set (i.e., if interrupts are disabled). See BRA instruction for further details of the execution of the branch.

## Condition Codes and Boolean Formulae:

| | | | H | I | N | Z | C |
|---|---|---|---|---|---|---|---|
| 1 | 1 | 1 | – | – | – | – | – |

## Source Forms, Addressing Modes, Machine Code, and Cycles:

| Source Forms | Addr Mode | Machine Code Opcode | Operand(s) | HCMOS Cycles |
|---|---|---|---|---|
| BMS  *rel* | REL | 2D | rr | 3 |

The following is a summary of all branch instructions.

| Branch | | | | Opposite Branch | | | Type |
|---|---|---|---|---|---|---|---|
| Test | Boolean | Mnemonic | Opcode | Test | Mnemonic | Opcode | |
| r > m | C + Z = 0 | BHI | 22 | r ≤ m | BLS | 23 | Unsigned |
| r ≥ m | C = 0 | BHS (BCC) | 24 | r < m | BLO (BCS) | 25 | Unsigned |
| r = m | Z = 1 | BEQ | 27 | r ≠ m | BNE | 26 | Unsigned |
| r ≤ m | C + Z = 1 | BLS | 23 | r > m | BHI | 22 | Unsigned |
| r < m | C = 1 | BLO (BCS) | 25 | r ≥ m | BHS (BCC) | 24 | Unsigned |
| Carry | C = 1 | BCS | 25 | No Carry | BCC | 24 | Simple |
| r = $00 | Z = 1 | BEQ | 27 | r ≠ $00 | BNE | 26 | Simple |
| Negative | N = 1 | BMI | 2B | Plus | BPL | 2A | Simple |
| I Mask | I = 1 | BMS | 2D | I Mask = 0 | BMC | 2C | Simple |
| H-Bit | H = 1 | BHCS | 29 | H = 0 | BHCC | 28 | Simple |
| IRQ High | - | BIH | 2F | IRQ Low | BIL | 2E | Simple |
| Always | - | BRA | 20 | Never | BRN | 21 | Uncond. |

r = register (ACCA or X)  m = memory operand

# BNE

### Branch if Not Equal

# BNE

**Operation:**     $PC \leftarrow (PC) + \$0002 + Rel \qquad if\ (Z) = 0$

**Description:**    Tests the state of the Z bit in the CCR and causes a branch if Z is clear. If the BNE instruction is executed immediately after execution of a CMP or SUB instruction, the branch will occur if the arguments were not equal. See BRA instruction for further details of the execution of the branch.

## Condition Codes and Boolean Formulae:

| | | | H | I | N | Z | C |
|---|---|---|---|---|---|---|---|
| 1 | 1 | 1 | – | – | – | – | – |

## Source Forms, Addressing Modes, Machine Code, and Cycles:

| Source Forms | Addr Mode | Machine Code Opcode | Operand(s) | HCMOS Cycles |
|---|---|---|---|---|
| BNE  *rel* | REL | 26 | rr | 3 |

The following is a summary of all branch instructions.

| Branch | | | | Opposite Branch | | | Type |
|---|---|---|---|---|---|---|---|
| Test | Boolean | Mnemonic | Opcode | Test | Mnemonic | Opcode | |
| r > m | C + Z = 0 | BHI | 22 | r ≤ m | BLS | 23 | Unsigned |
| r ≥ m | C = 0 | BHS (BCC) | 24 | r < m | BLO (BCS) | 25 | Unsigned |
| r = m | Z = 1 | BEQ | 27 | r ≠ m | BNE | 26 | Unsigned |
| r ≤ m | C + Z = 1 | BLS | 23 | r > m | BHI | 22 | Unsigned |
| r < m | C = 1 | BLO (BCS) | 25 | r ≥ m | BHS (BCC) | 24 | Unsigned |
| Carry | C = 1 | BCS | 25 | No Carry | BCC | 24 | Simple |
| r = \$00 | Z = 1 | BEQ | 27 | r ≠ \$00 | BNE | 26 | Simple |
| Negative | N = 1 | BMI | 2B | Plus | BPL | 2A | Simple |
| I Mask | I = 1 | BMS | 2D | I Mask = 0 | BMC | 2C | Simple |
| H-Bit | H = 1 | BHCS | 29 | H = 0 | BHCC | 28 | Simple |
| $\overline{\text{IRQ}}$ High | - | BIH | 2F | $\overline{\text{IRQ}}$ Low | BIL | 2E | Simple |
| Always | - | BRA | 20 | Never | BRN | 21 | Uncond. |

r = register (ACCA or X)   m = memory operand

# BPL
### Branch if Plus
# BPL

**Operation:**  $PC \leftarrow (PC) + \$0002 + Rel$    if $(N) = 0$

**Description:** Tests the state of the N bit in the CCR and causes a branch if N is clear. See BRA instruction for further details of the execution of the branch.

## Condition Codes and Boolean Formulae:

|   |   |   | H | I | N | Z | C |
|---|---|---|---|---|---|---|---|
| 1 | 1 | 1 | – | – | – | – | – |

## Source Forms, Addressing Modes, Machine Code, and Cycles:

| Source Forms | Addr Mode | Machine Code | | HCMOS Cycles |
|---|---|---|---|---|
| | | Opcode | Operand(s) | |
| BPL  *rel* | REL | 2A | rr | 3 |

The following is a summary of all branch instructions.

| Branch | | | | Opposite Branch | | | Type |
|---|---|---|---|---|---|---|---|
| Test | Boolean | Mnemonic | Opcode | Test | Mnemonic | Opcode | |
| r > m | C + Z = 0 | BHI | 22 | r ≤ m | BLS | 23 | Unsigned |
| r ≥ m | C = 0 | BHS (BCC) | 24 | r < m | BLO (BCS) | 25 | Unsigned |
| r = m | Z = 1 | BEQ | 27 | r ≠ m | BNE | 26 | Unsigned |
| r ≤ m | C + Z = 1 | BLS | 23 | r > m | BHI | 22 | Unsigned |
| r < m | C = 1 | BLO (BCS) | 25 | r ≥ m | BHS (BCC) | 24 | Unsigned |
| Carry | C = 1 | BCS | 25 | No Carry | BCC | 24 | Simple |
| r = \$00 | Z = 1 | BEQ | 27 | r ≠ \$00 | BNE | 26 | Simple |
| Negative | N = 1 | BMI | 2B | Plus | BPL | 2A | Simple |
| I Mask | I = 1 | BMS | 2D | I Mask = 0 | BMC | 2C | Simple |
| H-Bit | H = 1 | BHCS | 29 | H = 0 | BHCC | 28 | Simple |
| IRQ High | - | BIH | 2F | IRQ Low | BIL | 2E | Simple |
| Always | - | BRA | 20 | Never | BRN | 21 | Uncond. |

r = register (ACCA or X)  m = memory operand

# BRA                Branch                **BRA**

**Operation:**       PC ← (PC) + $0002 + Rel

**Description:**     Unconditional branch to the address given in the foregoing formula, in which "Rel" is the twos-complement relative offset in the last byte of machine code for the instruction and (PC) is the address of the opcode for the branch instruction.

A source program specifies the destination of a branch instruction by its absolute address, either as a numerical value or as a symbol or expression that can be numerically evaluated by the assembler. The assembler calculates the relative offset *rel* from this absolute address and the current value of the location counter.

## Condition Codes and Boolean Formulae:

|   |   |   | H | I | N | Z | C |
|---|---|---|---|---|---|---|---|
| 1 | 1 | 1 | – | – | – | – | – |

## Source Forms, Addressing Modes, Machine Code, and Cycles:

| Source Forms | Addr Mode | Machine Code | | HCMOS Cycles |
|---|---|---|---|---|
| | | Opcode | Operand(s) | |
| BRA   *rel* | REL | 20 | rr | 3 |

The table on the facing page is a summary of all branch instructions.

# BRCLR n    Branch if Bit n is Clear    BRCLR n

**Operation:**    PC ← (PC) + $0003 + Rel    if bit n of M = 0

**Description:**    Tests bit n (n = 7, 6, 5, ... 0) of location M and branches if the bit is clear. M can be any RAM or I/O register address in the $0000 to $00FF area of memory (i.e., direct addressing mode is used to specify the address of the operand).

The C bit is set to the state of the tested bit. When used with an appropriate rotate instruction, BRCLR n provides an easy method for performing serial-to-parallel conversions.

## Condition Codes and Boolean Formulae:

| | | | H | I | N | Z | C |
|---|---|---|---|---|---|---|---|
| 1 | 1 | 1 | – | – | – | – | Δ |

C:   Set if Mn = 1; cleared otherwise.

## Source Forms, Addressing Modes, Machine Code, and Cycles:

| Source Forms | Addr Mode | Machine Code Opcode | Machine Code Operands | HCMOS Cycles |
|---|---|---|---|---|
| BRCLR   0,*opr,rel* | DIR b0 | 01 | dd    rr | 5 |
| BRCLR   1,*opr,rel* | DIR b1 | 03 | dd    rr | 5 |
| BRCLR   2,*opr,rel* | DIR b2 | 05 | dd    rr | 5 |
| BRCLR   3,*opr,rel* | DIR b3 | 07 | dd    rr | 5 |
| BRCLR   4,*opr,rel* | DIR b4 | 09 | dd    rr | 5 |
| BRCLR   5,*opr,rel* | DIR b5 | 0B | dd    rr | 5 |
| BRCLR   6,*opr,rel* | DIR b6 | 0D | dd    rr | 5 |
| BRCLR   7,*opr,rel* | DIR b7 | 0F | dd    rr | 5 |

# BRN

**Branch Never**

**Operation:** PC ← (PC) + $0002

**Description:** Never branches. In effect, this instruction can be considered as a two-byte NOP (no operation) requiring three cycles for execution. Its inclusion in the instruction set is to provide a complement for the BRA instruction. The BRN instruction is useful during program debug to negate the effect of another branch instruction without disturbing the offset byte.

## Condition Codes and Boolean Formulae:

| | | | H | I | N | Z | C |
|---|---|---|---|---|---|---|---|
| 1 | 1 | 1 | – | – | – | – | – |

## Source Forms, Addressing Modes, Machine Code, and Cycles:

| Source Forms | Addr Mode | Machine Code Opcode | Operand(s) | HCMOS Cycles |
|---|---|---|---|---|
| BRN  *rel* | REL | 21 | rr | 3 |

The following is a summary of all branch instructions.

| Branch | | | | Opposite Branch | | | Type |
|---|---|---|---|---|---|---|---|
| Test | Boolean | Mnemonic | Opcode | Test | Mnemonic | Opcode | |
| r > m | C + Z = 0 | BHI | 22 | r ≤ m | BLS | 23 | Unsigned |
| r ≥ m | C = 0 | BHS (BCC) | 24 | r < m | BLO (BCS) | 25 | Unsigned |
| r = m | Z = 1 | BEQ | 27 | r ≠ m | BNE | 26 | Unsigned |
| r ≤ m | C + Z = 1 | BLS | 23 | r > m | BHI | 22 | Unsigned |
| r < m | C = 1 | BLO (BCS) | 25 | r ≥ m | BHS (BCC) | 24 | Unsigned |
| Carry | C = 1 | BCS | 25 | No Carry | BCC | 24 | Simple |
| r = $00 | Z = 1 | BEQ | 27 | r ≠ $00 | BNE | 26 | Simple |
| Negative | N = 1 | BMI | 2B | Plus | BPL | 2A | Simple |
| I Mask | I = 1 | BMS | 2D | I Mask = 0 | BMC | 2C | Simple |
| H-Bit | H = 1 | BHCS | 29 | H = 0 | BHCC | 28 | Simple |
| IRQ High | - | BIH | 2F | IRQ Low | BIL | 2E | Simple |
| Always | - | BRA | 20 | Never | BRN | 21 | Uncond. |

r = register (ACCA or X)  m = memory operand

# BRSET n         Branch if Bit n is Set         BRSET n

**Operation:**          $PC \leftarrow (PC) + \$0003 + Rel$          if bit n of M = 1

**Description:**        Tests bit n (n = 7, 6, 5, ... 0) of location M and branches if the
bit is set. M can be any RAM or I/O register address in the
$0000 to $00FF area of memory (i.e., direct addressing mode
is used to specify the address of the operand).

The C bit is set to the state of the tested bit. When used with
an appropriate rotate instruction, BRSET n provides an easy
method for performing serial to parallel conversions.

## Condition Codes and Boolean Formulae:

| | | | H | I | N | Z | C |
|---|---|---|---|---|---|---|---|
| 1 | 1 | 1 | – | – | – | – | Δ |

C:  Set if Mn = 1; cleared otherwise.

## Source Forms, Addressing Modes, Machine Code, and Cycles:

| Source Forms | Addr Mode | Machine Code Opcode | Operands | HCMOS Cycles |
|---|---|---|---|---|
| BRSET   0,*opr,rel* | DIR b0 | 00 | dd    rr | 5 |
| BRSET   1,*opr,rel* | DIR b1 | 02 | dd    rr | 5 |
| BRSET   2,*opr,rel* | DIR b2 | 04 | dd    rr | 5 |
| BRSET   3,*opr,rel* | DIR b3 | 06 | dd    rr | 5 |
| BRSET   4,*opr,rel* | DIR b4 | 08 | dd    rr | 5 |
| BRSET   5,*opr,rel* | DIR b5 | 0A | dd    rr | 5 |
| BRSET   6,*opr,rel* | DIR b6 | 0C | dd    rr | 5 |
| BRSET   7,*opr,rel* | DIR b7 | 0E | dd    rr | 5 |

# BSET n     Set Bit in Memory     BSET n

**Operation:**     Mn ← 1

**Description:**     Set bit n (n = 7, 6, 5, ... 0) in location M. All other bits in M are unaffected. M can be any RAM or I/O register address in the $0000 to $00FF area of memory (i.e., direct addressing mode is used to specify the address of the operand).

## Condition Codes and Boolean Formulae:

| | | | H | I | N | Z | C |
|---|---|---|---|---|---|---|---|
| 1 | 1 | 1 | – | – | – | – | – |

## Source Forms, Addressing Modes, Machine Code, and Cycles:

| Source Forms | Addr Mode | Machine Code Opcode | Operand(s) | HCMOS Cycles |
|---|---|---|---|---|
| BSET 0,*opr* | DIR b0 | 10 | dd | 5 |
| BSET 1,*opr* | DIR b1 | 12 | dd | 5 |
| BSET 2,*opr* | DIR b2 | 14 | dd | 5 |
| BSET 3,*opr* | DIR b3 | 16 | dd | 5 |
| BSET 4,*opr* | DIR b4 | 18 | dd | 5 |
| BSET 5,*opr* | DIR b5 | 1A | dd | 5 |
| BSET 6,*opr* | DIR b6 | 1C | dd | 5 |
| BSET 7,*opr* | DIR b7 | 1E | dd | 5 |

# BSR

## Branch to Subroutine

# BSR

**Operation:**

PC ← (PC) + $0002      Advance PC to return address
↓(PCL); SP ← (SP) – $0001      Push low half of return addr
↓(PCH); SP ← (SP) – $0001      Push high half of return addr
PC ← (PC) + Rel      Load PC with start address of
     requested subroutine

**Description:** The program counter is incremented by two from the opcode address (i.e., so it points to the opcode of the next instruction that will be the return address). The least significant byte of the contents of the program counter (low-order return address) is pushed onto the stack. The stack pointer is then decremented by one. The most significant byte of the contents of the program counter (high-order return address) is pushed onto the stack. The stack pointer is then decremented by one. A branch then occurs to the location specified by the branch offset. See BRA instruction for further details of the execution of the branch.

## Condition Codes and Boolean Formulae:

| | | | H | I | N | Z | C |
|---|---|---|---|---|---|---|---|
| 1 | 1 | 1 | – | – | – | – | – |

## Source Forms, Addressing Modes, Machine Code, and Cycles:

| Source Forms | Addr Mode | Machine Code | | HCMOS Cycles |
|---|---|---|---|---|
| | | Opcode | Operand(s) | |
| BSR  *rel* | REL | AD | rr | 6 |

# CLC

**Clear Carry Bit**

# CLC

**Operation:**     C bit ← 0

**Description:**     Clears the C bit in the CCR. CLC may be used to setup the C bit prior to a shift or rotate instruction that involves the C bit.

**Condition Codes and Boolean Formulae:**

| | | | H | I | N | Z | C |
|---|---|---|---|---|---|---|---|
| 1 | 1 | 1 | – | – | – | – | 0 |

C:   0 (cleared)

**Source Forms, Addressing Modes, Machine Code, and Cycles:**

| Source Forms | Addr Mode | Machine Code Opcode | HCMOS Cycles |
|---|---|---|---|
| CLC | INH | 98 | 2 |

# CLI

**Clear Interrupt Mask Bit**

# CLI

**Operation:**    I bit ← 0

**Description:**    Clears the interrupt mask bit in the CCR. When the I bit is clear, interrupts are enabled. There is one E-clock cycle delay in the clearing mechanism for the I bit, such that if interrupts were previously disabled, then the next instruction after a CLI will always be executed even if there was an interrupt pending prior to execution of the CLI instruction.

## Condition Codes and Boolean Formulae:

|   |   |   | H | I | N | Z | C |
|---|---|---|---|---|---|---|---|
| 1 | 1 | 1 | – | 0 | – | – | – |

I:    0 (cleared)

## Source Forms, Addressing Modes, Machine Code, and Cycles:

| Source Forms | Addr Mode | Machine Code Opcode | HCMOS Cycles |
|---|---|---|---|
| CLI | INH | 9A | 2 |

# CLR

**Clear**

# CLR

**Operation:** ACCA ← $00
or: X ← $00
or: M ← $00

**Description:** The contents of ACCA, X, or M are replaced by zeros.

**Condition Codes and Boolean Formulae:**

|   |   |   | H | I | N | Z | C |
|---|---|---|---|---|---|---|---|
| 1 | 1 | 1 | – | – | 0 | 1 | – |

N: 0 (cleared)

Z: 1 (set)

**Source Forms, Addressing Modes, Machine Code, and Cycles:**

| Source Forms | Addr Mode | Machine Code Opcode | Operand(s) | HCMOS Cycles |
|---|---|---|---|---|
| CLRA | INH (A) | 4F | | 3 |
| CLRX | INH (X) | 5F | | 3 |
| CLR  opr | DIR | 3F | dd | 5 |
| CLR  ,X | IX | 7F | | 5 |
| CLR  opr,X | IX1 | 6F | ff | 6 |

# CMP    Compare Accumulator with Memory    CMP

**Operation:**    $(ACCA) - (M)$

**Description:**    Compares the contents of ACCA to the contents of M and sets the condition codes, which may then be used for arithmetic and logical conditional branching. The contents of both ACCA and M are unchanged.

## Condition Codes and Boolean Formulae:

| | | H | I | N | Z | C |
|---|---|---|---|---|---|---|
| 1 | 1 | 1 | – | – | Δ | Δ | Δ |

N: R7
　　Set if MSB of result is one; cleared otherwise.

Z: $\overline{R7} \cdot \overline{R6} \cdot \overline{R5} \cdot \overline{R4} \cdot \overline{R3} \cdot \overline{R2} \cdot \overline{R1} \cdot \overline{R0}$
　　Set if the result is $00; cleared otherwise.

C: $\overline{A7} \cdot M7 + M7 \cdot \overline{R7} + R7 \cdot \overline{A7}$
　　Set if the unsigned contents of memory is larger than the unsigned value in the accumulator; cleared otherwise.

## Source Forms, Addressing Modes, Machine Code, and Cycles:

| Source Forms | Addr Mode | Machine Code Opcode | Operand(s) | HCMOS Cycles |
|---|---|---|---|---|
| CMP  #opr | IMM | A1 | ii | 2 |
| CMP  opr | DIR | B1 | dd | 3 |
| CMP  opr | EXT | C1 | hh  ll | 4 |
| CMP  ,X | IX | F1 | | 3 |
| CMP  opr,X | IX1 | E1 | ff | 4 |
| CMP  opr,X | IX2 | D1 | ee  ff | 5 |

# COM  Complement  COM

**Operation:**   $ACCA \leftarrow \overline{ACCA} = \$FF - (ACCA)$
or: $X \leftarrow \overline{X} = \$FF - (X)$
or: $M \leftarrow \overline{M} = \$FF - (M)$

**Description:**   Replace the contents of ACCA, X, or M with the ones complement. (Each bit of ACCA, X, or M is replaced with the complement of that bit).

## Condition Codes and Boolean Formulae:

| | | | H | I | N | Z | C |
|---|---|---|---|---|---|---|---|
| 1 | 1 | 1 | – | – | Δ | Δ | 1 |

N: R7
   Set if MSB of result is one; cleared otherwise.

Z: $\overline{R7} \cdot \overline{R6} \cdot \overline{R5} \cdot \overline{R4} \cdot \overline{R3} \cdot \overline{R2} \cdot \overline{R1} \cdot \overline{R0}$
   Set if the result is $00; cleared otherwise.

C: 1 (set)

## Source Forms, Addressing Modes, Machine Code, and Cycles:

| Source Forms | Addr Mode | Machine Code Opcode | Operand(s) | HCMOS Cycles |
|---|---|---|---|---|
| COMA | INH (A) | 43 | | 3 |
| COMX | INH (X) | 53 | | 3 |
| COM  opr | DIR | 33 | dd | 5 |
| COM  ,X | IX | 73 | | 5 |
| COM  opr,X | IX1 | 63 | ff | 6 |

# CPX

### Compare Index Register with Memory

# CPX

**Operation:**  (X) – (M)

**Description:**  Compares the contents of X to the contents of M and sets the condition codes, which may then be used for arithmetic and logical conditional branching. The contents of both X and M are unchanged.

## Condition Codes and Boolean Formulae:

| | | | H | I | N | Z | C |
|---|---|---|---|---|---|---|---|
| 1 | 1 | 1 | – | – | Δ | Δ | Δ |

N:  R7
Set if MSB of result is one; cleared otherwise.

Z:  $\overline{R7} \cdot \overline{R6} \cdot \overline{R5} \cdot \overline{R4} \cdot \overline{R3} \cdot \overline{R2} \cdot \overline{R1} \cdot \overline{R0}$
Set if the result is $00; cleared otherwise.

C:  $\overline{X7} \cdot M7 + M7 \cdot R7 + R7 \cdot \overline{X7}$
Set if the unsigned contents of memory is larger than the unsigned value in the accumulator; cleared otherwise.

## Source Forms, Addressing Modes, Machine Code, and Cycles:

| Source Forms | Addr Mode | Machine Code Opcode | Operand(s) | HCMOS Cycles |
|---|---|---|---|---|
| CPX  #opr | IMM | A3 | ii | 2 |
| CPX  opr | DIR | B3 | dd | 3 |
| CPX  opr | EXT | C3 | hh  ll | 4 |
| CPX  ,X | IX | F3 | | 3 |
| CPX  opr,X | IX1 | E3 | ff | 4 |
| CPX  opr,X | IX2 | D3 | ee  ff | 5 |

*M68HC05 Instruction Set Details*

# DEC                    Decrement                    DEC

**Operation:**     ACCA ← (ACCA) – $01

or: X ← (X) – $01

or: M ← (M) – $01

**Description:**   Subtract one from the contents of ACCA, X, or M. The N and Z bits in the CCR are set or cleared according to the results of this operation. The C bit in the CCR is not affected. Therefore, the BLS, BLO, BHS, and BHI branch instructions are not useful following a DEC instruction.

## Condition Codes and Boolean Formulae:

|   |   |   | H | I | N | Z | C |
|---|---|---|---|---|---|---|---|
| 1 | 1 | 1 | – | – | Δ | Δ | – |

N: R7
   Set if MSB of result is one; cleared otherwise.

Z: $\overline{R7} \cdot \overline{R6} \cdot \overline{R5} \cdot \overline{R4} \cdot \overline{R3} \cdot \overline{R2} \cdot \overline{R1} \cdot \overline{R0}$
   Set if the result is $00; cleared otherwise.

## Source Forms, Addressing Modes, Machine Code, and Cycles:

| Source Forms | Addr Mode | Machine Code Opcode | Operand(s) | HCMOS Cycles |
|---|---|---|---|---|
| DECA | INH (A) | 4A | | 3 |
| DECX | INH (X) | 5A | | 3 |
| DEC  opr | DIR | 3A | dd | 5 |
| DEC  ,X | IX | 7A | | 5 |
| DEC  opr,X | IX1 | 6A | ff | 6 |

(DEX is recognized by assemblers as being equivalent to DECX)

# EOR   Exclusive-OR Accumulator with Memory   EOR

**Operation:**   $ACCA \leftarrow (ACCA) \oplus (M)$

**Description:**   Performs the logical exclusive-OR between the contents of ACCA and the contents of M, and places the result in ACCA. (Each bit of ACCA after the operation will be the logical exclusive-OR of the corresponding bits of M and ACCA before the operation.)

## Condition Codes and Boolean Formulae:

| | | | H | I | N | Z | C |
|---|---|---|---|---|---|---|---|
| 1 | 1 | 1 | – | – | Δ | Δ | – |

N: R7
Set if MSB of result is one; cleared otherwise.

Z: $\overline{R7} \cdot \overline{R6} \cdot \overline{R5} \cdot \overline{R4} \cdot \overline{R3} \cdot \overline{R2} \cdot \overline{R1} \cdot \overline{R0}$
Set if the result is \$00; cleared otherwise.

## Source Forms, Addressing Modes, Machine Code, and Cycles:

| Source Forms | Addr Mode | Machine Code Opcode | Operand(s) | HCMOS Cycles |
|---|---|---|---|---|
| EOR  #opr | IMM | A8 | ii | 2 |
| EOR  opr | DIR | B8 | dd | 3 |
| EOR  opr | EXT | C8 | hh  ll | 4 |
| EOR  ,X | IX | F8 | | 3 |
| EOR  opr,X | IX1 | E8 | ff | 4 |
| EOR  opr,X | IX2 | D8 | ee  ff | 5 |

# INC

**Increment**

**Operation:**     ACCA ← (ACCA) + $01

**or:** X ← (X) + $01

**or:** M ← (M) + $01

**Description:**     Adds one to the contents of ACCA, X, or M. The N and Z bits in the CCR are set or cleared according to the results of this operation. The C bit in the CCR is not affected. Therefore, the BLS, BLO, BHS, and BHI branch instructions are not useful following an INC instruction.

## Condition Codes and Boolean Formulae:

|   |   |   | H | I | N | Z | C |
|---|---|---|---|---|---|---|---|
| 1 | 1 | 1 | – | – | Δ | Δ | – |

N: R7
   Set if MSB of result is one; cleared otherwise.

Z: $\overline{R7} \cdot \overline{R6} \cdot \overline{R5} \cdot \overline{R4} \cdot \overline{R3} \cdot \overline{R2} \cdot \overline{R1} \cdot \overline{R0}$
   Set if the result is $00; cleared otherwise.

## Source Forms, Addressing Modes, Machine Code, and Cycles:

| Source Forms | Addr Mode | Machine Code Opcode | Operand(s) | HCMOS Cycles |
|---|---|---|---|---|
| INCA | INH (A) | 4C | | 3 |
| INCX | INH (X) | 5C | | 3 |
| INC  opr | DIR | 3C | dd | 5 |
| INC  ,X | IX | 7C | | 5 |
| INC  opr,X | IX1 | 6C | ff | 6 |

(INX is recognized by assemblers as being equivalent to INCX)

# JMP

**Jump**

# JMP

**Operation:**    PC ← Effective Address

**Description:**    A jump occurs to the instruction stored at the effective address. The effective address is obtained according to the rules for extended, direct, or indexed addressing.

## Condition Codes and Boolean Formulae:

|   |   |   | H | I | N | Z | C |
|---|---|---|---|---|---|---|---|
| 1 | 1 | 1 | – | – | – | – | – |

## Source Forms, Addressing Modes, Machine Code, and Cycles:

| Source Forms | Addr Mode | Machine Code Opcode | Operand(s) | HCMOS Cycles |
|---|---|---|---|---|
| JMP  opr | DIR | BC | dd | 2 |
| JMP  opr | EXT | CC | hh  ll | 3 |
| JMP  ,X | IX | FC |  | 2 |
| JMP  opr,X | IX1 | EC | ff | 3 |
| JMP  opr,X | IX2 | DC | ee  ff | 4 |

*M68HC05 Instruction Set Details*

# JSR

**Jump to Subroutine**

# JSR

**Operation:**

$PC \leftarrow (PC) + n$      n = 1, 2, or 3 depending on address mode

$\downarrow$(PCL); $SP \leftarrow (SP) - \$0001$    Push low half of return addr

$\downarrow$(PCH); $SP \leftarrow (SP) - \$0001$    Push high half of return addr

$PC \leftarrow$ Effective Address     Load PC with start address of requested subroutine

**Description:**
The program counter is incremented by n so that it points to the opcode of the next instruction that follows the JSR instruction (n = 1, 2, or 3, depending on the addressing mode). The PC is then pushed onto the stack -- eight bits at a time, least significant byte first. Unused bits in the program counter high byte are stored as 1s on the stack. The stack pointer points to the next empty location on the stack. A jump occurs to the instruction stored at the effective address. The effective address is obtained according to the rules for extended, direct, or indexed addressing.

## Condition Codes and Boolean Formulae:

|   |   |   | H | I | N | Z | C |
|---|---|---|---|---|---|---|---|
| 1 | 1 | 1 | – | – | – | – | – |

## Source Forms, Addressing Modes, Machine Code, and Cycles:

| Source Forms | Addr Mode | Machine Code | | HCMOS Cycles |
|---|---|---|---|---|
| | | Opcode | Operand(s) | |
| JSR   *opr* | DIR | BD | dd | 5 |
| JSR   *opr* | EXT | CD | hh   ll | 6 |
| JSR   ,X | IX | FD | | 5 |
| JSR   *opr*,X | IX1 | ED | ff | 6 |
| JSR   *opr*,X | IX2 | DD | ee   ff | 7 |

# LDA

**Load Accumulator from Memory**

# LDA

**Operation:** ACCA ← (M)

**Description:** Loads the contents of the specified memory location into the accumulator. The N and Z condition codes are set or cleared according to the loaded data.

## Condition Codes and Boolean Formulae:

| | | H | I | N | Z | C |
|---|---|---|---|---|---|---|
| 1 | 1 | 1 | – | – | Δ | Δ | – |

N: R7
Set if MSB of result is one; cleared otherwise.

Z: $\overline{R7 \cdot R6 \cdot R5 \cdot R4 \cdot R3 \cdot R2 \cdot R1 \cdot R0}$
Set if the result is $00; cleared otherwise.

## Source Forms, Addressing Modes, Machine Code, and Cycles:

| Source Forms | Addr Mode | Machine Code Opcode | Operand(s) | HCMOS Cycles |
|---|---|---|---|---|
| LDA  #opr | IMM | A6 | ii | 2 |
| LDA  opr | DIR | B6 | dd | 3 |
| LDA  opr | EXT | C6 | hh  ll | 4 |
| LDA  ,X | IX | F6 | | 3 |
| LDA  opr,X | IX1 | E6 | ff | 4 |
| LDA  opr,X | IX2 | D6 | ee  ff | 5 |

*M68HC05 Instruction Set Details*

# LDX    Load Index Register from Memory    LDX

**Operation:**    $X \leftarrow (M)$

**Description:**    Loads the contents of the specified memory location into the index register. The N and Z condition codes are set or cleared according to the loaded data.

## Condition Codes and Boolean Formulae:

| | | | H | I | N | Z | C |
|---|---|---|---|---|---|---|---|
| 1 | 1 | 1 | – | – | Δ | Δ | – |

N: R7
  Set if MSB of result is one; cleared otherwise.

Z: $\overline{R7} \cdot \overline{R6} \cdot \overline{R5} \cdot \overline{R4} \cdot \overline{R3} \cdot \overline{R2} \cdot \overline{R1} \cdot \overline{R0}$
  Set if the result is $00; cleared otherwise.

## Source Forms, Addressing Modes, Machine Code, and Cycles:

| Source Forms | Addr Mode | Machine Code Opcode | Operand(s) | HCMOS Cycles |
|---|---|---|---|---|
| LDX   #opr | IMM | AE | ii | 2 |
| LDX   opr | DIR | BE | dd | 3 |
| LDX   opr | EXT | CE | hh   ll | 4 |
| LDX   ,X | IX | FE | | 3 |
| LDX   opr,X | IX1 | EE | ff | 4 |
| LDX   opr,X | IX2 | DE | ee   ff | 5 |

### Logical Shift Left
### (Same as ASL)

**Operation:**

$$C \leftarrow \boxed{b7 - - \quad - - b0} \leftarrow 0$$

**Description:** Shifts all bits of the ACCA, X, or M one place to the left. Bit 0 is loaded with a zero. The C bit in the CCR is loaded from the most significant bit of ACCA, X, or M.

## Condition Codes and Boolean Formulae:

| | | | H | I | N | Z | C |
|---|---|---|---|---|---|---|---|
| 1 | 1 | 1 | – | – | Δ | Δ | Δ |

N: R7
Set if MSB of result is one; cleared otherwise.

Z: $\overline{R7 \cdot R6 \cdot R5 \cdot R4 \cdot R3 \cdot R2 \cdot R1 \cdot R0}$
Set if the result is $00; cleared otherwise.

C: b7
Set if, before the shift, the MSB of the shifted value was set; cleared otherwise.

## Source Forms, Addressing Modes, Machine Code, and Cycles:

| Source Forms | Addr Mode | Machine Code | | HCMOS Cycles |
|---|---|---|---|---|
| | | Opcode | Operand(s) | |
| LSLA | INH (A) | 48 | | 3 |
| LSLX | INH (X) | 58 | | 3 |
| LSL  opr | DIR | 38 | dd | 5 |
| LSL  ,X | IX | 78 | | 5 |
| LSL  opr,X | IX1 | 68 | ff | 6 |

# LSR

**Logical Shift Right**

# LSR

**Operation:**

$$0 \rightarrow \boxed{\text{b7} - - \quad - - \text{b0}} \rightarrow \boxed{\text{C}}$$

**Description:** Shifts all bits of ACCA, X, or M one place to the right. Bit 7 is loaded with a zero. Bit 0 is shifted into the C bit.

## Condition Codes and Boolean Formulae:

| | | | H | I | N | Z | C |
|---|---|---|---|---|---|---|---|
| 1 | 1 | 1 | – | – | 0 | Δ | Δ |

N: 0 (cleared)

Z: $\overline{R7} \cdot \overline{R6} \cdot \overline{R5} \cdot \overline{R4} \cdot \overline{R3} \cdot \overline{R2} \cdot \overline{R1} \cdot \overline{R0}$
Set if the result is $00; cleared otherwise.

C: b0
Set if, before the shift, the LSB of the shifted value was set; cleared otherwise.

## Source Forms, Addressing Modes, Machine Code, and Cycles:

| Source Forms | Addr Mode | Machine Code | | HCMOS Cycles |
|---|---|---|---|---|
| | | Opcode | Operand(s) | |
| LSRA | INH (A) | 44 | | 3 |
| LSRX | INH (X) | 54 | | 3 |
| LSR  *opr* | DIR | 34 | dd | 5 |
| LSR  ,X | IX | 74 | | 5 |
| LSR  *opr*,X | IX1 | 64 | ff | 6 |

# MUL MUL

**Multiply Unsigned**

**Operation:**      X:ACCA ← X × ACCA

**Description:**      Multiplies the eight-bit value in the index register by the eight-bit value in the accumulator to obtain a 16-bit unsigned result in the concatenated index register and accumulator. After the operation, X contains the upper eight bits of the 16-bit result and ACCA contains the lower eight bits of the result.

## Condition Codes and Boolean Formulae:

|   |   |   | H | I | N | Z | C |
|---|---|---|---|---|---|---|---|
| 1 | 1 | 1 | 0 | – | – | – | 0 |

H:   0 (cleared)

C:   0 (cleared)

## Source Forms, Addressing Modes, Machine Code, and Cycles:

| Source Forms | Addr Mode | Machine Code Opcode | HCMOS Cycles |
|---|---|---|---|
| MUL | INH | 42 | 11 |

# NEG

### Negate (Twos Complement)

# NEG

**Operation:**

$ACCA \leftarrow -(ACCA) = \$00 - (ACCA)$

**or:** $X \leftarrow -(X) = \$00 - (X)$

**or:** $M \leftarrow -(M) = \$00 - (M)$

**Description:**

Replaces the contents of ACCA, X, or M with its twos complement. Note that the value \$80 is left unchanged.

## Condition Codes and Boolean Formulae:

|   |   | H | I | N | Z | C |
|---|---|---|---|---|---|---|
| 1 | 1 | 1 | – | – | Δ | Δ | Δ |

N: R7
Set if MSB of result is one; cleared otherwise.

Z: $\overline{R7} \cdot \overline{R6} \cdot \overline{R5} \cdot \overline{R4} \cdot \overline{R3} \cdot \overline{R2} \cdot \overline{R1} \cdot \overline{R0}$
Set if the result is \$00; cleared otherwise.

C: R7+R6+R5+R4+R3+R2+R1+R0
Set if there is a borrow in the implied subtraction from zero; cleared otherwise. The C bit will be set in all cases except when the contents of ACCA, X, or M was \$00 prior to the NEG operation.

## Source Forms, Addressing Modes, Machine Code, and Cycles:

| Source Forms | Addr Mode | Machine Code | | HCMOS Cycles |
|---|---|---|---|---|
| | | Opcode | Operand(s) | |
| NEGA | INH (A) | 40 | | 3 |
| NEGX | INH (X) | 50 | | 3 |
| NEG   *opr* | DIR | 30 | dd | 5 |
| NEG   ,X | IX | 70 | | 5 |
| NEG   *opr*,X | IX1 | 60 | ff | 6 |

# NOP                          No Operation                          NOP

**Operation:**      None

**Description:**    This is a single-byte instruction that does nothing except to
                    consume two CPU clock cycles while the program counter is
                    advanced to the next instruction. No register or memory
                    contents are affected by this instruction.

## Condition Codes and Boolean Formulae:

|   |   |   | H | I | N | Z | C |
|---|---|---|---|---|---|---|---|
| 1 | 1 | 1 | – | – | – | – | – |

## Source Forms, Addressing Modes, Machine Code, and Cycles:

| Source Forms | Addr Mode | Machine Code Opcode | HCMOS Cycles |
|--------------|-----------|---------------------|--------------|
| NOP          | INH       | 9D                  | 2            |

# ORA

# ORA

**Operation:**  ACCA ← (ACCA) + (M)

**Description:**  Performs the logical inclusive-OR between the contents of ACCA and the contents of M and places the result in ACCA. Each bit of ACCA after the operation will be the logical inclusive-OR of the corresponding bits of M and ACCA before the operation.

## Condition Codes and Boolean Formulae:

| | | | H | I | N | Z | C |
|---|---|---|---|---|---|---|---|
| 1 | 1 | 1 | – | – | Δ | Δ | – |

N: R7
   Set if MSB of result is one; cleared otherwise.

Z: $\overline{R7} \cdot \overline{R6} \cdot \overline{R5} \cdot \overline{R4} \cdot \overline{R3} \cdot \overline{R2} \cdot \overline{R1} \cdot \overline{R0}$
   Set if the result is $00; cleared otherwise.

## Source Forms, Addressing Modes, Machine Code, and Cycles:

| Source Forms | Addr Mode | Machine Code Opcode | Operand(s) | HCMOS Cycles |
|---|---|---|---|---|
| ORA  #opr | IMM | AA | ii | 2 |
| ORA  opr | DIR | BA | dd | 3 |
| ORA  opr | EXT | CA | hh  ll | 4 |
| ORA  ,X | IX | FA | | 3 |
| ORA  opr,X | IX1 | EA | ff | 4 |
| ORA  opr,X | IX2 | DA | ee  ff | 5 |

# ROL

# ROL

**Operation:**

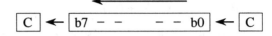

**Description:** Shifts all bits of ACCA, X, or M one place to the left. Bit 0 is loaded from the C bit. Bit 7 is shifted into the C bit. The rotate instructions include the carry bit to allow extension of the shift and rotate instructions to multiple bytes. For example, to shift a 24-bit value left one bit, the sequence {ASL LOW, ROL MID, ROL HIGH} could be used, where LOW, MID, and HIGH refer to the low-order, middle, and high-order bytes of the 24-bit value, respectively.

## Condition Codes and Boolean Formulae:

| H | I | N | Z | C |
|---|---|---|---|---|
| 1 | 1 | 1 | – | – | Δ | Δ | Δ |

N: R7
Set if MSB of result is one; cleared otherwise.

Z: $\overline{R7} \cdot \overline{R6} \cdot \overline{R5} \cdot \overline{R4} \cdot \overline{R3} \cdot \overline{R2} \cdot \overline{R1} \cdot \overline{R0}$
Set if the result is $00; cleared otherwise.

C: b7
Set if, before the shift, the MSB of the shifted value was set; cleared otherwise.

## Source Forms, Addressing Modes, Machine Code, and Cycles:

| Source Forms | Addr Mode | Machine Code Opcode | Operand(s) | HCMOS Cycles |
|---|---|---|---|---|
| ROLA | INH (A) | 49 | | 3 |
| ROLX | INH (X) | 59 | | 3 |
| ROL    opr | DIR | 39 | dd | 5 |
| ROL    ,X | IX | 79 | | 5 |
| ROL    opr,X | IX1 | 69 | ff | 6 |

*M68HC05 Instruction Set Details*

# ROR  Rotate Right thru Carry  ROR

**Operation:**

$$\xrightarrow{\hspace{3cm}}$$

$$\boxed{C} \rightarrow \boxed{b7 -- \quad --\ b0} \rightarrow \boxed{C}$$

**Description:** Shifts all bits of ACCA, X, or M one place to the right. Bit 7 is loaded from the C bit. Bit 0 is shifted into the C bit. The rotate instructions include the carry bit to allow extension of the shift and rotate instructions to multiple bytes. For example, to shift a 24-bit value left one bit, the sequence {LSR HIGH, ROR MID, ROR LOW} could be used, where LOW, MID, and HIGH refer to the low-order, middle, and high-order bytes of the 24-bit value, respectively.

## Condition Codes and Boolean Formulae:

| | | | H | I | N | Z | C |
|---|---|---|---|---|---|---|---|
| 1 | 1 | 1 | – | – | Δ | Δ | Δ |

N: R7
Set if MSB of result is one; cleared otherwise.

Z: $\overline{R7} \cdot \overline{R6} \cdot \overline{R5} \cdot \overline{R4} \cdot \overline{R3} \cdot \overline{R2} \cdot \overline{R1} \cdot \overline{R0}$
Set if the result is $00; cleared otherwise.

C: b0
Set if, before the shift, the LSB of the shifted value was set; cleared otherwise.

## Source Forms, Addressing Modes, Machine Code, and Cycles:

| Source Forms | Addr Mode | Machine Code Opcode | Operand(s) | HCMOS Cycles |
|---|---|---|---|---|
| RORA | INH (A) | 46 | | 3 |
| RORX | INH (X) | 56 | | 3 |
| ROR   opr | DIR | 36 | dd | 5 |
| ROR   ,X | IX | 76 | | 5 |
| ROR   opr,X | IX1 | 66 | ff | 6 |

# RSP

**Reset Stack Pointer**

# RSP

**Operation:**       SP ← $00FF

**Description:**     Resets the stack pointer to the top of the stack (address $00FF).

## Condition Codes and Boolean Formulae:

| | | | H | I | N | Z | C |
|---|---|---|---|---|---|---|---|
| 1 | 1 | 1 | – | – | – | – | – |

## Source Forms, Addressing Modes, Machine Code, and Cycles:

| Source Forms | Addr Mode | Machine Code Opcode | HCMOS Cycles |
|---|---|---|---|
| RSP | INH | 9C | 2 |

**Return from Interrupt**

**Operation:**

| | |
|---|---|
| SP ← SP + $0001; ↑ CCR | Restore CCR from stack |
| SP ← SP + $0001; ↑ ACCA | Restore ACCA from stack |
| SP ← SP + $0001; ↑ X | Restore X from stack |
| SP ← SP + $0001; ↑ PCH | Restore PCH from stack |
| SP ← SP + $0001; ↑ PCL | Restore PCL from stack |

**Description:**   The condition codes, the accumulator, the index register, and the program counter are restored to the state previously saved on the stack. The I bit will be cleared if the corresponding bit stored on the stack is 0 (this is the normal case).

## Condition Codes and Boolean Formulae:

| | | | H | I | N | Z | C |
|---|---|---|---|---|---|---|---|
| 1 | 1 | 1 | Δ | Δ | Δ | Δ | Δ |

Set or cleared according to the byte pulled from the stack into CCR.

## Source Forms, Addressing Modes, Machine Code, and Cycles:

| Source Forms | Addr Mode | Machine Code Opcode | HCMOS Cycles |
|---|---|---|---|
| RTI | INH | 80 | 9 |

# RTS        Return from Subroutine        RTS

**Operation:**    SP ← SP + $0001; ↑ PCH    Restore PCH from stack
                  SP ← SP + $0001; ↑ PCL    Restore PCL from stack

**Description:**   The stack pointer is incremented by one. The contents of the byte of memory that is pointed to by the stack pointer is loaded into the high-order byte of the program counter. The stack pointer is again incremented by one. The contents of the byte of memory that is pointed to by the stack pointer is loaded into the low-order eight bits of the program counter. Program execution resumes at the address that was just restored from the stack.

## Condition Codes and Boolean Formulae:

|   |   |   | H | I | N | Z | C |
|---|---|---|---|---|---|---|---|
| 1 | 1 | 1 | – | – | – | – | – |

## Source Forms, Addressing Modes, Machine Code, and Cycles:

| Source Forms | Addr Mode | Machine Code Opcode | HCMOS Cycles |
|---|---|---|---|
| RTS | INH | 81 | 6 |

# SBC

**Subtract with Carry**

# SBC

**Operation:**   ACCA ← (ACCA) – (M) – (C)

**Description:**   Subtracts the contents of M and the contents of the C bit of the CCR from the contents of ACCA, and places the result in ACCA.

## Condition Codes and Boolean Formulae:

| | | | H | I | N | Z | C |
|---|---|---|---|---|---|---|---|
| 1 | 1 | 1 | – | – | Δ | Δ | Δ |

N: R7
Set if MSB of result is one; cleared otherwise.

Z: $\overline{R7} \cdot \overline{R6} \cdot \overline{R5} \cdot \overline{R4} \cdot \overline{R3} \cdot \overline{R2} \cdot \overline{R1} \cdot \overline{R0}$
Set if the result is $00; cleared otherwise.

C: $\overline{A7} \cdot M7 + M7 \cdot R7 + R7 \cdot \overline{A7}$
Set if the unsigned contents of memory plus the previous carry is larger than the unsigned value in the accumulator; cleared otherwise.

## Source Forms, Addressing Modes, Machine Code, and Cycles:

| Source Forms | Addr Mode | Machine Code Opcode | Operand(s) | | HCMOS Cycles |
|---|---|---|---|---|---|
| SBC  #*opr* | IMM | A2 | ii | | 2 |
| SBC  *opr* | DIR | B2 | dd | | 3 |
| SBC  *opr* | EXT | C2 | hh | ll | 4 |
| SBC  ,X | IX | F2 | | | 3 |
| SBC  *opr*,X | IX1 | E2 | ff | | 4 |
| SBC  *opr*,X | IX2 | D2 | ee | ff | 5 |

# SEC

# SEC

**Operation:** C bit ← 1

**Description:** Sets the C bit in the CCR. SEC may be used to set up the C bit prior to a shift or rotate instruction that involves the C bit.

## Condition Codes and Boolean Formulae:

| | | | H | I | N | Z | C |
|---|---|---|---|---|---|---|---|
| 1 | 1 | 1 | – | – | – | – | 1 |

C: 1 (set)

## Source Forms, Addressing Modes, Machine Code, and Cycles:

| Source Forms | Addr Mode | Machine Code Opcode | HCMOS Cycles |
|---|---|---|---|
| SEC | INH | 99 | 2 |

# SEI      Set Interrupt Mask Bit      SEI

**Operation:**     I bit ← 1

**Description:**     Sets the interrupt mask bit in the CCR. The microprocessor is inhibited from responding to interrupts while the I bit is set.

## Condition Codes and Boolean Formulae:

|   |   |   | H | I | N | Z | C |
|---|---|---|---|---|---|---|---|
| 1 | 1 | 1 | – | 1 | – | – | – |

I:    1 (set)

## Source Forms, Addressing Modes, Machine Code, and Cycles:

| Source Forms | Addr Mode | Machine Code Opcode | HCMOS Cycles |
|---|---|---|---|
| SEI | INH | 9B | 2 |

# STA       Store Accumulator in Memory       STA

**Operation:**        M ← (ACCA)

**Description:**      Stores the contents of ACCA in memory. The value in ACCA remains unchanged. The N and Z condition codes are set or cleared according to the value stored.

## Condition Codes and Boolean Formulae:

|   |   |   | H | I | N | Z | C |
|---|---|---|---|---|---|---|---|
| 1 | 1 | 1 | – | – | Δ | Δ | – |

N: A7
   Set if MSB of result is one; cleared otherwise.

Z: $\overline{A7 \cdot A6 \cdot A5 \cdot A4 \cdot A3 \cdot A2 \cdot A1 \cdot A0}$
   Set if ACCA is $00; cleared otherwise.

## Source Forms, Addressing Modes, Machine Code, and Cycles:

| Source Forms | | Addr Mode | Machine Code | | HCMOS Cycles |
|---|---|---|---|---|---|
| | | | Opcode | Operand(s) | |
| STA | opr | DIR | B7 | dd | 4 |
| STA | opr | EXT | C7 | hh  ll | 5 |
| STA | ,X | IX | F7 | | 4 |
| STA | opr,X | IX1 | E7 | ff | 5 |
| STA | opr,X | IX2 | D7 | ee  ff | 6 |

# STOP

**Operation:**      I bit ← 0; Stop Oscillator

**Description:**      Reduces power consumption by eliminating all dynamic power dissipation. Timer interrupts are disabled and any existing timer interrupt flag is cleared. The external interrupt pin is enabled and the I bit in the CCR is cleared to enable the external interrupt. Finally, the oscillator is inhibited to put the MCU into the STOP condition.

When either the $\overline{\text{RESET}}$ or $\overline{\text{IRQ}}$ pin goes low, the oscillator is enabled. A delay of 1,920 processor clock cycles is imposed, allowing the oscillator to stabilize. The reset vector or interrupt request vector is fetched, and the associated service routine is executed.

External interrupts are enabled after a STOP command.

## Condition Codes and Boolean Formulae:

|   |   |   | H | I | N | Z | C |
|---|---|---|---|---|---|---|---|
| 1 | 1 | 1 | – | 0 | – | – | – |

I:    0 (cleared)

## Source Forms, Addressing Modes, Machine Code, and Cycles:

| Source Forms | Addr Mode | Machine Code Opcode | HCMOS Cycles |
|---|---|---|---|
| STOP | INH | 8E | 2 |

# STX

**Store Index Register in Memory**

# STX

**Operation:** $M \leftarrow (X)$

**Description:** Stores the contents of X in memory. The value in X remains unchanged. The N and Z condition codes are set or cleared, according to the value stored.

## Condition Codes and Boolean Formulae:

|   |   |   | H | I | N | Z | C |
|---|---|---|---|---|---|---|---|
| 1 | 1 | 1 | – | – | Δ | Δ | – |

N: X7
Set if MSB of result is one; cleared otherwise.

Z: $\overline{X7} \cdot \overline{X6} \cdot \overline{X5} \cdot \overline{X4} \cdot \overline{X3} \cdot \overline{X2} \cdot \overline{X1} \cdot \overline{X0}$
Set if X is $00; cleared otherwise.

## Source Forms, Addressing Modes, Machine Code, and Cycles:

| Source Forms | | Addr Mode | Machine Code | | HCMOS Cycles |
|---|---|---|---|---|---|
| | | | Opcode | Operand(s) | |
| STX | *opr* | DIR | BF | dd | 4 |
| STX | *opr* | EXT | CF | hh  ll | 5 |
| STX | ,X | IX | FF | | 4 |
| STX | *opr*,X | IX1 | EF | ff | 5 |
| STX | *opr*,X | IX2 | DF | ee  ff | 6 |

A-62

*M68HC05 Instruction Set Details*

# SUB

**Subtract**

# SUB

**Operation:**     ACCA ← (ACCA) – (M)

**Description:**     Subtracts the contents of M from ACCA and places the result in ACCA.

## Condition Codes and Boolean Formulae:

|   |   |   | H | I | N | Z | C |
|---|---|---|---|---|---|---|---|
| 1 | 1 | 1 | – | – | Δ | Δ | Δ |

N: R7
   Set if MSB of result is one; cleared otherwise.

Z: $\overline{R7} \cdot \overline{R6} \cdot \overline{R5} \cdot \overline{R4} \cdot \overline{R3} \cdot \overline{R2} \cdot \overline{R1} \cdot \overline{R0}$
   Set if the result is $00; cleared otherwise.

C: $\overline{A7} \cdot M7 + M7 \cdot R7 + R7 \cdot \overline{A7}$
   Set if the unsigned contents of memory is larger than the unsigned value in the accumulator; cleared otherwise.

## Source Forms, Addressing Modes, Machine Code, and Cycles:

| Source Forms | Addr Mode | Machine Code | | HCMOS Cycles |
|---|---|---|---|---|
| | | Opcode | Operand(s) | |
| SUB  #*opr* | IMM | A0 | ii | 2 |
| SUB  *opr* | DIR | B0 | dd | 3 |
| SUB  *opr* | EXT | C0 | hh  ll | 4 |
| SUB  ,X | IX | F0 | | 3 |
| SUB  *opr*,X | IX1 | E0 | ff | 4 |
| SUB  *opr*,X | IX2 | D0 | ee  ff | 5 |

# SWI                        Software Interrupt                        SWI

**Operation:**

| | |
|---|---|
| PC ← (PC) + $0001 | Move PC to return address |
| ↓(PCL); SP ← (SP) – $0001 | Push low half of return addr |
| ↓(PCH); SP ← (SP) – $0001 | Push high half of return address |
| ↓(X); SP ← (SP) – $0001 | Push index register on stack |
| ↓(ACCA); SP ← (SP) – $0001 | Push ACCA on stack |
| ↓(CCR); SP ← (SP) – $0001 | Push CCR on stack |
| I bit ← 1 | Mask further interrupts |
| PCH ← ($xxFC) | Vector fetch |
| PCL ← ($xxFD) | (xx=03, 1F, or 3F depending on M68HC05 device) |

**Description:** The program counter is incremented by one. The program counter, index register, accumulator, and condition code register are pushed onto the stack. The stack pointer is decremented by one after each byte of data is stored on the stack. The interrupt mask bit is then set. The program counter is then loaded with the address stored in the SWI vector (located at memory locations n minus 0002 and n minus 0003, where n is the address corresponding to a high state on all implemented lines of the address bus). The address of the SWI vector can be expressed as $xxFC:$xxFD, where xx is 03, 1F, or 3F, depending on the M68HC05 device being used. This instruction is not maskable by the I bit.

## Condition Codes and Boolean Formulae:

| | | H | I | N | Z | C |
|---|---|---|---|---|---|---|
| 1 | 1 | 1 | – | 1 | – | – | – |

I:   1 (set)

## Source Forms, Addressing Modes, Machine Code, and Cycles:

| Source Forms | Addr Mode | Machine Code Opcode | HCMOS Cycles |
|---|---|---|---|
| SWI | INH | 83 | 10 |

# TAX

**Transfer Accumulator to Index Register**

# TAX

**Operation:** $X \leftarrow (ACCA)$

**Description:** Loads the index register with the contents of the accumulator. The value in the accumulator is unchanged.

## Condition Codes and Boolean Formulae:

|   |   |   | H | I | N | Z | C |
|---|---|---|---|---|---|---|---|
| 1 | 1 | 1 | – | – | – | – | – |

## Source Forms, Addressing Modes, Machine Code, and Cycles:

| Source Forms | Addr Mode | Machine Code Opcode | HCMOS Cycles |
|--------------|-----------|---------------------|--------------|
| TAX | INH | 97 | 2 |

# TST

**Test for Negative or Zero**

# TST

**Operation:**        (ACCA) − $00
or: (X) − $00
or: (M) − $00

**Description:**      Sets the N and Z condition codes according to the contents of ACCA, X, or M. The value in the tested register or memory location is not altered.

## Condition Codes and Boolean Formulae:

| | | H | I | N | Z | C |
|---|---|---|---|---|---|---|
| 1 | 1 | 1 | – | – | Δ | Δ | – |

N: M7
   Set if MSB of the tested value is one; cleared otherwise.

Z: $\overline{M7} \cdot \overline{M6} \cdot \overline{M5} \cdot \overline{M4} \cdot \overline{M3} \cdot \overline{M2} \cdot \overline{M1} \cdot \overline{M0}$
   Set if ACCA, X, or M contains $00; cleared otherwise.

## Source Forms, Addressing Modes, Machine Code, and Cycles:

| Source Forms | Addr Mode | Machine Code Opcode | Operand(s) | HCMOS Cycles |
|---|---|---|---|---|
| TSTA | INH (A) | 4D | | 3 |
| TSTX | INH (X) | 5D | | 3 |
| TST    opr | DIR | 3D | dd | 4 |
| TST    ,X | IX | 7D | | 4 |
| TST    opr,X | IX1 | 6D | ff | 5 |

# TXA     Transfer Index Register to Accumulator     **TXA**

**Operation:**     ACCA ← (X)

**Description:**     Loads the accumulator with the contents of the index register. The value in the index register is not altered.

## Condition Codes and Boolean Formulae:

| | | | H | I | N | Z | C |
|---|---|---|---|---|---|---|---|
| 1 | 1 | 1 | – | – | – | – | – |

## Source Forms, Addressing Modes, Machine Code, and Cycles:

| Source Forms | Addr Mode | Machine Code Opcode | HCMOS Cycles |
|---|---|---|---|
| TXA | INH | 9F | 2 |

# WAIT

# WAIT

**Operation:**    I bit ← 0;  Inhibit CPU clocking until interrupted

**Description:**    Reduces power consumption by eliminating dynamic power dissipation in some portions of the MCU. The timer, the timer prescaler, and the on-chip peripherals continue to operate because they are potential sources of an interrupt. Wait causes enabling of interrupts by clearing the I bit in the CCR, and stops clocking of processor circuits.

Interrupts from on-chip peripherals may be enabled or disabled by local control bits prior to execution of the WAIT instruction.

When either the $\overline{\text{RESET}}$ or $\overline{\text{IRQ}}$ pin goes low, or when any on-chip system requests interrupt service, the processor clocks are enabled, and the reset, IRQ, or other interrupt service request is processed.

## Condition Codes and Boolean Formulae:

| | | H | I | N | Z | C |
|---|---|---|---|---|---|---|
| 1 | 1 | 1 | – | 0 | – | – | – |

I:    0 (cleared)

## Source Forms, Addressing Modes, Machine Code, and Cycles:

| Source Forms | Addr Mode | Machine Code Opcode | HCMOS Cycles |
|---|---|---|---|
| WAIT | INH | 8F | 2 |

# Reference Tables

This appendix includes the following conversion-lookup tables...

- Hexadecimal to ASCII
- Hexadecimal to Decimal
- Hexadecimal to M68HC05 Instruction Mnemonics

# ASCII-to-Hexadecimal Conversion

The American Standard Code for Information Interchange (ASCII) provides a widely accepted standard for encoding alphanumeric information as binary numbers. The original code was designed as a seven-bit code with an additional *parity* bit. Since most modern computers work best with eight-bit values, the code has been adapted slightly and expressed as eight-bit values. The low-order seven bits are the original ASCII code and the eighth bit is usually zero.

The first 32 codes contain device-control codes, such as carriage return and the audible bell code. Many of these are special for archaic teletype transmissions that have similar meanings on a modern terminal or have slipped into disuse.

**Table B-1.**
Hexadecimal-to-ASCII Conversion

| Hex | ASCII | Hex | ASCII | Hex | ASCII | Hex | ASCII |
|-----|-------|-----|-------|-----|-------|-----|-------|
| $00 | NUL | $20 | SP space | $40 | @ | $60 | ` grave |
| $01 | SOH | $21 | ! | $41 | A | $61 | a |
| $02 | STX | $22 | " | $42 | B | $62 | b |
| $03 | ETX | $23 | # | $43 | C | $63 | c |
| $04 | EOT | $24 | $ | $44 | D | $64 | d |
| $05 | ENQ | $25 | % | $45 | E | $65 | e |
| $06 | ACK | $26 | & | $46 | F | $66 | f |
| $07 | BEL beep | $27 | ' apost. | $47 | G | $67 | g |
| $08 | BS back sp | $28 | ( | $48 | H | $68 | h |
| $09 | HT tab | $29 | ) | $49 | I | $69 | i |
| $0A | LF linefeed | $2A | * | $4A | J | $6A | j |
| $0B | VT | $2B | + | $4B | K | $6B | k |
| $0C | FF | $2C | , comma | $4C | L | $6C | l |
| $0D | CR return | $2D | -- dash | $4D | M | $6D | m |
| $0E | SO | $2E | . period | $4E | N | $6E | n |
| $0F | SI | $2F | / | $4F | O | $6F | o |
| $10 | DLE | $30 | 0 | $50 | P | $70 | p |
| $11 | DC1 | $31 | 1 | $51 | Q | $71 | q |
| $12 | DC2 | $32 | 2 | $52 | R | $72 | r |
| $13 | DC3 | $33 | 3 | $53 | S | $73 | s |
| $14 | DC4 | $34 | 4 | $54 | T | $74 | t |
| $15 | NAK | $35 | 5 | $55 | U | $75 | u |
| $16 | SYN | $36 | 6 | $56 | V | $76 | v |
| $17 | ETB | $37 | 7 | $57 | W | $77 | w |
| $18 | CAN | $38 | 8 | $58 | X | $78 | x |
| $19 | EM | $39 | 9 | $59 | Y | $79 | y |
| $1A | SUB | $3A | : | $5A | Z | $7A | z |
| $1B | ESC | $3B | ; | $5B | [ | $7B | { |
| $1C | FS | $3C | < | $5C | \ | $7C | | |
| $1D | GS | $3D | = | $5D | ] | $7D | } |
| $1E | RS | $3E | > | $5E | ^ | $7E | ~ |
| $1F | US | $3F | ? | $5F | _ under | $7F | DEL delete |

# Hexadecimal-to-Decimal Conversion

To convert a hexadecimal number (up to four hexadecimal digits) to decimal, look up the decimal equivalent of each hexadecimal digit in table B-2. The decimal equivalent of the original hexadecimal number is the sum of the weights found in the table for all hexadecimal digits.

Example: Find the decimal equivalent of $3E7.

The decimal equivalent of the 3 in the third (from the right) hex digit is 768.
The decimal equivalent of the E in the second hex digit is 224.
The decimal equivalent of the 7 in the first hex digit is 7.

$$
\begin{aligned}
&\phantom{+}\ 768 \\
&\phantom{+}\ 224 \\
+\ &\phantom{++}\underline{7} \\
=\ &\phantom{+}\ 999
\end{aligned}
$$

$$\$3E7 = 999_{10}$$

**Table B-2.**
Hexadecimal to Decimal Conversion

| 15 | Bit | | 8 | 7 | Bit | | 0 |
|----|-----|----|----|----|----|----|----|
| 15 | 12 | 11 | 8 | 7 | 4 | 3 | 0 |
| **4th Hex Digit** | | **3rd HexDigit** | | **2nd Hex Digit** | | **1st Hex Digit** | |
| **Hex** | **Decimal** | **Hex** | **Decimal** | **Hex** | **Decimal** | **Hex** | **Decimal** |
| 0 | 0 | 0 | 0 | 0 | 0 | 0 | 0 |
| 1 | 4,096 | 1 | 256 | 1 | 16 | 1 | 1 |
| 2 | 8,192 | 2 | 512 | 2 | 32 | 2 | 2 |
| 3 | 12,288 | 3 | 768 | 3 | 48 | 3 | 3 |
| 4 | 16,384 | 4 | 1,024 | 4 | 64 | 4 | 4 |
| 5 | 20,480 | 5 | 1,280 | 5 | 80 | 5 | 5 |
| 6 | 24,576 | 6 | 1,536 | 6 | 96 | 6 | 6 |
| 7 | 28,672 | 7 | 1,792 | 7 | 112 | 7 | 7 |
| 8 | 32,768 | 8 | 2,048 | 8 | 128 | 8 | 8 |
| 9 | 36,864 | 9 | 2,304 | 9 | 144 | 9 | 9 |
| A | 40,960 | A | 2,560 | A | 160 | A | 10 |
| B | 45,056 | B | 2,816 | B | 176 | B | 11 |
| C | 49,152 | C | 3,072 | C | 192 | C | 12 |
| D | 53,248 | D | 3,328 | D | 208 | D | 13 |
| E | 57,344 | E | 3,484 | E | 224 | E | 14 |
| F | 61,440 | F | 3,840 | F | 240 | F | 15 |

# Decimal-to-Hexadecimal Conversion

To convert a decimal number (up to $65,535_{10}$) to hexadecimal, find the largest decimal number in table B-2 that is less than or equal to the number you are converting. The corresponding hexadecimal digit is the most significant hexadecimal digit of the result. Subtract the decimal number found from the original decimal number to get the *remaining decimal value*. Repeat the procedure using the remaining decimal value for each subsequent hexadecimal digit.

Example: Find the hexadecimal equivalent of $777_{10}$.

The largest decimal number from table B-2, that is less than or equal to $777_{10}$, is $768_{10}$. This corresponds to a $3 in the third hexadecimal digit.

Subtract this $768_{10}$ from $777_{10}$ to get the *remaining decimal value* $9_{10}$.

Next look in the column for the next lower order hexadecimal digit (second hex digit in this case). Find the largest decimal value that is less than or equal to the *remaining decimal value*. The largest decimal value in this column that is less than or equal to $9_{10}$ is 0, so you would place a zero in the second hex digit of your result.

$9_{10}$ minus 0 is the *remaining decimal value* $9_{10}$.

Next look in the column for the next lower order hexadecimal digit (first hex digit in this case). Find the largest decimal value that is less than or equal to the *remaining decimal value*. The largest decimal value in this column that is less than or equal to $9_{10}$ is 9, so you would place a 9 in the first hex digit of your result.

$$\boxed{777_{10} = \$309}$$

# Hexadecimal Values vs. M68HC05 Instructions

Table B-3 lists all hexadecimal values from $00 to $FF and the equivalent M68HC05 instructions with their addressing modes. Since there are only 210 M68HC05 instructions, 46 of the hexadecimal values do not correspond to legal instructions.

**Table B-3. (1 of 4)**
Hexadecimal-to-M68HC05 Instruction Mnemonics

| Op | Instruc | Address Mode | Op | Instruc | Address Mode |
|------|---------|--------------|------|---------|--------------|
| $00 | BRSET0 | direct | $20 | BRA | relative |
| $01 | BRCLR0 | direct | $21 | BRN | relative |
| $02 | BRSET1 | direct | $22 | BHI | relative |
| $03 | BRCLR1 | direct | $23 | BLS | relative |
| $04 | BRSET2 | direct | $24 | BCC | relative |
| $05 | BRCLR2 | direct | $25 | BCS | relative |
| $06 | BRSET3 | direct | $26 | BNE | relative |
| $07 | BRCLR3 | direct | $27 | BEQ | relative |
| $08 | BRSET4 | direct | $28 | BHCC | relative |
| $09 | BRCLR4 | direct | $29 | BHCS | relative |
| $0A | BRSET5 | direct | $2A | BPL | relative |
| $0B | BRCLR5 | direct | $2B | BMI | relative |
| $0C | BRSET6 | direct | $2C | BMC | relative |
| $0D | BRCLR6 | direct | $2D | BMS | relative |
| $0E | BRSET7 | direct | $2E | BIL | relative |
| $0F | BRCLR7 | direct | $2F | BIH | relative |
| $10 | BSET0 | direct | $30 | NEG | direct |
| $11 | BCLR0 | direct | $31 | — | — |
| $12 | BSET1 | direct | $32 | — | — |
| $13 | BCLR1 | direct | $33 | COM | direct |
| $14 | BSET2 | direct | $34 | LSR | direct |
| $15 | BCLR2 | direct | $35 | — | — |
| $16 | BSET3 | direct | $36 | ROR | direct |
| $17 | BCLR3 | direct | $37 | ASR | direct |
| $18 | BSET4 | direct | $38 | LSL | direct |
| $19 | BCLR4 | direct | $39 | ROL | direct |
| $1A | BSET5 | direct | $3A | DEC | direct |
| $1B | BCLR5 | direct | $3B | — | — |
| $1C | BSET6 | direct | $3C | INC | direct |
| $1D | BCLR6 | direct | $3D | TST | direct |
| $1E | BSET7 | direct | $3E | — | — |
| $1F | BCLR7 | direct | $3F | CLR | direct |

| Op | Instruc | Address Mode | Op | Instruc | Address Mode |
|----|---------|--------------|----|---------|--------------|
| $40 | NEGA | inherent | $60 | NEG | indexed 1 |
| $41 | — | — | $61 | — | — |
| $42 | — | — | $62 | — | — |
| $43 | COMA | inherent | $63 | COM | indexed 1 |
| $44 | LSRA | inherent | $64 | LSR | indexed 1 |
| $45 | — | — | $65 | — | — |
| $46 | RORA | inherent | $66 | ROR | indexed 1 |
| $47 | ASRA | inherent | $67 | ASR | indexed 1 |
| $48 | LSLA | inherent | $68 | LSL | indexed 1 |
| $49 | ROLA | inherent | $69 | ROL | indexed 1 |
| $4A | DECA | inherent | $6A | DEC | indexed 1 |
| $4B | — | — | $6B | — | — |
| $4C | INCA | inherent | $6C | INC | indexed 1 |
| $4D | TSTA | inherent | $6D | TST | indexed 1 |
| $4E | — | — | $6E | — | — |
| $4F | CLRA | inherent | $6F | CLR | indexed 1 |
| $50 | NEGX | inherent | $70 | NEG | indexed 0 |
| $51 | — | — | $71 | — | — |
| $52 | — | — | $72 | — | — |
| $53 | COMX | inherent | $73 | COM | indexed 0 |
| $54 | LSRX | inherent | $74 | LSR | indexed 0 |
| $55 | — | — | $75 | — | — |
| $56 | RORX | inherent | $76 | ROR | indexed 0 |
| $57 | ASRX | inherent | $77 | ASR | indexed 0 |
| $58 | LSLX | inherent | $78 | LSL | indexed 0 |
| $59 | ROLX | inherent | $79 | ROL | indexed 0 |
| $5A | DECX | inherent | $7A | DEC | indexed 0 |
| $5B | — | — | $7B | — | — |
| $5C | INCX | inherent | $7C | INC | indexed 0 |
| $5D | TSTX | inherent | $7D | TST | indexed 0 |
| $5E | — | — | $7E | — | — |
| $5F | CLRX | inherent | $7F | CLR | indexed 0 |

| Op | Instruc | Address Mode | Op | Instruc | Address Mode |
|------|---------|----------|------|---------|-----------|
| $80 | RTI | inherent | $A0 | SUB | immediate |
| $81 | RTS | inherent | $A1 | CMP | immediate |
| $82 | — | — | $A2 | SBC | immediate |
| $83 | SWI | inherent | $A3 | CPX | immediate |
| $84 | — | — | $A4 | AND | immediate |
| $85 | — | — | $A5 | BIT | immediate |
| $86 | — | — | $A6 | LDA | immediate |
| $87 | — | — | $A7 | — | — |
| $88 | — | — | $A8 | EOR | immediate |
| $89 | — | — | $A9 | ADC | immediate |
| $8A | — | — | $AA | ORA | immediate |
| $8B | — | — | $AB | ADD | immediate |
| $8C | — | — | $AC | — | — |
| $8D | — | — | $AD | BSR | relative |
| $8E | STOP | inherent | $AE | LDX | immediate |
| $8F | WAIT | inherent | $AF | — | — |
| $90 | — | — | $B0 | SUB | direct |
| $91 | — | — | $B1 | CMP | direct |
| $92 | — | — | $B2 | SBC | direct |
| $93 | — | — | $B3 | CPX | direct |
| $94 | — | — | $B4 | AND | direct |
| $95 | — | — | $B5 | BIT | direct |
| $96 | — | — | $B6 | LDA | direct |
| $97 | TAX | inherent | $B7 | STA | direct |
| $98 | CLC | inherent | $B8 | EOR | direct |
| $99 | SEC | inherent | $B9 | ADC | direct |
| $9A | CLI | inherent | $BA | ORA | direct |
| $9B | SEI | inherent | $BB | ADD | direct |
| $9C | RSP | inherent | $BC | JMP | direct |
| $9D | NOP | inherent | $BD | JSR | direct |
| $9E | — | — | $BE | LDX | direct |
| $9F | TXA | inherent | $BF | STX | direct |

| Op | Instruc | Address Mode | Op | Instruc | Address Mode |
|------|---------|--------------|------|---------|--------------|
| $C0 | SUB | extended | $E0 | SUB | indexed 1 |
| $C1 | CMP | extended | $E1 | CMP | indexed 1 |
| $C2 | SBC | extended | $E2 | SBC | indexed 1 |
| $C3 | CPX | extended | $E3 | CPX | indexed 1 |
| $C4 | AND | extended | $E4 | AND | indexed 1 |
| $C5 | BIT | extended | $E5 | BIT | indexed 1 |
| $C6 | LDA | extended | $E6 | LDA | indexed 1 |
| $C7 | STA | extended | $E7 | STA | indexed 1 |
| $C8 | EOR | extended | $E8 | EOR | indexed 1 |
| $C9 | ADC | extended | $E9 | ADC | indexed 1 |
| $CA | ORA | extended | $EA | ORA | indexed 1 |
| $CB | ADD | extended | $EB | ADD | indexed 1 |
| $CC | JMP | extended | $EC | JMP | indexed 1 |
| $CD | JSR | extended | $ED | JSR | indexed 1 |
| $CE | LDX | extended | $EE | LDX | indexed 1 |
| $CF | STX | extended | $EF | STX | indexed 1 |
| $D0 | SUB | indexed 2 | $F0 | SUB | indexed 0 |
| $D1 | CMP | indexed 2 | $F1 | CMP | indexed 0 |
| $D2 | SBC | indexed 2 | $F2 | SBC | indexed 0 |
| $D3 | CPX | indexed 2 | $F3 | CPX | indexed 0 |
| $D4 | AND | indexed 2 | $F4 | AND | indexed 0 |
| $D5 | BIT | indexed 2 | $F5 | BIT | indexed 0 |
| $D6 | LDA | indexed 2 | $F6 | LDA | indexed 0 |
| $D7 | STA | indexed 2 | $F7 | STA | indexed 0 |
| $D8 | EOR | indexed 2 | $F8 | EOR | indexed 0 |
| $D9 | ADC | indexed 2 | $F9 | ADC | indexed 0 |
| $DA | ORA | indexed 2 | $FA | ORA | indexed 0 |
| $DB | ADD | indexed 2 | $FB | ADD | indexed 0 |
| $DC | JMP | indexed 2 | $FC | JMP | indexed 0 |
| $DD | JSR | indexed 2 | $FD | JSR | indexed 0 |
| $DE | LDX | indexed 2 | $FE | LDX | indexed 0 |
| $DF | STX | indexed 2 | $FF | STX | indexed 0 |

# Glossary

*1K* — One kilobyte or $1,024_{10}$ bytes. Similar to the use of the prefix in kilogram, which means 1,000 grams in the decimal numbering system. 1,024 is $2^{10}$.

*A* — Abbreviation for "accumulator" in the M68HC05 MCU.

*accumulator* — An eight-bit register in the CPU of the M68HC05. The contents of this register may be used as an operand of an arithmetic or logical instruction.

*address bus* — The set of conductors that are used to select a specific memory location so the CPU can write information into the memory location, or read its contents. If a computer has 10 wires in its address bus, it can address $2^{10}$ or $1,024_{10}$ memory locations. In most M68HC05 MCUs, the address bus is not accessible on external pins.

*addressing mode* — The way that the CPU obtains (addresses) the information needed to complete an instruction. The M68HC05 CPU has six addressing modes:
- Inherent - The CPU needs no additional information from memory to complete the instruction.
- Immediate - The information needed to complete the instruction is located in the next memory location(s) after the opcode.
- Direct - The low-order byte of the address of the operand is located in the next memory location after the opcode, and the high-order byte of the operand address is assumed to be $00.
- Extended - The high-order byte of the address of the operand is located in the next memory location after the opcode, and the low-order byte of the operand address is located in the next memory location after that.
- Indexed - The address of the operand depends upon the current value in the X index register and a zero-, eight-, or 16-bit instruction-provided value.
- Relative - Used for branch instructions to specify the destination address where processing will continue if the branch condition is true.

*ALU* — See arithmetic logic unit.

*analog* — A signal that can have voltage-level values that are neither the $V_{SS}$ level or the $V_{DD}$ level. In order for a computer to use such signals, they must be converted into binary values that correspond to the voltage levels of the signal. An analog-to-digital converter can be used to perform this conversion. By contrast, a digital signal has only two possible values, 1 ($\approx V_{DD}$) or 0 ($\approx V_{SS}$).

*application programs* — Software programs that instruct a computer to solve an application problem.

*arithmetic logic unit or ALU* — This is the portion of the CPU of a computer where mathematical and logical operations take place. Other circuitry decodes each instruction and configures the ALU to perform the necessary arithmetic or logical operations at each step of an instruction.

*ASCII* — American Standard Code for Information Interchange. A widely accepted correlation between alphabetic and numeric characters and specific seven-bit binary numbers. Refer to Table B-1 in Appendix B.

*assembler* — A software program that translates source-code mnemonics into opcodes that can then be loaded into the memory of a microcontroller.

*assembly language* — Instruction mnemonics and assembler directives that are meaningful to programmers and can be translated into an object code program that a microcontroller understands. The CPU uses opcodes and binary numbers to specify the operations that make up a computer program. These numbers are not meaningful to people, so they use assembly language mnemonics instead to represent instructions. Assembler directives provide additional information, such as the starting memory location for a program. Labels are used to indicate an address or binary value.

*base 2* — Binary numbers that use only the two digits, zero and one. Base 2 is the numbering system used by computers.

*base 10* — Decimal numbers that use the 10 digits, zero through nine. This is the customary numbering system used by people.

*base 16* — The hexadecimal numbering system. The sixteen characters (0 through 9 and the letters A through F) represent hexadecimal values. One hexadecimal digit can exactly represent a four-bit binary value. Hexadecimal is used by people to represent binary values because it is easier to use a two-digit number than the equivalent eight-digit binary number. Refer to Table 2-1.

*BCD* — Binary-Coded Decimal is a notation that uses binary values to represent decimal quantities. Each BCD digit uses four binary bits. Six of the possible 16 binary combinations are considered illegal.

*binary* — The numbering system used by computers because any quantity can be represented by a series of ones and zeros. Electrically, these 1s and 0s are represented by voltage levels of approximately $V_{DD}$ and $V_{SS}$, respectively.

*bit* — A single binary digit. A bit can represent a single value of either 0 or 1.

***black box*** — A hypothetical block of logic or circuitry that performs some input-to-output transformation. A black box is used when the input-to-output relationship is known but the means to achieve this transformation is not known or is not important to the discussion.

***branch instructions*** — Computer instructions that cause the CPU to continue processing at a memory location other than the next sequential address. Most branch instructions are conditional. That is, the CPU will continue to the next sequential address (no branch) if a condition is false, or continue to some other address (branch) if the condition is true.

***breakpoint*** — During debugging of a program, it is useful to run instructions until the CPU gets to a specific place in the program, and then enter a "debugger" program. A breakpoint is established at the desired address by temporarily substituting a software interrupt (SWI) instruction for the instruction at that address. In response to the SWI, control is passed to a debugging program.

***byte*** — A set of exactly eight binary bits.

***C*** — Abbreviation for "carry/borrow" in the condition codes register of the M68HC05. When adding two unsigned eight-bit numbers, the C bit is set if the result is greater than 255 ($FF).

***CCR*** — See condition codes register.

***central processor unit or CPU*** — The part of a computer that controls execution of instructions.

***checksum*** — A value that results from adding a series of binary numbers. When exchanging information between computers, a checksum gives an indication of the integrity of the data transfer. If values were transferred incorrectly, it is highly unlikely that the checksum would match the value that was expected.

***clock*** — A square-wave signal that sequences events in a computer.

***CMOS*** — Complementary metal-oxide semiconductor. A silicon semiconductor processing technology that allows fabrication of both N-type and P-type transistors on the same integrated circuit. Most modern microcontrollers use CMOS technology.

***computer program*** — A series of instructions that cause a computer to operate productively.

*computer system* — A CPU plus other components needed to perform a useful function. A minimum computer system includes a CPU, a clock, memory, a program, and input/output interfaces.

*condition codes register* — The CCR has five bits (H, I, N, Z, and C) that control conditional branch instructions. The values of the bits in the CCR are determined by the results of previous operations. For example, after a load accumulator (LDA) instruction, Z will be set if the loaded value was $00.

*CPU* — See central processor unit.

*CPU cycle* — One period of the internal bus-rate clock. Normally, this clock is derived by dividing a crystal oscillator source frequency by two or more. The length of time required to execute an instruction is measured in CPU clock cycles.

*CPU registers* — Memory locations that are wired directly into the CPU logic instead of being part of the addressable memory map. The CPU always has direct access to the information in these registers. The CPU registers in an M68HC05 are:
- A - eight-bit accumulator
- X - eight-bit index register
- CCR - condition codes register containing the H, I, N, Z, and C bits
- SP - stack pointer
- PC - program counter

*CRT* — Cathode ray tube. Also used as an informal expression to refer to a complete communication terminal that has a keyboard and a video display.

*cycle* — See CPU cycle.

*data bus* — A set of conductors that convey binary information from a CPU to a memory location, or from a memory location to a CPU. In the M68HC05, the data bus is eight bits.

*decimal* — Base-ten numbers use the digits zero through nine. This is the numbering system normally used by humans.

*development tools* — Software or hardware devices that are used to develop computer programs and application hardware. Examples of software development tools include text editors, assemblers, debug monitors, and simulators. Examples of hardware development tools include emulators, logic analyzers, and PROM programmers. An in-circuit simulator combines a software simulator with hardware interfaces.

*digital* — A binary logic system where signals can have only two states: zero ($\approx V_{SS}$) or one ($\approx V_{DD}$).

*direct address* — Any address within the first 256 addresses of memory ($0000 through $00FF). The high order byte of these addresses is always $00. Special instructions allow these addresses to be accessed using only the low-order byte of their address. These instructions automatically fill in the assumed $00 value for the high-order byte of the address.

*direct addressing mode* — Direct addressing mode uses a program-supplied value for the low-order byte of the address of an operand. The high-order byte of the operand's address is assumed to be $00, so it does not have to be explicitly specified.

*direct page* — The first 256 bytes of memory ($0000 through $00FF).

*EEPROM* — Electrically erasable, programmable read-only memory. A nonvolatile type of memory that can be erased and reprogrammed by program instructions. Since no special power supplies or ultra-violet light source are needed, the contents of this kind of memory can be changed without removing the MCU from the application system.

*effective address* — The address where an instruction operand is located. The addressing mode of an instruction determines how the CPU calculates the effective address of the operand.

*eight-bit MCU* — A microcontroller where data is communicated over a data bus made up of eight separate data conductors. Members of the M68HC05 family of microcontrollers are eight-bit MCUs.

*embedded* — When an appliance contains a microcontroller, the MCU is said to be an "embedded controller." Often, the end user of the appliance is not aware (or does not care) that there is a computer inside.

*EPROM* — Erasable, programmable read-only memory. A nonvolatile type of memory that can be erased by exposure to an ultraviolet light source. MCUs that have EPROM are easily recognized because the package has a quartz window to allow exposure to the uv light. If an EPROM MCU is packaged in an opaque plastic package, it is called a "one-time-programmable" (OTP) MCU, because there is no way to expose the EPROM to uv light.

*extended addressing mode* — In this addressing mode, the high-order byte of the address of the operand is located in the next memory location after the opcode. The low-order byte of the operand's address is located in the second memory location after the opcode.

*fetching a vector* — When the CPU is reset or responds to an interrupt, the contents of a specific pair of memory locations is loaded into the program counter and processing continues from the loaded address. The process of reading these two locations is called "fetching the vector."

*flowchart* — A symbolic means to show the sequence of steps required to perform an operation. A flowchart not only tells *what* needs to be done, but also the *order* in which the steps should be done.

*H* — Abbreviation for "half-carry" in the condition codes register of the M68HC05. This bit indicates a carry from the low-order four bits of an eight-bit value to the high-order four bits. This status indicator is used during BCD calculations.

*half flip flop* — A half flip flop (HFF) has a transparent condition and a latched condition. In the transparent condition (clock input equal logic one), the Q output is always equal to the logic level presented at the input. In the latched condition (clock input equals logic 0), the output maintains the logic level that was present when the flip flop was last in the transparent condition.

*hexadecimal* — The base-16 numbering system. The sixteen characters (0 through 9 and the letters A through F) are used to represent hexadecimal values. One hexadecimal digit can exactly represent a four-bit binary value. Hexadecimal is used by people to represent binary values because it is easier to use a two-digit number than the equivalent eight-digit binary number. (Refer to Table 2-1.)

*HFF* — See half flip flop.

*high order* — The leftmost digit(s) of a number. Five is the high-order digit of the number 57.

*I* — Abbreviation for "interrupt mask bit" in the condition codes register of the M68HC05.

*I/O* — See input/output.

*immediate addressing mode* — In immediate addressing mode, the operand is located in the next memory location(s) after the opcode.

*in-circuit simulator* — A simulator with hardware interfaces that allows connection into an application circuit. The in-circuit simulator replaces the MCU and behaves as a real MCU. The developer has greater control and visibility of internal MCU operations because they are being simulated by instructions in the host computer. An in-circuit simulator, like other simulators, is not as fast as a real MCU.

*indexed addressing mode* — In indexed addressing mode, the current value of the index register is added to a zero-, eight-, or 16-bit value in the instruction to get the effective address of the operand. There are separate opcodes for zero-, eight-, and 16-bit variations of indexed mode instructions, so the CPU knows how many additional memory locations to read after the opcode.

*index register* — An eight-bit CPU register in the M68HC05 that is used in indexed addressing mode. X can also be used as a general purpose eight-bit register (in addition to the eight-bit accumulator).

*inherent addressing mode* — In inherent addressing mode, the CPU already inherently has everything it needs to complete the instruction. The operands (if there are any) are in the CPU registers.

*input-output or I/O* — Interfaces between a computer system and the external world. A CPU reads an input to sense the level of an external signal and writes to an output to change the level on an external signal.

*instruction decoder* — The portion of a CPU that receives an instruction opcode and produces the necessary control signals so that the rest of the CPU will perform the desired operations.

*instruction set* — The instruction set of a CPU is the set of all operations that the CPU is able to perform. One way to represent an instruction set is with a set of shorthand mnemonics, such as LDA meaning "load A." Another representation of an instruction set is the set of opcodes that is recognized by the CPU.

*instructions* — Instructions are operations that a CPU can perform. Instructions are expressed by programmers as assembly language mnemonics. A CPU interprets an opcode and its associated operand(s) as an instruction.

*inverter* — A simple logic circuit that produces an output logic level that is the opposite of the level presented to its input.

*kilobyte* — One kilobyte is $1,024_{10}$ bytes. Similar to the use of the prefix in kilogram, which means 1,000 grams in the decimal numbering system. 1,024 is $2^{10}$.

*label* — A name that is assigned (by a programmer) to a specific address or binary value. When a program containing a label is assembled, the label is replaced by the binary value it represents. Programs typically include many labels.

*latch* — A logic circuit that maintains a stable output state even after the input has been removed or changed. A clock control input determines when the latch will capture the input state and apply it to the output.

**least significant bit** — The rightmost digit of a binary value.

**LED** — Light emitting diode. A solid-state device that emits light when dc current passes through it.

**listing** — A program listing shows the binary numbers that the CPU needs alongside the assembly language statements that the programmer wrote. The listing is generated by an assembler in the process of translating assembly language source statements into the binary information that the CPU needs.

**logic 1** — A voltage level approximately equal to the $V_{DD}$ power supply.

**logic 0** — A voltage level approximately equal to $V_{SS}$ (ground).

**low order** — The rightmost digit(s) of a number. Seven is the low-order digit of the number 57.

**LSB** — Least significant bit. The rightmost digit of a binary value.

**machine codes** — The binary codes that are processed by the CPU as instructions. Machine code includes both opcodes and operand data.

**mainframe computer** — A large computer system that is usually confined to a special room. Mainframe computers are used for large information processing jobs like checking the tax returns for all taxpayers in a region.

**mass storage** — A very large capacity storage device such as a magnetic disk. Information in a mass storage device takes longer to access than information in the memory map of a CPU.

**MCU** — Microcontroller unit. See microcontroller.

**memory location** — In the M68HC05, each memory location holds one byte of data and has a unique address. To store information into a memory location, the CPU places the address of the location on the address bus, the data information on the data bus, and asserts the write signal. To read information from a memory location, the CPU places the address of the location on the address bus and asserts the read signal. In response to the read signal, the selected memory location places its data onto the data bus.

**memory map** — A pictorial representation of all memory locations in a computer system. A memory map is similar to a city street map in that it shows where items are located.

*memory-mapped I/O* — In this type of system, I/O and control registers are accessed in the same way as RAM or ROM memory locations. Any instruction that can be used to access memory can also be used to access I/O registers.

*microcontroller* — A complete computer system, including a CPU, memory, a clock oscillator, and I/O, on a single integrated circuit.

*microprocessor* — A microprocessor is similar to a microcontroller, except that one or more of the subsystems needed to make a complete computer system is not included on the same chip with the CPU. A microprocessor typically includes a CPU and a clock oscillator but does not include program memory or I/O registers.

*mnemonic* — Here, three to five letters that represent a computer operation. For example, the mnemonic form of the "load accumulator" instruction is LDA.

*monitor program* — A software program that is intended to assist in system development. A typical monitor program allows a user to examine and change memory or CPU register contents, set breakpoints, and selectively execute application programs.

*most significant bit or MSB* — The leftmost digit of a binary value.

*MSB* — See most significant bit.

*N* — Abbreviation for "negative," a bit in the condition codes register of the M68HC05. In twos-complement computer notation, positive signed numbers have a 0 in their MSB; negative numbers, a 1. The N condition code bit reflects the sign of the result of an operation. After a load accumulator instruction, the N bit will be set if the MSB of the loaded value was a 1.

*NAND gate* — A basic logic circuit. The output of a NAND gate is a logic 0 when all of its inputs are logic 1s. The output of a NAND gate is a logic 1 if any of its inputs are logic 0.

*nonvolatile* — A type of memory that does not forget its contents when power is turned off. ROM, EPROM, and EEPROM are all nonvolatile memories.

*NOR gate* — A basic logic circuit. The output of a NOR gate is a logic 0 when any of its inputs are logic 1s. The output of a NOR gate is a logic 1 if all of its inputs are logic 0.

*object code file* — A text file containing numbers that represent the binary opcodes and data of a computer program. An object code file can be used to load binary information into a computer system. Motorola uses the S-record file format for object code files. See Figure 7-5.

*octal* — Base-8 numbers that use the characters 0 through 7 to represent sets of three binary bits. Octal is seldom used in modern computer work.

*one* — A logic high level ($\approx V_{DD}$).

*ones-complement* — To get the logical ones-complement of a binary value, invert each bit.

*opcode* — A binary code that instructs the CPU to do a specific operation in a specific way. The M68HC05 CPU recognizes 210 unique eight-bit opcodes that represent addressing mode variations of 62 basic instructions.

*operand* — An input value to a logical or mathematical operation.

*oscillator* — A circuit that produces a constant-frequency square wave that is used by the computer as a timing and sequencing reference. A microcontroller typically includes all elements of this circuit except the frequency-determining component(s) (the crystal or R-C components) [R-C = resistor-capacitor].

*OTP* — See OTPROM.

*OTPROM* — A nonvolatile type of memory that can be programmed but cannot be erased. An OTPROM is an EPROM MCU that is packaged in an opaque plastic package. It is called a "one-time-programmable" MCU because there is no way to expose the EPROM to uv light.

*parity* — An extra bit in a binary word that is intended to indicate the validity of the remaining bits in the word. In "even" parity, the parity bit is set or cleared as needed to make the total number of logic ones in the word (including the parity bit) equal to an even number (0, 2, 4, etc.).

*PC* — See program counter.

*personal computer* — A small computer system that is normally used by a single person to process information.

*playing computer* — A learning technique in which you pretend to be a CPU that is executing the instructions of a program.

*pointer register* — An index register is sometimes called a pointer register because its contents are used in the calculation of the address of an operand. A straightforward example is an indexed—no offset instruction where the X register contains the direct address of (points to) the operand.

*program* — A set of computer instructions that causes a computer to perform an application task.

*program counter* — The program counter (PC) is the CPU register that holds the address of the next instruction or operand that the CPU will use.

*programming model* — The registers of a particular CPU. The programming model of the M68HC05 CPU is shown in Figure 5-2.

*PROM* — Programmable read-only memory. A nonvolatile type of memory that can be programmed after it is manufactured. EPROM and EEPROM are two types of PROM memory.

*pulled* — The act of reading a value from the stack. In the M68HC05, a value is pulled by the following sequence of operations: First, the stack pointer register is incremented so that it points at the last value that was saved on the stack. Next, the value that is at the address contained in the stack pointer register is read into the CPU.

*pushed* — The act of storing a value at the address contained in the stack pointer register, and then decrementing the stack pointer so it points at the next available stack location.

*PWM* — Pulse-width modulation. A system where the duty cycle (percentage of on-time) of a waveform is varied.

*RAM* — Random access memory. Any RAM location can be read or written (to) by the CPU. The contents of a RAM memory location remain valid until the CPU writes a different value or until power is turned off.

*read* — Transfer the contents of a memory location to the CPU.

*record* — One line of an object code text file.

*registers* — Memory locations that are wired directly into the CPU logic instead of being part of the addressable memory map. The CPU always has direct access to the information in these registers. The CPU registers in an M68HC05 are:

- A - eight-bit accumulator
- X - eight-bit index register
- CCR - condition codes register containing the H, I, N, Z, and C bits
- SP - stack pointer
- PC - program counter

Memory locations that hold status and control information for on-chip peripherals are called I/O and control registers.

*relative addressing mode* — Relative addressing mode is used to calculate the destination address for branch instructions. If the branch condition is true, the signed eight-bit value after the opcode is added to the current value of the program counter to get the address where the CPU will fetch the next instruction.

*relative offset* — An eight-bit signed twos-complement value that is added to the program counter when a branch condition is true. The relative offset is located in the byte after a branch opcode.

*reset* — Reset forces a computer system to a known starting point and on-chip peripherals to known starting conditions.

*reset vector* — The contents of the last two memory locations in an M68HC05 MCU are called the reset vector. As the MCU leaves reset, the program counter is loaded with the contents of these two locations so the first instruction after reset will be fetched from that address.

*ROM* — Read-only memory. A type of memory that can be read but cannot be changed (written). The contents of ROM must be specified before manufacturing the MCU.

*S-record* — A Motorola standard format used for object code files. See Figure 7-5.

*simulator* — A computer program that copies the behavior of a real MCU.

*source code* — See source program.

*source program* — A text file containing instruction mnemonics, labels, comments, and assembler directives. The source file is processed by an assembler to produce a composite listing and an object file representation of the program.

*SP* — Abbreviation for "stack pointer," a CPU register in the M68HC05 MCU.

*stack* — A mechanism for temporarily saving CPU register values during interrupts and subroutines. The CPU maintains this structure with the stack pointer register that contains the address of the next available storage location on the stack. When a subroutine is called, the CPU pushes (stores) the low-order and high-order bytes of the return address on the stack before starting the subroutine instructions. When the subroutine is done, a return from subroutine (RTS) instruction causes the CPU to recover the return address from the stack and continue processing where it left off before the subroutine. Interrupts work in the same way, except all CPU registers are saved on the stack instead of just the program counter.

*stack pointer* — A CPU register that holds the address of the next available storage location on the stack.

*subroutine* — A sequence of instructions that need to be used more than once in the course of a program. The last instruction in a subroutine is a return from subroutine (RTS) instruction. At each place in the main program where the subroutine instructions are needed, a jump or branch to subroutine (JSR or BSR) instruction is used to call the subroutine. The CPU leaves the flow of the main program to execute the instructions in the subroutine. When the RTS instruction is executed, the CPU returns to the main program where it left off.

*three-state buffer* — The output of a three-state buffer can be a logic 0, a logic 1, or a high impedance (as if connected to nothing). An enable input controls the high impedance (off) state vs. the low impedance (on) state. When the buffer is on, the output has the same logic level as the input (1 or 0). When the buffer is off, the output acts like an open circuit.

*transducer* — A device that converts some physical property, such as pressure, into electrical signals that can be used by a computer.

*transmission gate* — A basic logic circuit used in microcontrollers. A transmission gate works like a series switch that is controlled by a logic level signal. When the control input is a logic 0, the transmission gate acts like an open circuit. When the control input is a logic 1, the transmission gate acts like a short circuit.

*twos-complement* — A means of performing binary subtraction using addition techniques. The most significant bit of a twos-complement number indicates the sign of the number (1 indicates negative). The twos-complement negative of a number is obtained by inverting each bit in the number and then adding 1 to the result. For example, the twos-complement negative of 0000 0011 ($3_{10}$) is 1111 1100 + 0000 0001 = 1111 1101.

*variable* — A value that changes during the course of executing a program.

$V_{DD}$ — The positive power supply to a microcontroller (typically 5 volts dc).

*vector* — A pointer (address) that indicates where the CPU should continue processing instructions after an interrrupt or reset.

*volatile* — A type of memory that loses its contents when power is turned off. RAM is a type of volatile memory. In modern microcontrollers, it takes very little power to maintain the contents of a RAM, under good conditions. In some cases, the contents of RAM and registers may be unchanged after a short interruption of power.

$V_{SS}$ — The 0 volt dc power supply return for a microcontroller.

*word* — A group of binary bits. Some larger computers consider a set of 16 bits to be a word, but this is not a universal standard.

*write* — The transfer of a byte of data from the CPU to a memory location.

*X* — Abbreviation for "index register", a CPU register in the M68HC05 MCU.

*Z* — Abbreviation for "zero", a bit in the condition codes register of the M68HC05. A compare instruction subtracts the contents of the tested value from a register. If the values were equal, the result of this subtraction would be zero, so the Z bit would be set. After a load accumulator instruction, the Z bit will be set if the loaded value was $00.

*zero* — A logic low level ($\approx V_{SS}$).

*zero crossings* — When an alternating-current signal goes from a positive to a negative or from a negative to a positive value, crossing the zero level, it is called a zero crossing. The 60 Hz ac power line crosses zero every 8.33 milliseconds (twice each cycle).

# Index

Page numbers in boldface indicate primary references.